SEMANTICS AND SOCIAL SCIENCE

# SEMANTICS AND SOCIAL SCIENCE

Graham Macdonald
*Senior Lecturer in Philosophy, University of Bradford*

Philip Pettit
*Professor of Philosophy, University of Bradford*

ROUTLEDGE & KEGAN PAUL
LONDON, BOSTON AND HENLEY

*First published in 1981*
*by Routledge &Kegan Paul Ltd*
*39 Store Street,*
*London WC1E 7DD,*
*Broadway House,*
*Newtown Road,*
*Henley-on-Thames,*
*Oxon RG9 1EN and*
*9 Park Street,*
*Boston, Mass. 02108, USA*
*Printed in Great Britain by*
*Billing &Sons Limited,*
*Guildford, London, Oxford and Worcester*


*British Library Cataloguing in Publication Data*

*MacDonald, Graham*
*Semantics and social science.*
*1. Semantics*
*2. Meaning (Psychology)*
*I. Title II. Pettit, Philip*
*412 P325*

*ISBN 0-7100-0783-3*
*ISBN 0-7100-0784-1 Pbk*

# CONTENTS

# INTRODUCTION

1

This book is an exploration of the four major questions that are raised by philosophical reflection on social science. Social science covers all the attempts to make systematic sense of human beings in society: thus it includes anthropology and history, the sciences of the exotic, as well as the more domestic disciplines of social psychology or micro-sociology, macro-sociology, political science and economics. The four issues which philosophy raises in connection with social science are the following: each is dealt with in a separate chapter of the book and they are here given in the order treated. 1. The cross-cultural question: how far can we hope as social scientists to be able to encompass all cultures in a single scheme, making sense of what is done in other societies on the same pattern that we make sense of what is done in our own? 2. The humanism-scientism question: how far can we expect the explanation of what people say and do to conform to the model of explanation suggested by the natural sciences? 3. The individualism-collectivism question: in accounting for the institutional features of a society how far can we expect to succeed with the resources that do for explaining the actions of individuals? 4. The fact-value question: in characterising and accounting for social patterns how far can we hope to remain neutral on the matter of evaluative commitments?

Our primary purpose in this text is to set out and defend a distinctive set of views on these issues, charting a not uncontentious course for the future of social inquiry. Like any two philosophers we are subject to differences of opinion, including differences on some of the topics treated in the text. However, on the broad questions just distinguished we find ourselves able to present a common front. We argue against cultural relativism, for humanism and (with reservations) individualism, and against the view that social science is undermined by evaluative commitments: such commitments as it may have to make are not subversive of the enterprise. But what of the differences between us, and the problem which these raise in a collaborative production? Our solution has been to allocate the responsibility for each chapter to an individual author. Graham Macdonald is responsible for the first and fourth chapters, which deal respectively with the cross-cultural question and the fact-value one. Philip Pettit is responsible for Chapter 2, which discusses the humanism-scientism issue, and Chapter 3, which covers the issue between individualism and collectivism. This introduction was penned by Philip Pettit but is sponsored fully by both authors. The four chapters of the book are standardised in substance and style, so as to make what we hope is a cohesive text. However, they can also be treated as more or less independent essays. They all presuppose some understanding of the matter treated in this introduction, especially Chapters 1 and 4, but we have left sufficient overlap between the different chapters to make it possible for them to be read separately.

The viewpoint from which we approach the problems of social science is as distinctive as the set of answers for which we argue. It is provided by semantics, or more specifically by philosophical inquiry into the semantic enterprise. Semantics is understood here in a sense promoted in recent theory of language, not in the common sense of a pedantic concern with connotations. To idealise somewhat, it is the discipline which would give the meaning of each sentence in a language, as the parallel syntactic discipline would give its structure. As native speakers of English, it appears that we are each able to see how any of an indefinite number of sentences is structured - what is the subject, what the verb, and so on - and what any of the sentences means. The aim of linguistics is to make this competence intelligible, explaining in particular how we as finite minds can have a grasp of an indefinitely extended range of sentences, including sentences that we have never heard or seen before. The strategy which linguists follow in pursuit of this goal is to try to construct for a given language a finite set of rules, a finite theory, which would be able to assign a correct structure and meaning to any sentence that we care to construct within the language. At the very least, such a theory would show that there is nothing mysterious in the competence which finite minds have in the language, this competence being paralleled by the ability of the finite theory to assign structure and meaning to any of the indefinite number of sentences which the language allows us to construct. The syntactic theory of the language, at least on our idealised version, is the part of that overall theory which would assign structure to each sentence; the semantic is the part that would assign meaning.

No linguist has yet provided a satisfactory syntactic or semantic theory for a natural language but it is agreed almost on all sides that great progress has been made in the past quarter-century on the problem of how such theories are to be pursued, and what form they may be expected to take (see Lyons 1968, for a survey). In syntactic theory the work of the linguist, Noam Chomsky, has been particularly enlightening and influential and this work has inspired similar efforts in the semantic area - efforts, it must be admitted, which are often out of line with Chomsky's own semantic views. Our focus in the present text is provided by just such an investigation of the nature of semantic theory: specifically, an investigation pursued by a number of contemporary philosophers, among whom the foremost is the American thinker, Donald Davidson (see Davidson entries, also Evans and McDowell 1976, and Platts 1979

We believe that the elaboration of Davidson's understanding of semantics, the pursuit of the so-called Davidsonian programme, has thrown new light on the old project of making sense of people, and that in this light we can gain fresh insight into the issues raised by the philosophy of social science. Whether or not that belief is sound will be borne out by the discussion in the chapters that follow. In this introduction we do not attempt to defend it, since that would be to anticipate our arguments. Instead we concentrate on two related tasks. First, we offer a rudimentary account, accessible to non-philosophers, of what semantics is on Davidson's understanding of it. And second, we sum up in a set of five principles the main lessons for the project of making sense of people that we identify in the elaboration of that understanding, both by Davidson himself and by others. The lessons are independently derived in the text but a summary statement of them may serve as a useful check-list: it is given in section 3 below.

## 2

To the first task, then. In order to understand what semantics is it is useful to imagine that we are concerned with providing within our home language a semantic theory for some foreign tongue. The foreign medium is the object-language, as it is sometimes called: the language which forms the topic of our discussions. The home medium, in parallel, is the meta-language: the language from within which we look at the language that constitutes the object of our inquiry. We may take it that the meta-language is English and imagine that the object-language is any other natural tongue: say Irish, a language that happens to be known to one of the present authors. Our job as semantic theorists will be to provide within English a meaning for each of the sentences that may be constructed within Irish, a job which supposes that we have already succeeded in developing a syntactic theory whereby we can assign a structure to each such sentence. Put otherwise, the job is that of elaborating in English a theory for the interpretation of each Irish sentence. We say 'interpretation' and not 'translation' for the following reason. The interpretative project is envisaged on the presupposition that English is understood, and can be used to give the meanings of Irish sentences. A translational enterprise might be undertaken in respect of two languages, neither of which is understood by the investigator. To interpret is to give the meaning of a sentence, to translate is only to say that two sentences have the same meaning, and where the interpreting language must be understood, the translating language may not be.

On Davidson's understanding of things, and so far it is shared with many opponents, there are three aspects to the project of understanding, and ultimately interpreting, a foreign language. First of all it is necessary to be able to distinguish the well-formed units of speech in the foreign language: this is the syntactic aspect of the enterprise. We must be able to say that in Irish 'Is fear . . .', and 'Bhfuil tú . . .', while they are combinations of significant words, are not significant sentences, any more than their literal equivalents '. . . is a man' and 'Are you . . .'. The syntactic theory of Irish should ideally tell us, for every possible string of words, whether it is a well-formed sentence and, if so, what structure it has. But whether or not we have a fully formalised theory at our disposal, we must be able to identify and analyse such sentences intuitively if we are to be able to get on with the business of interpretation.

But apart from having a syntactic grasp of a language we wish to understand, the present account holds that we must also have a pragmatic one. To understand a language pragmatically is to recognise that certain types of sentences have the same content but lend themselves to being uttered with different force, and that some types are capable of being uttered with one or another force, depending on circumstance. It is to be able to see for example that 'Tá tú ciúin', 'Bhfuil tú ciúin' and 'Bí ciúin' are Irish sentences normally used to express different attitudes, indicative, interrogative and imperative, in respect of the same state of affairs, just like their equivalents 'You are quiet', 'Are you quiet' and 'Be quiet'. And it is to be able to tell that 'Tá tú ciúin', like 'You are quiet', although it is normally used with an indicative attitude, takes on an interrogative significance when stressed in a certain way. What it is that sentences such as those given have in common is usefully called their content, what it is that distinguishes them their force. A pragmatic theory of a foreign language would ideally give us the cues for determining the force of an uttered sentence, and would enable us to recognise that certain sentence types have the same content, although typically used with different force. But whether or not we have a rigorous theory to deal with the matter, we certainly must be able to handle such questions intuitively if we are to have any hope of interpreting the language successfully.

The third and final aspect to understanding a foreign language is that which bears properly on interpretation: the semantic one. Imagine that we are syntactic and pragmatic masters of Irish, without being also semantic masters; the prospect is not a plausible one but we may allow ourselves some speculative licence. We can identify sentences in Irish and we can say with what force each of the sentences is liable to be uttered, whether with the intention of making a statement, asking a question, giving an order, or whatever. What more is needed, then, if we are to be able fully to understand the language? Well if we accept the picture so far, the natural answer is: a grasp of that state of affairs which is (normally) asserted to obtain in each indicative sentence. If we understand what the state of affairs is which corresponds to each indicative sentence, then we will also be in a position to understand sentences which have the same content but different force.[1]

We are speaking loosely in referring to the state of affairs corresponding to each indicative sentence. What is in question is that condition in the actual world which warrants the assertion of the sentence if it is fulfilled, and only if it is fulfilled: the condition whose fulfilment is necessary and sufficient for the truth of the sentence.[2] Subject to other constraints which will be discussed shortly, the truth-condition for a sentence 'S' is given by a formula of the following sort, a formula known from the work of Alfred Tarski as a T-sentence: ' "S" is true in language L if and only if p'. The idea is that in interpreting Irish within English we would need, for each indicative sentence of Irish, something like a T-sentence of this kind.[3] Suppose our syntactic sense of the language tells us that 'Tá Séan ciúin' is a well-formed sentence, and our pragmatic sense that it is an indicative sentence normally used to make an assertion. What is also required by the present understanding of the semantic aspect is a grasp of a T-sentence expressing the truth-condition of the sentence. We must be given, or be enabled to construct, a formula such as '"Tá Séan ciúin" is true in Irish if and only if John is quiet'. This formula is a bi-conditional, something which makes the truth-value of each side conditional on that of the other. On the left-hand side it quotes or mentions an Irish indicative sentence and on the right-hand side it uses an English sentence, 'John is quiet', in order to give the condition under which the Irish sentence is uniquely true. (It is important that the English sentence is used and not just mentioned, for this marks the difference between interpretation and translation. The T-formula carries us outside of the Irish language, giving by the use of English the condition with which the Irish sentence is correlated. If the English sentence on the right-hand side were just mentioned, the formula would at best serve the translational purpose of giving two sentences which are correlated with the same condition; it would not actually give that condition, for no sentence would be used to pick the condition out.)

The Davidsonian account of what is involved in understanding a foreign language, even as it has been presented so far, is not uncontentious. Two aspects of it in particular represent currently controversial options and these we will notice, even though we cannot provide a full justification of them here. First of all it is contentious to maintain that pragmatic force and semantic content can generally be divorced in the manner envisaged within the account. There are some sentences in any natural language which must be admitted by everyone not to lend themselves to a distinction between content and force, the content not being informatively identifiable independently of the force. Take the English one-word sentences 'Hello', 'Gosh', and 'Alas'. It would be procrustean of us to insist that the pragmatic-semantic distinction be imposed on these in interpreting the language. We would do better to treat them as exceptions to the usual frame, holding them to be wholly explicable under their pragmatic aspect, by reference to the force with which they are uttered under normal circumstances. So far so good. What is controversial about the account which we have given however is the assumption that the pragmatic-semantic frame does not fail more systematically and pervasively of being fulfilled.

The assumption is quite natural since with sentences of greater complexity than our one-word examples, it is almost always possible to construct sets of counterparts which appear to have the same content and different force. We cannot think of an interrogative or imperative which corresponds to the presumably indicative 'Hello', but we do not generally find such a problem with longer sentences: we can always envisage at least one counterpart, at least one other sentence that seems to display the same content while having a distinct force. However the assumption has been challenged among a substantial number of philosophers who, worried about the difficulty of giving an informative account of the truth conditions of certain sentences, have suggested that the sentences should be understood, so far at least as they are troublesome, in wholly pragmatic terms. These philosophers claim that such a sentence, although a sentence in indicative mood, should be understood, like the sentence 'Hello', in terms of the effect it is typically used to produce: that is, in terms of its force. Our assumption is that while the force of the sentence is something that certainly needs to be understood, there is in the general case a semantic content that calls for independent understanding. Examples of analyses which reject the pragmatic-semantic frame are: the explanation of saying that something is good as commending it, of saying that someone acted voluntarily as putting him forth for praise or blame, and of saying that a thesis is true as endorsing it (see respectively, Hare 1952, Hart 1948-9 and Strawson 1950).

The first controversial aspect of the account we have sketched is defended by Peter Geach on the grounds that with the sentences which opponents construe in wholly pragmatic terms, it is always possible to construct conditionals, putting the sentences in antecedent place, and that this is hard to understand if the sentences do not have semantic content (Geach 1972, Chapter 8). A sentence like 'Hello' cannot be put in the antecedent place of a conditional: we cannot say 'If hello, then . . .'. This fits with the view that the sentence does not have a semantic content or truth-condition, for a conditional seems to give expression to a relationship between the truth condition of the antecedent sentence and whatever it is that the consequent expresses. However, we can place sentences about such matters as goodness, voluntariness and truth within the antecedent of conditional and this fact is difficult to square with the analysis of them on the same lines as 'Hello'. Geach's argument needs further elaboration and support, particularly in view of the rebuttal published by Michael Dummett (Dummett 1973, Chapter 10). It will do however, to render plausible the line which we have taken in our account of the relationship between syntactic, pragmatic and semantic theory. We cannot hope to provide a full justification of that account in this introduction: our aim is merely to present it and to make it seem reasonably persuasive.

The second respect in which the account that we have given is controversial is in the assumption that the truth-condition for an indicative sentence is adequately represented as a condition that obtains in the actual world: an absolute truth-condition, as it is called, rather than a truth-condition relativised to possible worlds. The absolute truth-condition is given in a T-sentence of the kind '"S" is true in language L if and only if p'; a relativised truth-condition would go '"S" is true in language L in the actual world W if and only if . . .'. The relativised T-sentence, unlike the absolute variety, is not confined to using a sentence on the right-hand side which bears on how things actually are. It can speak equally well of how things are in certain worlds possible relative to W. Take the Irish sentence 'Ní féider nach bhfuil Séan ciúin': literally, 'It's impossible that John is not quiet'. A relativised T-sentence for this might be: '"Ní féider nach bhfuil Séan ciúin" is true in Irish in the actual world W if and only if in every world possible relative to W John is quiet'.

The reason why it might be suggested that we ought to forsake absolute truth-conditions in favour of relativised ones is that the relativised T-sentence is richer in content, seeming to offer on the right-hand side a decomposition and not just an interpretation of the sentence mentioned on the left. The bilingual in Irish and English might learn something from the formula just given, where he would not be enlightened in any way by the absolute counterpart: '"Ní féider nach bhfuil Séan ciúin" is true in Irish if and only if it is impossible that John is not quiet'. The decompositional benefit of the relative truth-condition cannot be denied but, it seems to us, it also gives reason for thinking that in constructing a semantic theory for a language we do right to restrict ourselves to the more austere truth-condition. Our job in semantics is to assign to each indicative sentence of the object-language a condition under which it is uniquely true and if the meta-language in which we are constructing our theory allows us to do this without reference to ersatz theoretical entities such as possible worlds, there is no reason why we should not take this easier way. We have no interest as semantic theorists in deepening our philosophical grasp of the nature of what is said in the sentences which we are concerned to interpret (for other considerations see Davidson 1973b).

So much then by way of an outline account of the understanding of semantic theory sponsored by Donald Davidson. Semantics or the theory of meaning is distinct from pragmatics or the theory of force and semantics is concerned with assigning an absolute truth-condition to each indicative sentence of the language under interpretation. With this outline account clear, we can indicate the problem at the heart of the semantic enterprise. The best way towards an understanding of the problem is to recognise that the constraint on a semantic theory, for all we have said so far, can be satisfied uninformatively. The constraint can be summed up as follows: that the semantic theory for a language must be able to produce a true T-sentence for every indicative sentence in the language.[4] But consider now that in order to be true a T-sentence is required only to contain clauses that are both true or both false, a requirement that is very easily met. This consideration may well give us pause for it shows that for any language we will get what passes as a semantic theory by pairing any old true sentence with each true sentence in the language, and any old false sentence with each false one. Thus if we could separate out the true and false sentences of Irish, we would satisfy our constraint by writing for every true sentence 'St' the T-sentence, '"St" is true in Irish if and only if two and two are four' and for every false sentence 'Sf' the T-sentence '"Sf" is true in Irish if and only if two and two are five'. By taking this line we would guarantee that for every indicative sentence in Irish we had a true T-sentence and, for all that has been said so far, we might make the bizarre claim to have thereby provided a semantic theory for Irish.

It may surprise non-philosophers to be told that all that is required for a T-sentence to be true is that both of its clauses be true or both false. A T-sentence is a biconditional which makes each of its clauses conditional on the other, meeting the form 'P if and only if Q'. Such a biconditional can be seen as formed from two conditions, 'P if Q' and 'Q if P'. The standard or extensional understanding of such a conditional, although it is not an account that can easily be squared with ordinary usage, represents the conditional as being true so long as the following case is ruled out: that the antecedent is true and the consequent false; thus any two true sentences, any two false ones, or any pair of which the first is false and the second true, can be combined in a true conditional. When we say 'P if and only if Q', asserting conditionals both ways, we rule out two cases: that P is true and Q false, and that Q is true and P false. Thus the biconditional is true under either of two circumstances: that both P and Q are true, or that both P and Q are false.

But to return to the main line of discussion, we must put some extra conditions on a successful semantic theory besides the constraint that it should produce a true T-sentence for every indicative sentence of the object-language. There are two constraints to be imposed, the one formal and the other empirical. The formal constraint, and it was implicit in some of our earlier remarks, is that the theory must generate the T-sentences from a finite base, deriving each as a theorem from a finite set of rules or axioms. If we were dealing with an artificial scrap of language that had only a finite list of sentences Sl to Sn, then our theory might simply consist in a set of T-sentences, one for each sentence of the object language. With a natural language such as Irish however, there is an indefinite number of sentences for which truth-conditions must be provided. If we are to provide T-sentences in an informative way for this indefinite number, we can only hope to do so by having a finite bunch of rules or axioms with the help of which, given a sentence of Irish, we can derive a T-sentence.

These rules or axioms, we may presume, would assign denotations to referring expressions of Irish, extensions to predicates, and so on, and would indicate the conditions under which components such as referring expressions and predicates are combined into true sentences.

The addition of the formal constraint, important though the constraint is, is not enough to ensure that the semantic theory which generates true T-sentences for the indicative sentences of the object-language is a satisfactory one. Suppose we have a semantic theory for Irish which is more or less satisfactory, generating among other theorems the T-sentence '"Tá Séan ciúin" is true in Irish if and only if John is quiet'. What can be shown is that if such a theory passes the formal constraint then so will a variant which produces on the right hand side of each T-sentence a conjunction of the sentence given in the existing theory and any true sentence: for example it may yield a T-sentence such as '"Tá Séan ciúin" is true in Irish if and only if John is quiet and two plus two equals four'. It is not enough then to guarantee the acceptability of a semantic theory for Irish that the theory produces a true T-sentence for each indicative Irish sentence, even if it produces the T-sentences from a common finite base. We need some further constraint which a satisfactory semantic theory must meet.

The required constraint is an empirical one. It must specify conditions in the observed speech and behaviour of Irish speakers which any semantic theory for Irish must fulfil. One such condition would certainly be the following: that Irish speakers must generally be disposed to assent to the sentence mentioned on the left-hand side of a T-sentence under the circumstances which would lead us to assent to the sentence used on the right-hand side, and that if they are not there must be some independently plausible explanation of why this is so. Another likely condition would be: that Irish speakers must not act in a way which is hard to square with the beliefs that our semantic theory has us assign to them in suggesting interpretations of their utterances, and that if they do act in such a way there must be some independently compelling account of why they do so. But in mentioning conditions such as these we are anticipating what we have to say in the first chapter. Granted a Davidsonian account of what it is to interpret speech, what it is to provide a semantic theory for a language, the possibility of cross-cultural understanding turns on how we constrain our theory empirically: what tests we decide that it should meet. Thus in the discussion of cross-cultural understanding in the first chapter we investigate at some length the nature of the empirical constraint appropriate to semantics.

We have said sufficient in elucidation of the project of semantics. The account which we have presented is taken mainly from the work of Donald Davidson but it is not just the product of one man's reflection: it is a distillation out of a half-century of philosophical work on the nature of meaning and the structure of language, work in which the great figures are Frege and Tarski, Russell and

Wittgenstein, Carnap and Quine. We take the account as given in the remainder of our text, our interest being in general insights which the pursuit of the Davidsonian programme has sponsored. It should be mentioned, however, that even if Davidson's understanding of how to do semantics is demolished, this need not undermine the lessons sponsored by the attempt to implement his programme. Thus we hope that what we have to say about social science may be found convincing even by those who reject the account given of the nature of semantic theory.

3

The pursuit of the Davidsonian programme has meant two things. First of all it has meant the attempt to paraphrase various problematic types of sentence in natural language in such a way that we can see how they might be handled within a truth-conditional semantics. This enterprise merges with traditional philosophical attempts to reveal the logical form of such problematic propositions as causal statements, statements of belief and desire, modal statements expressing necessity or possibility, and so on. Second, however, the pursuit of the Davidsonian programme has meant the investigation of just when we would take a semantic theory for a foreign language to be satisfactory, just when we would say that we have achieved the true interpretation of utterances within that language. This project links up with established philosophical attempts to say what guides us in our understanding of other minds, particularly in the understanding of the minds of people from very different backgrounds. The two enterprises involved in the pursuit of the Davidsonian programme correspond with the two constraints, formal and empirical, which we saw that a truth-conditional semantics must meet. The one has to do with showing how the formal constraint can be satisfied in respect of certain structurally difficult sentence types, the other with how exactly the empirical constraint should be elaborated and imposed.

Most of the lessons that bear on social science come from the more empirical of the two projects. They are worked out within the text since, in dealing with the topic of cross-cultural understanding, we begin our considerations with precisely this empirical project. In the remainder of this introduction however we would like to present the lessons in the form of five general principles. We shall not be referring later to the list but it may serve to give the reader a useful idea of the sort of views that we shall be pressing. The principles, then, are as follows:

(i) *The mental nature of meaning*

In order to assign meanings to the utterances of a speaker we must make assumptions about his mental states. In identifying an utterance as an assertion, we assume that the speaker has an assertoric intention in making the utterance. And, more important, in putting an interpretation on the assertion we assume that the agent is of a state of belief and desire which explains his saying what we interpret him as saying: in the normal case we assume that he believes what we take the assertion to say and that he sincerely desires to communicate that belief. The mental nature of meaning is important because it entails that in the semantic project of interpreting the utterances of a speaker or group of speakers, we must ensure that the interpretations we offer fall in with an overall plausible story about the things they believe and pursue, and the practices they follow. The task of semantic interpretation is part of a larger task of making comprehensive sense of the speakers (see McDowell 1976).

(ii) *The homogeneity of interpretation*
What follows from the first principle is that the interpretation of utterances connects with the interpretation of non-linguistic actions, in so far as the mental states which it assumes must be ones that do not render the explanation of the non-verbal behaviour of the speakers problematic. But we can go even further than saying that the two sorts of interpretation are connected. We have reason also to say that they are essentially of a kind: that they are homogeneous. In each we are concerned with ascribing to the speaker a complex of beliefs and desires such that granted that complex the utterance or action is behaviourally rational: it is an event which the agent believed would bring about, or at least make likely, a state of affairs that he desired. The state of affairs desired in the case of an utterance is normally that the speaker's audience believe something about what he holds or wants; in the case of a non-linguistic action it may be any circumstance under the sun that he envisages its realising or occasioning. To interpret the utterance or action, tracing it to an appropriate state of belief and desire, is always in a certain sense to rationalise it: to represent it as what it was rational of the agent to say or do, granted what he there and then assumed and aspired after.

(iii) *The underdetermination of the mental*
The mental states crucially involved in interpretation are, in a catch-all phrase, states of belief and desire. The trouble however with such states is that we cannot say what an agent believes or desires just by looking at the noises or movements he makes. A given piece of behaviour, or even a pattern of pieces, may be associated with any of a number of mental states: it may be taken to issue from this set of beliefs or that, for example, depending on what desires are ascribed to the agent. This means that behaviour, both linguistic and non-linguistic, leaves slack in the interpretation of the mental. It may be thought that the slack is taken up by the reference to other public factors such as circumstances or involuntary cues. However we learn to associate these factors with mental states only so far as we have presumed to interpret some behaviour as betokening those states and the uncertainty of the latter exercise is bound to pass into the associa-

tions that we take ourselves to have learned.

(iv) *The rational nature of the mental*
Beliefs, like their propositional objects, are capable of being true and false and it would make no sense to ascribe beliefs to an agent without assuming that he was disposed to make moves appropriate to ensure that his beliefs were true. To assume this is to take it that the agent is attitudinally rational, where to take his utterances and actions as the rational issue of beliefs and desires was to assume behavioural rationality. The assumption plays a vital role in the ascription of beliefs, and also as we shall see in the ascription of desires, and it serves to guide us in the interpretation of what the agent says and does. We will not ascribe beliefs of such a kind that we must then admit that the agent seems to be quite unresponsive to manifest counterexamples or inconsistencies. In view of dimness and obduracy, we will be prepared to acknowledge a certain lack of responsiveness in the agent but there are severe limits on the tolerance we can exercise. Thus the assumption of attitudinal rationality serves to take up some of the slack left by behaviour in the divination of what an agent believes.[5]

(v) *The social nature of the mental*
We are not guided just by the assumption of attitudinal rationality in taking up the interpretative slack left by behaviour. Tyler Burge has recently argued that we are also influenced, or at least ought to be influenced, by certain subtle social considerations (Burge 1979). Suppose that an agent in our own language community is held on the basis of what he says and does to believe that arthritis is a disease manifested in various rheumatoid pains and that he himself has the disease, a view corroborated by his doctor; and suppose that on the same grounds he is held to fear arthritis, to desire to be rid of it, and to hope that it will not spread in his body. Imagine now that he says one morning that the arthritis has spread to his thigh. Since arthritis is a disease of the joints, we have before us the following interpretative option: to say that the man believes wrongly that he has arthritis in the thigh, or to say that as he understands arthritis it is a disease of the joints or thigh - 'tharthritis', let us call it - and he believes that he now has tharthritis in the thigh. We would unhesitatingly opt for the first reading in such a case, and what this shows is that we pay attention to social matters as well as personal ones in ascribing mental states. The tharthritis interpretation would make the agent out to be as rational, and more canny, than the orthodox one but we naturally reject it none the less. We assume that the agent would want to be taken to have beliefs about what is known in his community as 'arthritis', and so we consider how the term is used in the community at large in attributing beliefs about arthritis to the agent. Were the linguistic community changed on the other hand, and it happened that 'arthritis' was used in the manner of 'tharthritis', then our inter-

pretation of the agent's beliefs would alter in correspondence. In divining the mental we look to the society as well as to the individual: in a sense, the community at large, and not the individual agent, is the subject of interpretation.

This, then, must suffice by way of introduction to our text. In conclusion we would each like to express gratitude to those colleagues and students who have directed us, as we think for well, in our ruminations. We are both in the debt of our philosophical colleagues at Bradford, Roger Fellows, Gregory des Jardins and Richard Lindley, and of a close colleague from Manchester, Cindy Macdonald. Philip Pettit would also like to express his gratitude to a number of other people who read his part of the typescript and offered comments on it: Desmond Clarke, Susan James, Martin Hollis, David Papineau and Ian Steedman, and to the critical members of seminars at which extracts were read at the universities of Cambridge, Columbia, Connecticut, Cork, East Anglia, Essex, Manchester, Sheffield and Wales (Aberystwyth). Denise Martin, Susan Wilday and, especially, Beverley Toulson helped us in typing and preparing the script. However, in this regard our major debt is to Vera Hawley: without her patience and perseverance, the task of finalising the text would have been immeasurably more difficult.

# 1 CROSS-CULTURAL UNDERSTANDING

## 1 THE SIGNIFICANCE OF TRANSLATION AND INTERPRETATION

Much recent work in the philosophy of language, particularly in semantics, has been inspired by W.V. Quine's reflections on the problems of translation (Quine 1960, Ch.2). These reflections gain their significance from the broader issues concerning meaning and the nature of mind which surround the more specific matter of translation. At the same time there has been considerable controversy within anthropology concerning the methodological problems posed by the investigation of alien cultures. Some of the questions raised in that discussion are: 'Is translation possible?', 'Can I judge the truth/falsity of the beliefs of members of an alien culture?', 'Is rationality only a "modern" phenomenon?', 'Is rationality relative?'. That there is a convergence of interest between the anthropologist and the philosopher is masked only by the contrast between the abstractions of the philosophical approach and the more practical concerns of the anthropologist and linguist. For the anthropologist, translation is a means to the end of understanding the customs and behaviour of people in different societies; for the philosopher of language, reflection on translation illuminates issues which have their base in the theory of meaning and the philosophy of mind. Our aim in this chapter is to outline the points of contact and to use recent discussions in semantics to clarify some of the recurrent problems of the philosophy of anthropology.

That the questions concerning translation are central to anthropological field work is indubitable: Evans-Pritchard claims that they are 'the major problem we are confronted with in the subject we are discussing' (Evans-Pritchard 1965, p.12). The example he gives to illustrate the difficulties involved will serve to introduce us to the position of Quine's radical translator. A language in Central Africa has a word, 'anzo', which we translate as 'dog': For Evans-Pritchard, the trouble is that there is an extremely rough equivalence between the aliens' use of 'anzo' and our use of 'dog', the significance which dogs have in the alien society is very different from that which they have in England. Thus there is no real identity of meaning between the terms, only a partial overlap: we might say that while the terms have the same reference, they have a different connotation. Such difficulties raise the possibility that we will never be able to provide a precise translation of the language of a society radically different from our own, suggesting that a full understanding of those societies is impossible.

This suggestion is strengthened when we consider that the interpretation of utterances is only part of the project of understanding a culture and that it must be carried on hand in hand with the explanation of non-linguistic actions. The utterance of sentences, whether in assertions, questions, commands, or whatever, is intertwined with non-linguistic behaviour and sense must be made of both forms of action at once. Specifically, to take up a theme from the introduction, utterance interpretation involves the assignment of mental states of belief and desire and the states which are assigned must be more or less consistent with the beliefs and desires ascribed in the explanation of non-linguistic behaviour. This interconnection makes a problem for translation when the non-linguistic behaviour in question is to our eyes peculiar or bizarre. In that case the translator will be forced to try at once to map the foreigners' terms on to words in our language and to embed those terms in a representation of the foreign mind which makes sense of the peculiar behaviour. Under just such circumstances practising anthropologists have often despaired of straightforward translation of the alien language, denying the applicability of one or more of the standard assumptions we make in interpretation. Different positions may be adopted. One suggests that the foreigners operate with a fundamentally divergent categorial scheme or that they have a variant logic. Another challenges the linguistic appearances and claims that apparently assertoric acts are not really assertions which display the beliefs of their utterers. They are said rather to be acts which are explained by their expressive or symbolic significance or by their role in promoting some important social function such as the maintenance of social cohesion.

In what follows we shall be approaching the problems raised in the philosophy of anthropology from a consideration of the constraints that ought to bind the radical translator or interpreter. This sort of consideration will lead us eventually to an assessment of the various positions just outlined, although it belongs itself to the province of semantics: what place it has in semantics should be clear from the introduction. In analysing the constraints on interpretation it should be mentioned that we shall employ a familiar philosophical tactic: that of taking our starting point in idealised, homespun examples, venturing away from such examples only to link the discussion with the concerns of the anthropologist. The a priori character of our meditations is not accidental: it has its basis in the fact that problems of interpretation begin at home and that the principles of their resolution must apply to the familiar as well as to the foreign. Neither, however, is the character absolute: we do not think that philosophers have nothing to learn from anthropologists and we hope that our reflections are not anthropologically uninformed.

Before proceeding to the analysis of constraints on interpretation it must be said that there are some respects in which the discussion of radical translation among philosophers such as Quine diverges from discussions among anthropologists and those who reflect on anthropology. The position of Quine's radical translator is more extreme than that envisaged for the anthropologist in Evans-Pritchard's example. It is not one of considering possible differences of connotation once it has been agreed that a word like 'anzo' has the same application or extension as our 'dog'. The concerns of the radical translator run beyond the recondite resonance of words to the very matter of how their reference is fixed. The problem is how it can be known that 'anzo' refers to dogs, how even this much determinancy in translation can be achieved. Unlike Evans-Pritchard, Quine conceives of the environment in which his translator is placed in extremely austere terms. All that the translator has to go on are the noises made by her subjects, noises with which she is assumed to be quite unfamiliar. The only concessions are that she is taken to be able to distinguish assertions from other utterance types and she is assumed to be able to identify the native signs of assent and dissent.

Given the austerity of the radical translator's environment of inquiry it is not surprising that, as Quine sees it, the translator will be forced to a conclusion which no practising anthropologist is likely to reach. The conclusion is that there is no reason to suppose that there cannot be more than one translation and that there is no way of telling which of the theories as to the correct translation is the best one: 'manuals for translating one language into another can be set up in divergent ways, all incompatible with one another' (Quine 1960, p.27). As against this, the practising anthropologist will say that, far from there being any different possible ways of translating foreign utterances, the investigator in the field will be lucky to identify a single one. The conflict, however, need not be a matter for particular concern. Someone intent on defending Quine's conclusions, but sympathetic none the less with the anthropologist's complaint, can reasonably argue as follows: that the radical translator is embarrassed with the variety of translations available only because so little is assumed in the way of constraint on translation, whereas the practising anthropologist suffers the complementary embarrassment only because so much is taken for granted as background constraint. In the case of radical translation very few assumptions about the speakers are allowed and so there may be a great variety of translation manuals conceivable. In the more realistic case assumptions naturally teem - the speakers for example, will be taken to be of a certain language group or culture type - and these assumptions will crowd out many of the radical translational alternatives.

So much by way of explaining respects in which the discussion of radical translation diverges from the discussion of anthropology. In passing we should add that although the environment allowed by Quine to the radical translator is comparatively austere, it is not as impoverished as it might at first sight seem. Two points need to be made. The first is that the evidence which is said to be at the disposal of the radical translator already presupposes a good deal of hypothesising and interpretation. Strange noises from the mouths of strangers do not come neatly parcelled into segmented sentences, each with a label indicating the mood and mode of its utterance. In order for the noises to be taken as part of a language they have to be assumed to be intentionally uttered with the aim of making an assertion, asking a question, giving a command, or whatever. Quine is at least unstinting in allowing that his translator may make this assumption and in ascribing to the translator the ability to identify the different types of utterance made. His generosity is not of course gratuitous. The radical translator tries to explore the mind of the speakers by discovering the meaning of the sentences they utter but in order to do this she needs already to know something about this mind: in particular, something about the intentions behind utterances. Quine lifts this block to translational progress by his act of generosity but by that act he makes the evidence available to the radical translator richer than some might like to have it.

The second point to be made about Quine's characterisation of the environment of radical translation is that while it has a behaviouristic quality, the behaviourism assumed is not as strong as it might have been. When Quine speaks of the translator being presented with the noises, and perhaps marks, made by foreigners, someone may want to object that the data available do not reduce to such physically describable phenomena, that the data assume meaningful configurations which fail to correlate with physically characterised sorts of events. The idea behind the objection is that when a certain sort of act, for example the act of assent, is identified in the data, there is no reason to believe that the particular actions which come to be recognised as being of this character will share any salient physical property: any physical property by which we might be guided in the recognition of such acts. As against this objection however it must be said in defence of Quine that the sort of behaviourism he assumes need not be reductionist. Quine takes it that any meaning in the minds of speakers, or at least any meaning which is worth bothering about, must be reflected in this physical reality: the totality of dispositions to behaviour in the community in question. More generally, he thinks that any psychological characteristic ascribed to an individual must be justified via the different physically characterised behaviour which that characteristic would lead us to expect, in specified circumstances, from that individual. This doctrine has the following consequence: that if two individuals are physically alike, their physical pasts and futures indiscernible, then they share the same mental constitution. However, it does not have the stronger reductionist consequence that for every mental characteristic there is an identifiable type of physical property which is realised just when that characteristic is present. A psychological difference may be taken always to make a physical difference, without the extra assumption being intruded that the difference it makes is always the same, or always of a recognisable sort.[2]

We have seen why translation and interpretation have a special significance in the work of the anthropologist and why discussions of radical translation may be expected to be relevant to the anthropological enterprise. Our task now is to look at the constraints which we may expect to guide radical translation or interpretation, for a grasp of those constraints ought to give us an interesting line on the problems that beset anthropology: that is, on the problems of cross-cultural understanding. Before we leave this section, however, a terminological remark. Up to now we have been speaking as if translations were interpretations: as if, in translating from language A into language B, we always already understood language B. As we saw in the introduction, translation is possible without the translating language being understood. All that is necessary is that terms and sentences from the translated language are paired with terms and sentences from the translating one and this may be done in total ignorance as to the meaning of the translating expressions. In interpretation this possibility of ignorance is necessarily closed, for the concern is not to 'mention' or 'quote' expressions of the translating language which happen to have the same meaning as expressions 'mentioned' or 'quoted' from the translated, it is rather to 'use' the former expressions in such a way as to give the meaning of the latter, this use presupposing understanding. If the translator says that 'TA', a term or sentence from language A, has the same reference or truth condition as 'TB', a term or sentence from language B, the interpreter says that 'TA' refers to TB or that 'TA' is true if and only if TB. Like Quine we are only concerned with translation insofar as the translating language is understood: that is, insofar as it is tantamount to interpretation. In what follows therefore we shall give up all talk of translation and identify our topic simply as interpretation.

## 2 CHARITY IN INTERPRETATION

Our favoured theory of meaning is, as indicated in the introduction, Davidsonian. One of the prime motivating forces for any theory which calls itself a theory of meaning must be the observation that language-users are able to construct and understand a large variety of sentences which they have never encountered before. Whether this large variety amounts to infinity is not of immediate concern; the point remains that our understanding of novel sentences must depend upon the understanding of their parts, and of the ways in which such parts can be combined. The Davidsonian approach suggests that the meaning of the sentences is given by stating their truth-conditions, and that the meaning of the elements (semantic primitives) is identified by the way in which those elements contribute to the truth-conditions of the sentences in which they can appear. Thus from a finite vocabulary we can construct perhaps infinitely many novel sentences via the combinatory rules of the theory.

This exceptionally brief outline indicates the following programme for radical interpretation. First, one identifies, somehow, the truth-conditions of sentences uttered by the foreigner. Second, one notices which elements reappear in which sentences, and by process of trial and error manages to specify the contributions made to the truth-conditions of those sentences, and so on. One-word sentences are obviously the most useful, as the two stages combine effortlessly. Having decided that 'Anzo' means that a dog is in the vicinity, one can use the information in interpreting longer sentences in which 'anzo' appears. The outcome will (eventually) be a theory of truth for the language, specifying under what conditions all the indicative sentences of the language are true. The hope is to be able to understand what information is being conveyed by the aliens in their assertions.

We have already indicated that one of the problems is whether the project can get off the ground. Can we distinguish assertions from other speech acts, and can we identify signs of assent and dissent, prior to the interpretation of sentences? Davidson suggests that the attitude of 'holding-true' may be amenable to such prior identification, that we may be able, behaviourally, to discern that some of the sentences uttered, being sincere assertions, are held to be true by the utterer (Davidson 1974a). It will be these sentences which will form the evidential base for the interpretative theory. Leaving aside the difficulty of such prior identification, the problem that remains is to identify the truth-conditions of the held-true sentences. (The 'holding-true' is relativised to time, so we want to find the truth-conditions of a sentence held-true at a time.) This splits into two problems:
(a) There are too many truths consistent with the utterance of the sentence at that time for the process of elimination to be easy. 'Anzo' is uttered when it is true that a dog is in the vicinity; but it is also true at that time that tables, people, chairs, trees, houses are in the vicinity, and that Manchester is north of London.
(b) It may be that the sentence uttered is false.

The first problem has already been discussed in the introduction. We saw there that in order to identify the truth condition of a foreign sentence such as 'Anzo' it was not sufficient to say: it is the condition picked out by any home sentence which yields a truth when inserted in the formula '"Anzo" is true in Central Africaneese (for speaker s at time t) if and only if . . .'. The trouble is that on the standard, extensional understanding of such a formula - it is what Tarski calls a T-sentence - we get a truth whenever the sentence mentioned on the left-hand side and the sentence used on the right are both true or whenever they are both false. It will not be enough then for us to require that the theory of truth which we arrive at in interpreting some foreign language should yield a true T-sentence for every indicative sentence in that language. This would not ensure that the theory would give the truth condition of every such sentence, since the T-sentences yielded might be utterly bizarre. The formal constraint on a theory of truth, that it should be able to generate the required T-sentences from a finite set of axioms, will diminish the bizarreness that is liable to appear in the T-sentences but, as we saw, it cannot succeed in eliminating it.

How then is the radical interpreter going to select the home sentence which she thinks expresses the condition that ought to be correlated with a foreign sentence in a satisfactory theory of meaning? How does she decide which of the true T-sentences mentioning 'Anzo' on the left-hand side is the T-sentence that ought to be generated by that theory of meaning? The winning candidate will have to be a true T-sentence, and it will have to be one that can be derived within a finitely axiomatised theory of truth for the whole language. But what other features must it possess, what other constraints must it satisfy?

One further constraint must certainly be a constraint of accessibility. Whatever English sentence 'Anzo' is paired with, it must be the case that when foreigners say 'Anzo' they are in a position which, if they knew English, would allow them equally to assert that sentence. The constraint will assure us for example, if the formal constraints had not already done so, that in saying 'Anzo' they are not declaring that Manchester is north of London: this, assuming that they do not know of Manchester or London. However, the accessibility constraint is still going to leave too many truths as candidates for what is asserted in the indicative sentence 'Anzo'. It may not enable us to decide whether the foreigners are speaking about the dog or the ever present cat; or it may leave open the possibility that they are reporting some standing condition by the use of the sentence rather than a variable circumstance such as the presence of the dog.[3]

In face of the problem that there are too many truths which may be expressed by a foreign indicative sentence, one proposal which has been made is that the radical interpreter should be charitable in assigning truth conditions across the indicative sentences of the language which are held true by the person interpreted: this, in addition to satisfying the formal constraints on the assignment of truth conditions, and perhaps also the constraint of accessibility (see N.L. Wilson 1959). The much-discussed principle of charity is sometimes rendered, uncharitably, as follows: maximise the number of truths which one takes the foreigner to uphold. It is characterised more plausibly in the words of one commentator as: 'choose that translation which maximises agreement (at least of certain sorts) between ourselves and our translatees' (Grandy 1973, p. 440). Understood in either way, the principle of charity would represent a very powerful constraint on interpretation. Even in its weaker form however it is scarcely persuasive, since it would seem to counsel neglect of considerations as to whether the foreigners are likely to have attained knowledge of truths maintained by us. We shall be urging a very deep-running modification of the principle in the next section, a modification which takes account of this objection, but our further discussions in this section will tend to give it some support.

We have been discussing the first of two problems which we

identified a little while ago. The second of those problems may now be introduced, especially since it seems to raise a particular difficulty for anyone tempted by the first problem to endorse charity as a principle of interpretation. The second problem is that any foreign sentence which the interpreter finds to be held true may turn out in actual fact to be false. If 'Anzo' is true when asserted by one of the foreigners it is difficult enough, as we have seen, to say how we would work out its truth-condition: what it is that the sentence is being used to express. If 'Anzo' is false, however, the problem is exacerbated.

The second problem may be posed in different forms. If we assume with Davidson that the radical interpreter can identify those sentences which foreigners hold true then we distinguish these possibilities: (1) the speech-community is such that all or most of the speakers hold true certain sentences which are false and (2) the interpreter's informant holds such sentences true, by reason of individual error. However, we may lift the Davidsonian assumption and replace it by the weaker supposition that while the interpreter can identify those sentences which foreigners assert she cannot tell straight off whether they assert them sincerely, and hold them to be true. In this case two further possibilities call to be considered: (3) the speech-community is such that all or most of the speakers continually affirm certain false sentences in order to mislead others and (4) the interpreter's informant continually affirms false sentences, by reason of individual deceitfulness. The four cases may be described respectively as cases of communal and individual error on the one hand, communal and individual deceitfulness on the other. In what follows we shall consider them in reverse order. It may be mentioned that cases of error or deceitfulness involving sub-groups of the society can be assimilated to the individual or communal cases: to the individual, if the sub-group is comparatively insignificant and is naturally seen as deviant against a wider social context; to the communal, if the sub-group is significant enough to call for consideration as a society in its own right.

We assume that in pursuing her task the interpreter is concerned with making intelligible the utterances of a majority of the speakers of the language. We ignore the tricky problem of giving the identity conditions of the language, making the pragmatic supposition that members of a community who are in constant contact and interaction communicate by using a common tongue. If case 4 arises, and the interpreter is dealing with a distinctively deceitful informant, this fact should be detectable and should not cause insuperable problems. It will be detectable because the interpreter will be in a position to compare her informant's assertions with those of other members of the community and to notice divergences. If the interpreter tries to exercise charity in respect of the informant's assertions, and to construct a theory of meaning for the language on that basis, she will find that the theory will not be suitable for the language as it is used generally across the community.

But what of the case of communal as distinct from individual deceitfulness? As interpreter, would I be able to detect such deceitfulness? Let us assume first of all that the speakers are deceitful only towards me: that they speak misleadingly only when addressing me or when conversing in my presence. The point which needs to be made here is that if the deceitfulness is sustained it ceases to be clear that I am in any significant sense deceived. If a foreigner tells me that she is going to her house and then proceeds to go to someone else's I will be deceived about the meaning of her words only if the dissimulation is maintained, the appearance being kept up that the house she enters really is her house. She will have to be there when I call, she will have to have the use of the clothes, books and utensils in the house, and so on; and this deception will have to be supported by the connivance of the rest of the community. In that case however I will not be badly mistaken after all: the house which I identify as hers will in an extended sense be hers. The pattern can be made clearer if we consider another example. Suppose that women in the community are identified as 'leti' and men as 'meti' and that speakers deceive me about the use of the terms, leading me to refer to the women as 'meti' and the men as 'leti'. One can imagine my being deceived in this fashion but not in a way that would really matter. The foreigners would understand me in my use of the language, as they would understand one another, and I too would understand them. If they made sure to adjust their terminology whenever in my company, I would have a serviceable theory for the purposes of communication. One might suggest that two languages were being spoken by the deceivers, one in my presence as investigator and one in my absence, and that I had the correct theory for the first medium of communication.

But it is a fiction in any case to suppose that a whole community might be deceitful towards me in regard to certain terms, without also being deceitful towards one another. As interpreter my evidence, serving both in discovery and justification of hypotheses, may include the communications of aliens with one another as well as their attempts to communicate with me and I might surely have unobtrusive access to those communications. In the situation, however, where everybody deceives everybody in certain respects, one has to ask after the point of the activity. The normal point of deception is to mislead an audience, but in systematic deception the system would appear to defeat that aim. If a community uses certain terms in a particular way then no sense can be given to the idea that this is not the correct way and that the terms really have a different meaning. The fact reflects a general truth about matters conventional, of which we take language to be one: that the convention used by the majority just is the convention. It points to the primacy of practice in establishing which convention operates. There may be a complex set of beliefs in the community about what the convention is but if the practice does not accord with those beliefs, if it flouts the beliefs without disrupting social life and without inviting sanction, then the operative convention is that which is exemplified by the actions of the people involved. This is not to deny the possibility of a community of pranksters who take delight in misleading one another, giving wrong bus times, incorrect routes, and so on. It is only to say that such deception has to take place against a background of agreement, a background against which the interpreter will be able, if only with difficulty, to sort out truth from falsehood.

With these remarks on individual and communal deceitfulness, we may return to the assumption, not just that the radical interpreter can identify assertions and other utterance types, but also that she can distinguish sincere assertions: in Davidson's terms, that she can discern among the sentences asserted those which the foreigners hold true. Returned to this assumption, however, we still have to consider whether the interpreter may have her efforts undermined through individual or communal error. Individual error, case 2 in our list of possibilities above, does not raise a severe problem. Like individual deceitfulness, it should be detectable from the fact of divergences between the informant's assertions and those of other members of the community. The interpreter may not be able to say whether she is dealing with a deceitful or a mistaken informant but she will certainly be in a position to learn that it would be folly to build an interpretation of the language on the basis of the informant's assertions. Exercising charity in respect of those assertions, she could not construct a theory that would be suitable for the language as it is used generally in the community.

Finally we come to case 1 in the list of possible ways in which a foreigner's assertion may be false: the case of communal error. We need concern ourselves only with wholesale communal error since limited error will be explicable and will not cause the interpreter any particular problem. Anthropologists and philosophers of anthropology have distinguished at least two ways in which what we would take as massive communal error may come about among an alien people. First, as it is put, they may inhabit a different world, operate with a different conceptual scheme, have categorially different minds; second, they may share our conceptual scheme but have a different logic. The first view is associated with the relativism of Sapir and Whorf, the second with the approach taken by Levy-Bruhl when he ascribes a 'pre-logical' mind to certain so-called primitive peoples: 'pre-logical', we are assuming, does not mean 'a-logical'. Both views suggest that, judged by our standards - the only standards by which we can judge them - the beliefs of foreigners may turn out to be mainly false: this, at least if we insist on cross-cultural comparison, against the wishes of Sapir and Whorf. The situation, if realised, would appear to undermine the possibility of uncovering meaning by the procedure outlined earlier, it would seem to confound the charitable assumption that assertions held true by foreigners are indeed, for the most part, true.

Is the situation a serious possibility? Davidson, for one, has suggested that it is not. 'What makes interpretation possible, then, is the fact that we can dismiss *a priori* the chance of massive error. A theory of interpretation cannot be correct that makes a man assent to very many false sentences: it must generally be the case that a sentence is true when a speaker holds it to be. . . . In the end, what must be counted in favour of a method of interpretation is that it puts the interpreter in general agreement with the speaker' (Davidson 1975, p.21). The supposed necessity of agreement is explained as follows. 'We can, however, take it as given that *most* beliefs are correct. The reason for this is that a belief is identified by its location in a pattern of beliefs; it is this pattern that determines the subject matter of the belief, what the belief is about. Before some object in, or object of, the world can become part of the subject matter of a belief (true or false) there must be endless true beliefs about the subject matter' (Davidson 1975, p.20).

The picture is this. Suppose that someone says 'Die hund is root' and that we take her to be speaking about the dog and to be saying, perhaps falsely, that the dog is red. We take her to be saying that the dog is red because of how we interpret 'root' as it occurs in other assertions, assertions which that interpretation generally makes out to be true; if it made them out to be mainly false, the interpretation would be suspect and we would not feel pressurised into characterising our speaker as saying that the dog is red. On the other hand we take the speaker to be speaking about the dog because we assume that she holds true various sentences about that entity in which we would concur: that it has a fluffy coat, that it bites postmen, and so on. If we found that the speaker did not hold these things to be true but believed on the contrary that the dog was round and smooth, and served as a toy, we would be brought up short in our construal; in all likelihood, assuming these collateral beliefs to be true, we would conclude that she was speaking, not about the dog, but about the local soccer ball.

Applied to certain singular terms in language, in particular proper names, Davidson's view amounts to a form of the so-called description theory of reference. There are a variety of description accounts, primarily due to Frege, Strawson and Searle, but the most succinct of all is Neil Wilson's. 'We select as designation that individual which will make the largest possible number of . . . statements true' (Wilson 1959, p.532). This account of how reference is fixed is a description theory because it supposes that in identifying the X which speakers describe as A and B and C, we should assume that a maximum number of those descriptions are true and we should then use the descriptions as guidelines to the identification: the X in question is whatever it is that satisfies description as A and as B and as C. Such an account is tied up with Davidson's general view, as we can see if we consider what referent ought to be ascribed to 'Fido' in the case where the speakers from our example hold, so far as we can see, that Fido is a dog but also that it is round and smooth, that it is a toy and that it is kicked around by the local schoolchildren. Both Davidson and Wilson would presumably take the term to denote the soccer ball in such an instance, ascribing a novel, and perhaps non-standard, meaning to the term previously translated as 'dog': this, assuming at least that the speakers do not evince the beliefs associated with holding that Fido is a dog, such as that he barks, has four legs, and so on.

If the description theory of reference is an application of Davidson's general view on how the subject matter of assertion is identified, it may well be thought relevant that this theory has come in for criticism in recent years. Saul Kripke has put forward as an alternative the 'rigid designation' view, according to which proper names have their reference fixed independently of what associated descriptions speakers may hold true; the names designate rigidly, insofar as they would denote the same things even if all the differences possible in associated descriptions were realised (Kripke 1972). Kripke's idea is that a name achieves reference through being used to baptise an object and that this reference is sustained through other speakers' having a certain causal relation to that baptism: they intend to use the term with that same reference, however false such a reference ascription may turn out to make the various sentences involving the name which they hold true.

This novel theory of reference would suggest that in one area of interpretation, the assignment of denotata to proper names, the interpreter should not be guided by charity, she should not set out, in the manner of the description theorist, to ascribe such denotata as will make true a maximum of the associated statements held true by speakers. The fact has suggested to some thinkers that charity has no special claims and that it might be dispensed with altogether in interpretation. Colin McGinn speculates as follows: 'we may equally provide a basis for deriving the meanings of sentences held-true by uncharitably imparting false beliefs to our speaker. We simply suppose, with or without good reason, that he has made a mistake and is expressing a false belief with a corresponding false sentence' (McGinn 1977, p.523).

This response seems to us to be an over-reaction. Even if we should take the proper names, and perhaps some other singular terms, of a foreign language as rigid designators, we are not yet exempted from taking charitable considerations into account. McGinn seems to suppose that assigning denotata to singular terms can be isolated from assigning ranges of application, extensions, to predicates, and this supposition is highly questionable. If we assigned denotata without any thought for truth, we might discover that predicates which otherwise we would have spontaneously taken as certain predicates of colour or weight or size or shape had extensions which cast doubt on such an interpretation: the assignment might force us to represent the speakers as believing that inappropriate objects were all green, or of the same weight, or whatever, if we held onto the natural reading of the predicates. In such a case it is doubtful if the sensible interpretative line would prescribe neglect of charity. More generally, in the ascription of extensions to at least some predicates we are certainly not released from the obligation of charity by any consideration arising from the rigid designation theory of reference. If the interpretees use qualitative and comparative expressions, for example, it is difficult to see how any adequate interpretation could represent them as having a preponderance of associated false beliefs: a preponderance of false beliefs about such matters as whether one person is taller than another, whether it is a shorter distance to the river or to the forest, whether beaver fur is soft or rough, whether certain flowers are blue or green, and so on.

In making his case McGinn mentions as an example of uncharitable interpretation our imputation to the ancients of the belief that the stars are apertures in a heavenly dome, apertures through which light shines (McGinn 1977, p.525). His thought is that we naturally find it reasonable to interpret the ancients as speaking about what we know as the stars, even when this means attributing to them a great variety of what we must take as false beliefs. In connection with this example, and the point is of general importance, what needs to be mentioned is the difficulty in counting beliefs. It might well be argued that in taking the ancients to have been speaking about the stars we are actually making more of their beliefs true than we would have done had we sought to represent them as holding forth on some other matter in their discourse about apertures and the like. We take them to believe, correctly, that the stars are up above us, that they emit light, that the light comes as if from comparatively tiny apertures, and so on. Since we lack a firm method for identifying and counting beliefs, it is not clear how we can say for sure that the interpretation actually adopted is not in fact the most charitable one. Here we come upon a general weakness in the method of seeking to maximise agreement in interpretation, a weakness which is overcome in the method characterised in the next section, but it need not detain us at the moment. All that we are presently concerned to notice is that however difficult it may be to apply the method of charity in practice, there is no short way of undermining it by appeal to the rigid designation theory of reference.

What are we to say then about the possibility of massive error: the possibility that on a certain range of topics a whole community is mistaken? In general we are in sympathy with the line taken by Davidson but we do not think it is necessary to rest the case on contentions as to what is required for fixing the subject matter of assertion. A better approach to the topic, it seems to us, is to distinguish among the beliefs of speakers between those that inform their practical activity and those which are unrelated to everyday needs and actions, and to press the view that, whatever about the second category, we cannot seriously consider representing the first as significantly mistaken. By the beliefs which inform practical activity we mean those beliefs which we are forced to postulate by way of explaining the things that the people do in their unproblematic, everyday negotiation of their environment. The assumption is that some such beliefs will find expression in the sentences held true by speakers and with sentences of the kind we think that there will be little option but to take them as indeed true.

There are two grounds on which the beliefs which inform practical activity should recommend themselves for consideration by the interpreter. The first is that there is no doubt but that the beliefs in question should indeed be ascribed to the speakers: or at least none independently of any question about the action explanations in which they appear. This may not seem to be much of a benefit until we reflect that often there is a difficulty about what beliefs to assign to people. The difficulty appears when we ask whether a tribe who are ascribed true beliefs about the spatial relationships of their huts, should also be attributed corresponding true beliefs about the spatial relationships of islands in a lake or constellations in the sky. If in the one case they have grasped the applications, and the implications of applying, such concepts as those of what is to the right, what to the left, what in between, and so on, should they be taken to have a similar grasp in the other cases and should this assumption guide the interpretation of what they say? We get over such a difficulty by concentrating on beliefs involved in everyday action. In taking any piece of behaviour as an action we assume that it issues from a desire to achieve a certain outcome and a belief that the course of behaviour in question at least stands a good chance of realising that outcome: we assume, as we may say, that the event is behaviourally rational. This means that what agents do dictates to us what beliefs we should ascribe to them in the relevantly associated matters: these will include beliefs about the alternatives on offer, the outcomes foreseeable, the relative desirability of the outcomes, and so on. Thus in the area of beliefs informing practical activity we can achieve a significant determinancy about what it is that people actually maintain.

The second ground on which the beliefs which inform practical activity should recommend themselves to the interpreter is that for the main part we must take them to be true. The actions which the beliefs are invoked to explain are people's everyday, more or less successful exchanges with one another and with their environment: actions such as those of finding food, making deals, building huts, and so on. The success of these exchanges cannot be generally put down to coincidence and fortune. But if we are to make the success intelligible without invoking the forces of accident, we must suppose that the beliefs underlying the actions are true: were they false, success would have to be the product of accident. Thus we find in the beliefs informing practical activity a set of beliefs in which the interpreter may safely assume a preponderance of truth.

This line of thought suggests then that at least with respect to one class of beliefs it is reasonable to assume with Davidson that massive communal error is out of the question. So far as we support it, however, the conclusion is conditional. It says that if a society of foreigners is to be taken as a group of agents many of whose doings are behaviourally rational, and if we are to understand them in a manner akin to our understanding of one another, then we must be able to sustain the assumption that the beliefs informing their practical activity are for the most part true. This conclusion does not close the possibility that we may come across a tribe whose actions are so chaotic and incoherent from our point of view that we cannot identify persistent beliefs which would represent them as rational. Were that possibility realised we might well come to doubt that the individuals were properly agents or we might continue to assume agency but despair of ever understanding their mentality: in this second case we might postulate a deep difference in conceptual scheme or logic. Thus we do not think that the possibility of communal error of a massive kind can be ruled out unconditionally: there is no a priori argument which can show that it is incoherent.

Although it is conditional however, the conclusion which we have reached about massive communal error is not inconsequential. The only effective way we have of understanding human beings is to take the doings which we describe as actions to be the behaviourally rational outcome of beliefs and desires and to use those doings therefore as a token of the agents' mental states. What we have concluded is that if in this sense we are to come to understand a society of aliens, then we must be able to see most of the beliefs informing their practical activity as true. To return to the specific matter of linguistic interpretation, this conclusion would have bite in forcing us to take assertions expressing such practical beliefs as mainly true. It would prohibit us from adopting the uncharitable line mentioned by McGinn, whereby we would assume that most of the assertions were false. Were we to take that line then the beliefs - the states of holding sentences true - employed to explain certain assertions would be at variance with the beliefs invoked to make sense of practical everyday behaviour. We would have to translate as 'My hut is to the left of the tree' an assertion associated with the action of walking in the other direction to the hut, an action which forces us to conclude the person believes the hut is to the right of the tree.

We began this section by raising two problems which the radical interpreter must confront. The first of these was that for any alien assertion there will be too many truths that it may be taken to express, the second that we have no guarantee in any case that the assertion is not false. A solution to the first problem is suggested by Neil Wilson's method of charity: the method of assuming that one pattern of interpretation is better than another if, at least with respect to certain sorts of belief, it represents the foreigners as agreeing with us in a higher degree that the other. Having mentioned this possible solution we turned to the second problem, our particular concern being to see whether the possibility of falsehood would confound the exercise of charity in interpretation. We distinguished four ways in which an alien assertion may come to be false: through individual or communal deceitfulness or through individual or communal error. The real problem comes up with the possibility of communal error, specifically error of a wholesale kind. Even in face of this possibility however we have found reason to think that charity is not as misplaced as might have been thought. At least with respect to beliefs which inform practical activity, it seems reasonable to try to work with the assumption that communal error is out of the question.

Having seen that charity has its virtues, the next stage in our investigation will be to see how we may refine the method that it represents. Before leaving this section however it may be worth remarking that we are not committed to the view that the only possible way to attempt radical interpretation is first to identify the sentences held true by the foreigners - a procedure which, as we noted, has its own problems - next to try to work out the truth-conditions that ought to be assigned to those sentences and only finally to see whether the beliefs thereby attributed can be squared with the non-linguistic behaviour of the people in question. That strategy may turn out to be the most straightforward one but we have nothing in principle against such alternatives as that which would recommend starting with the non-linguistic behaviour or perhaps the evidential situation of the foreigners, using one or both of these to develop a view of their beliefs, and only coming later to the identification of the sentences held true and of the truth-conditions of those sentences. The interpreter must be concerned at once with the identification of sentences held-true, the assignment of truth-conditions, and the ascription of belief on a non-linguistic basis, and there is no reason in principle why she has to prefer one or another point of entry to this system of elements (for a discussion see D. Lewis 1974). In what follows we shall be concerning ourselves with how the interpreter may fix the beliefs, and the desires, of agents but we shall leave open the question of which strategy she should follow.

## 3 FROM CHARITY TO HUMANITY

In introducing the principle of charity in the last section we mentioned that it was scarcely persuasive: the reason given was that in advocating maximisation of agreement in interpretation it counsels neglect of considerations as to whether the interpretees are likely to have attained knowledge of the truths on which they are construed as agreeing. That objection gives us a cue for proposing an alternative to the principle of charity: an alternative which is related sufficiently closely to it to gain support from the reasons given in defence of charity. The alternative, which Richard Grandy has christened 'the principle of humanity', says that the interpreter should not so much maximise agreement, whatever the cost, as minimise a certain sort of disagreement, specifically disagreement which we find unintelligible.[4] Where charity would have us recoil from the ascription of any disagreement or, as we are going to see it, error, humanity would only have us do so when we cannot explain how such disagreement or error could have come about. Thus while the principle of humanity would evade the complaint we made against its counterpart, it still succeeds in engaging with the considerations that we mentioned in the last section in support of charity. That we should expect beliefs which inform practical activity to be true gives at least as much reason for endorsing humanity as it does charity. The reason is that it is precisely in such everyday matters as those covered by these beliefs that we would find error scarcely intelligible.

The principle of humanity clearly requires that we have some criteria of intelligibility by which to guide the ascription of belief. One such criterion is given by the assumption of behavioural rationality mentioned in the last section. If we are to relate to agents as persons then we must treat at least some pieces of their behaviour as actions in the proper sense: we must take them as events that each issue from a desire to achieve a certain outcome and a belief that the behaviour at least stands a good chance of realising that outcome. This means that we must ascribe such beliefs as make sense of those actions that we impute to our subjects and we must not ascribe any that are incompatible with the actions. Here we have our first constraint on belief ascription, our first criterion as to what beliefs it is intelligible to attribute to people. As a constraint it will only have a cutting edge when it is clear what desires the people are liable to have but we postpone that topic until later in the section.

A second criterion of intelligibility in belief ascription derives from the assumption, not just that people are behaviourally rational, but that they are also attitudinally so. This assumption will be discussed in the next chapter. It means at a minimum that we expect our subjects to conform to certain inductive and deductive standards in the beliefs they form and maintain. The expectation of inductive sensitivity appears at a first level in the fact that we cannot envisage ascribing perceptual beliefs to people about matters with which they have not been brought into causal connection: this was mentioned in section 2 in relation to the so-called accessibility constraint; at a second, in our disposition to find people concerned about what we see as counterexamples to the beliefs we have imputed to them; and at a third in our assumption that people have views systematically related to their experience about what effects their future behaviour will have. We may be prepared to find that people are often inductively fairly stupid, and certainly we should be ready to recognise the possibility of variation in inductive standards, but it is hardly conceivable that we should ascribe beliefs without assuming some sort of responsiveness to what we take as relevant evidence. If we attributed a certain belief and then found that the agent to whom the belief was attributed was quite insensitive to evidential considerations, that she tended to assert it or question it in a pattern uncorrelated with the evidence on hand, we would be given reason by that very fact to wonder about whether we had got the attribution right in the first place.

We must expect people to be deductively sensitive on the other hand insofar as we ascribe to them a disposition to draw consequences from what they come to believe, a disposition without which human planning and organisation is scarcely conceivable.[5] We may find reasons for ascribing to certain foreigners a deductive logic which differs in some way from our own: this will be discussed in section 5. However the natural line will be to assume that in their reasoning they follow familiar principles. If they believe P, we will certainly take it that they do not believe not-P, if they believe P and believe Q, that they do not believe not-(P and Q), and so on. The principles are constraints on the ideal believer and may not be followed in all cases but we will expect them to serve as norms, and we look for explanations by reference to disturbing influences of departures from them. The disturbing influence may be laziness, or dimness, some psychological pressure or some sort of social conditioning.

The assumptions of behavioural and attitudinal rationality form the core of a sort of theory of persons. To call it a theory is to aggrandise it: better perhaps to characterise it as 'nothing more than a mass of platitudes of common sense, though these may be reorganised in perspicuous and unfamiliar ways' (D. Lewis 1974, p.335). So far we have mentioned as part of the content of this theory only platitudes about people's common inductive and deductive propensities: that is, about their sensitivity to evidence and consistency. In addition we should recognise that we may also count as part of the theory platitudes about how such propensities are sharpened and developed. David Lewis points out that we naturally acknowledge dispositions to sharpen and develop those propensities under certain conditions: dispositions to give them precise expression as tools for the assessment of scientific evidence. In applying the principle of humanity we will want to put our beliefs about these dispositions into play, as well as our lower order beliefs about the propensities themselves. Thus if certain aliens have not been exposed to the conditions required for the development of refined tools of evidence assessment, we would denounce as implausible any interpretation that assigned beliefs which presupposed the operation of such instruments. The crucial question will be: if we had been placed in their circumstances and given their training, would we have developed such and such inductive and deductive habits, and would we have been led to form beliefs based on those habits?

It is clear from what has been said earlier that the principle of humanity represents a refinement of the principle of charity. One important respect in which it is continuous with that principle is that it rests on a belief in the unity of human nature: a belief that people in different cultures are essentially similar. Understood in accordance with the principle of humanity the thesis is that any differences there are across cultures, or at least any differences central to the attitudes and actions of people, should be explicable by reference to different circumstances. The point was already made by Hume. 'The philosopher, if he be consistent, must apply the same reasoning to the actions and volitions of intelligent agents. The most irregular and unexpected resolutions of men may frequently be accounted for by those who know every particular circumstance of their character and situation' (Hume 1902, p.88). The belief in the unity of human nature which both the principle of charity and the principle of humanity suppose is an essential precondition of interpretation. Were it rejected then there would be no point in that exercise, for what interpretation means is coming to understand our interpretees in the way in which we understand one another in our personal exchanges: it involves gaining access 'to the conceptual world in which our subjects live so that we can, in some extended sense of the term, converse with them' (Geertz 1975, p.24).

While the principle of humanity is parallel in many ways to the principle of charity, one point of difference which needs to be mentioned is this. The principle invites the interpreter to perform the thought experiment of working out what she would come to believe, and ultimately do, if she were put in the circumstances of her interpretees, the assumption being that it is those circumstances which will explain any differences between her beliefs and theirs.[6] The invitation pre-supposes that the interpreter knows a lot about the circumstances in question and here a problem arises which is specific to the principle of humanity. The problem is that what appears to be inexplicable error on the part of certain foreigners, and what would count therefore against certain interpretations, might become explicable in the light of some special theory about the social and psychological situation of the interpretees, but that such special theory is vindicated only through making possible an adequate theory of interpretation. If the factors by reference to which the error becomes explicable are physical, if they have to do with the technological state of the community for example, then the difficulty is not serious. If social or psychological structures are involved however, it appears that we may have to move in a circle.

The dilemma is unavoidable and the only solution is to grasp both horns simultaneously. Assuming some special theory concerning psychological and sociological determinants of belief, we make a first attempt to understand the utterances and actions of our subjects and if this attempt is less than fully satisfying we change our assumptions in some measure and have a second go: and so on until satisfaction is attained. In this exercise we have to make use of special theories of which we have some knowledge as a starting point but it must be admitted that if we start off with Freudian theory as one of our interpretative instruments, for example, we are liable to go in a very different direction from that which we would have taken had we adopted a Skinnerian theory. The exercise is not a straightforward matter of starting off with a theory such as the Freudian one, seeing if it fits the facts available to one as interpreter and, if it does not, rejecting the theory or at least denying its unversal application. What the facts are deemed to be will partly depend on the theory assumed as starting point and so they cannot be expected to offer a base for questioning the theory. The circle however need not be regarded as hopeless. The interpreter will be in a position, at least in principle, to work out, not just what the facts come to when interpretation is guided by Freudian theory, but also what they consist in when the interpretation has a Skinnerian or some other starting point. A comparison between the rival interpretative patterns may enable her then to decide the question as to which theory ought to underlie her enterprise.

The comparison, to be somewhat more specific, may give an interpreter one or both of at least two reasons for preferring one pattern of interpretation to another. First of all it may show that one pattern represents as intentional and intelligible more of the interpretees' behaviour than does the other: it may indicate that one pattern is more comprehensive than the other. Second, the comparison may reveal that one pattern is able to make sense of the things done and said by interpretees without such reliance as the other on special ad hoc assumptions: it may make it clear that one pattern is simpler than the other. Comprehensiveness and simplicity seem to us to be grounds on which an interpreter may rationally make a preference as between different ways of construing what is said, and done, by her subjects.

The problem of theory choice in interpretation is more serious, it should be noticed, than the sort of problem in natural science which is often nowadays described as the theory-ladenness of data. In interpretation the data are theory-laden in the strong sense that how they are characterised may depend in part on which of the very theories under competition is adopted. In natural science the data may be theory-laden in the sense that perception is directed by a certain encompassing theory of what there is, but usually their characterisation will not depend on which of the competing theories is embraced. This may be overlooked because what certainly does depend on which of those theories is accepted is the scientist's reaction to how the data turn out to be: as Kuhn shows, this may determine for example whether the scientist sees a certain negative test result as a refutation of the theory or as a more or less insignificant anomaly (see Kuhn 1970).

Leaving aside the problem of theory choice to which the principle of humanity gives rise, it will be useful now if we make some connections between the application of the principle and the concrete practice of anthropologists. In particular we would like to mention two cases where the principle would yield contrary advice to that which is given by Evans-Pritchard. To take up the first case, Evans-Pritchard, whilst inveighing against atheistic anthropologists attempting to explain away 'primitive' religion (and implicitly, with it, Christianity) as an 'intellectual aberration, as a mirage induced by emotional stress, or by its social function . . .', still wants to maintain that the anthropologist, qua anthropologist, is not concerned with the truth or falsity of religious thought. 'The beliefs are for him sociological facts, not theological facts, and his sole concern is with their relation to each other and to other social facts. . . . It was precisely because so many anthropological writers did take up a theological position, albeit a negative and implicit one, that they felt that an explanation of primitive religious phenomena in causal terms was required' (Evans-Pritchard 1965, pp.15-17).

Our contention as against this is that one's own opinion about the truth or falsity of the aliens' beliefs will affect the kind of explanation one gives of them. A long-standing problem in anthropology for example is the longevity of beliefs that appear to be manifestly false. This is a problem precisely because the beliefs are taken to be obviously incorrect: it would not arise if they were true, or were not so clearly false. An explanation of why a Westerner goes to the doctor when ill will be framed in terms of that person's belief in the efficacy of the prescribed medicine. If the medicine is efficacious, then no further explanation of the belief or the behaviour seems to be required. If the medicine is consistently useless in remedying the ailment, however, the persistence of the belief, and the behaviour, immediately requires explaining. It is the same with some of the rituals of a variety of tribespeople. If these are interpreted as attempts to control the environment (e.g. to bring rain), then the truth or falsity of the conditional 'If we do this dance now, then rain will fall' will determine the kind of explanation given of their beliefs and actions.

This is a fairly simple example of the way in which judgments about truth-values may be relevant to understanding aliens. That they have to be so is evident if the principle of humanity is to be used in selecting an interpretation. Minimising inexplicable error depends upon identifying error, and this will always be relative to our own beliefs. None of this should be taken to imply that when true belief is at issue there is no room for causal explanation. In some cases the true belief may be acquired 'accidentally', i.e. in a manner in which the truth-conditions played no part, or did not play the 'correct' causal role. And even in cases where the true belief is properly acquired, causation still plays a role; in these cases the causal factors are usually sufficiently transparent not to require emphasis. What remains are cases where the mistaken nature of the belief is very much evident (in our opinion); here explanations by reference to social function or psychological pressure may be worth exploring.

A second case where the principle of humanity pits us against Evans-Pritchard is in relation to the so-called 'If I were a horse' fallacy. In criticising, amongst others, Frazer, he argues that the introspectionist bias in Frazer's method accounted for some of his errors. 'How often have we been warned not to try to interpret the thought of ancient or primitive peoples in terms of our own psychology. . . . it is all too easy, when translating the conceptions of the simpler peoples into our own, to transplant our thought into theirs' (Evans-Pritchard 1965, p.109).

The accusation of introspectionist method does not necessarily carry against someone who applied the principle of working out what it would be like to be in the position of others. The self-knowledge required for the application of that principle may be attained in a non-introspective manner. It may be derived for example from what others say about one or it may be acquired through reflection on the nature of the society one lives in and one's position within it. Granted this, is there any basis for criticising the use of the principle: are there any grounds for speaking of a fallacy in connection with its interpretative employment? We do not think so. The only charge which it may be sensible to bring against interpreters who follow the procedure is that they have not been careful enough in building the basis of self-knowledge on which they pursue their interpretations. If Evans-Pritchard has reason to complain about Frazer's method, it may be found here. The interpretations put forward by Frazer may well fail to be informed by what we would regard nowadays as the most reliable theories as to the effects on belief of different psychological or sociological circumstances. Such a criticism however should not be inflated into a wholesale rejection of the interpretative method of putting oneself in the position of one's interpretees.

Compelling though our reflections may have made it seem, it appears nonetheless that the principle of humanity may put us in conflict with the received wisdom of much practising anthropology. We shall not develop that theme further in this section but it will appear again in the next two. In the remainder of the present section we would like to mention a class of platitudes within our everyday theory of persons which we have so far ignored. This bears, not on the beliefs which people are likely to form, but rather on their desires. We cannot afford to neglect desires in the enterprise of interpretation for the belief or beliefs which we invoke to explain any linguistic or non-linguistic action is a plausible explanatory candidate only so far as appropriate desires are assumed to have been present in the agent. What desires then ought we to expect to guide people in different circumstances, even when the people are from another culture? We might reasonably expect certain second order desires always to operate, such as the desire to achieve whatever end is proposed by the most efficient means available: this desire gives expression to what is often called instrumental rationality. But can we form reasonable expectations about the content of lower order desires? The issue will be dealt with in detail in the final chapter of this book but it will be useful to give a preliminary survey of it here.

The question comes down to the following. When we explain the actions of aliens by postulating certain desires that weigh with them, have we any way of telling whether it is reasonable to ascribe those desires, and in particular whether it is more reasonable to ascribe them than it is to ascribe a set which is associated with a different pattern of action explanation? The answer to which the principle of humanity points should be obvious. In parallel to the belief case, the test will be whether differences in the desires attributed are plausible in the light of our own views concerning the formation of our own desires. The effect of social conditioning, the knowledge of esteemed behaviour, the functional needs of the society and the like will all have to be taken into account in attributing to members of a foreign society a certain set of desires. We need not make the alien 'a lover of the good (all by our own lights . . .)' (Davidson 1970, p.97); but where goodness departs from 'our own lights' then we must have a unifying explanation of the departure, i.e. an explanation which is able to give an account of the evaluative scheme of both the aliens and ourselves.

It is clear that our understanding of others will need to take into account not only what they spontaneously desire, but also what they find admirable for ethical reasons and the like. This necessitates a description of them as moral agents, with an accompanying moral code which informs many of their actions. Even the morally blighted society of the Ik still recognises (in a passive fashion) certain moral rules, norms of behaviour transgression of which invites blame and sanction (see Turnbull 1974). This identification of a people's moral attitudes however is a particularly tricky interpretative issue, since the relation of moral beliefs and the perceptible environment is far less 'obvious' than in other cases. The attribution of a classifying scheme of actions (as good, virtuous, cowardly and so on) requires more interpretation than attribution of beliefs to do with one's relationship to the river, other people, one's house, and so on. This is reflected in the belief that there is a smaller degree of consensus on such a classification within one's speech community than exists with respect to other matters which are more closely connected to environmental conditioning. Nevertheless there is still a prima facie case for using our moral dispositions as a first guide to the dispositions of foreigners. This case rests on the assumption that there is something common to the actions or states-of-affairs we and the aliens describe using corresponding evaluative terms and that, even if the extensions of the terms vary, there must at least be a common attitude maintained towards the members of the extensions.

Such an assumption may of course be confounded. For example a divergence in action, attitude, or expression of attitude will leave us undecided as to what term is best suited. Thus, apparently, classification of West African 'jokes' is rather hazardous. 'What is *said* is "we insult" - but they laugh rather than take offence so the foreign observer calls it joking' ('Times Literary Supplement', 30 April 1976). This argues for a certain indeterminacy in interpretative conclusions: one way of describing the situation will be better than another, depending on which features are taken to be more important. In the above example the response - laughing - is taken to be more indicative of the type of speech act performed than is the description of it given by the agent; this, presumably, is because an insult is a successful speech act only when there is 'uptake' on the part of the person insulted, and laughing indicates that such uptake has not been realised. The situation will be similar with the more obviously evaluative predicates; the problematic cases will be determined by those criteria of application we deem more important. If we think of some actions as clearly desirable, or some states of affairs as those that ought, in these circumstances, to be realised, then a failure on the part of the aliens to behave in the suggested manner can be explained as due either to their 'blindness' with respect to those value-impregnated features of the situation, or as due to their recognition of what is good but refusal to act accordingly, or as due to their perception of a good not recognised as such by ourselves.

If we take behaviour as a central indicator of the evaluative scheme accepted by the agent, then the second course will not be inviting. This leaves us with the first or third options, either of which would mean explaining how the alien has adopted a different framework. How we explain the difference will depend upon the theory we adopt concerning moral predicates: whether we take them to be descriptive of reality or not, i.e. whether we are realist or not concerning them. The realist view would need to explain why it is that these people are ignorant of aspects of their environment which are apparent to us; or why it is that we have been mistaken for so long concerning our own evaluations. The opposing view can explain the differences as arising from the relativist nature of morality; there is not, on this view, a correct moral viewpoint, so differences need not be described as deviations from rectitude.

The question of how far the principle of humanity limits the attribution of desires is clearly a complex one and will be taken up again in the final chapter. In concluding the discussion of that principle which we have conducted in this section it may be useful to summarise the main points which have been made. We have seen that rather than taking charity to the lengths of minimising all disagreement, it would seem to be a more sensible interpretative strategy only to be concerned with minimising unintelligible disagreement. In applying such a strategy we saw that the interpreter would have to rely on a theory of persons which would give her some idea of when disagreement is intelligible and when it is not. This theory, filled out with more recondite speculations from psychology and sociology will be vindicated as an interpretative tool to the extent to which it facilitates a more comprehensive and simpler pattern than is otherwise available. As to what we might expect to find intelligible and what unintelligible, the following points emerged. (a) A piece of behaviour is an intelligible action only if it is behaviourally rational, issuing from an appropriate set of beliefs and desires. (b) Beliefs are intelligible only if they satisfy certain constraints of attitudinal rationality: in particular, only if they accord with recognised inductive and deductive patterns or accord with patterns the existence of which we can explain in the circumstances of the believers. (c) Desires are intelligible only if something similar obtains: the desires, whether spontaneously or ethically motivated, must either be ones that we ourselves might uphold on the occasions in question or ones the existence of which we can explain, granted the experience and conditioning of the people in question. In view of the parallel between the two we might well speak of desires being subject like beliefs to constraints of attitudinal rationality but if we do so we must keep in mind the issue which we are postponing until the last chapter: that of whether desires, or more properly judgments of desirability, should be taken in a realist manner or not; the question of how seriously the parallel between beliefs and desires ought to be taken turns in great part on this issue.

## 4 THE REPUDIATION OF RATIONALITY

The constraints on interpretation involved in applying the principle of humanity may seem so obvious as scarcely to be worth stating. Obvious though they are, however, anthropologists have often despaired of finding interpretations which will satisfy them. This despair leads to the denial that the utterances and actions in question are rational in our sense of that term or, more radically, to the denial that they are rational at all. The one approach would sponsor a relativisation of rationality and we will look at it in the next section. The other would propose the repudiation of rationality: it would refuse to consider the events in question as the behaviourally rational outcome of attitudinally rational mental states. This second route, which we will examine in the present section, may take the form either of explaining the sayings and doings in functionalist terms, or of explaining them by reference to their symbolic significance.

We shall be looking at functionalism in some detail in the third chapter of this book but it is necessary to examine it in the present context to see whether it represents a reasonable interpretative recourse. In general functionalism views society as an integrated whole, the parts of which survive and flourish insofar as they serve to maintain the whole. Thus the functionalist's presumption on being presented with some social pattern or practice is, regardless of the apparent point or lack of point in the behaviour, to show that it has some socially useful role, a role which accounts for its appearance or at least its persistence. Functionalism serves well the anthropologist who despairs of making rational sense of a certain stretch of linguistic or non-linguistic behaviour, for it suggests that the behaviour may be explicable, even if it fails of being rationally comprehensible. To mention a stock example, the Hopi rain dances may be manifestly ineffective in bringing about precipitation but they may serve for all that to promote group identity, providing an occasion on which members of the society assemble for co-ordinated activity.

In order to get a better grasp on the nature of the functionalist approach it may be useful, following Jon Elster, to spell out some necessary and jointly sufficient conditions for an explanation to be functional (see Elster 1979, p.28).

(1) The function, Y, of the institution (or behavioural regularity), X, must be an effect of X.
(2) Y must be beneficial for the society (or group) Z.
(3) Y is unintended by the actors producing X.
(4) Y (or the causal relationship between X and Y) is unrecognised by the actors in Z.
(5) Y maintains X by a causal feedback loop passing through Z.

Some features of this outline may appear questionable if they are taken as definitional of functional explanation in general: in particular, the stipulation that Y is unintended, and that the causal connection between X and Y is unrecognised, may seem unnecessary. However, as Elster indicates, the non-recognition by the actors of Y is what has given some functionalist analyses their point. For our purposes, such non-awareness is necessary: functionalism is being put forward as a way of avoiding strange interpretations which some actions appear to require. In effect, what it does is to specify a function (e.g. reinforcement of group-identity) which is a by-product of the intentional activity. If this by-product was recognised as such by agents, and recognised to be beneficial, then they would have every reason to achieve the same ends by direct means, rather than the presently-practised indirect method. It is also clear that non-recognition is implied by Merton's distinction between manifest and latent functions, the latent (real) function being hidden from view (Merton 1957, Ch. 1).

The question to which functionalism was posed as a solution was: why does manifestly irrational activity persist? Its answer is in terms of the unintended effects of the behaviour. There are a number of grounds on which fault can be found with functionalism - we shall be considering one important ground in Chapter 3 - but here we would like to mention just one problem with the approach. The problem is that if, as seems necessary, the functional aspect of the activity remains unrecognised by the actors, then we have not answered the original question. If the agents perceive their actions in terms of attempts to bring rain, and the continued presence of this behaviour in the community is manifestly irrational (no rain is consequent upon the rain-dance), then why do they persist in acting 'stupidly'? That the behaviour serves another function is, ex hypothesi, not known to them, so their own reasons for acting in this way cannot include reference to this function. We are left with the interpretative problem with which we started: how do we explain this behaviour in terms of the beliefs and desires of the agents in such a way as to render their set of propositional attitudes intelligible? The functionalist attempt to bypass the problem does just that without removing the need for a solution. (For an account of ritual which stresses the agents recognition of its significance, see G. Lewis 1980).

This objection, it will be noticed, assumes that the behaviour in question should be taken as action: that is, should be viewed as rational in the minimal sense of issuing from appropriate beliefs and desires. Could the functionalist not reject this assumption and claim that what is given is merely an explanation of certain bodily movements and that there is no need to take those brute events as meaningful actions? We do not think so. The issue will come up in the next chapter but here we can say that the rejection of the assumption in question would be inconsistent with functionalist practice and would be empirically implausible. The starting point for the functionalist is not mere behaviour, but action. The ritual performers in the rain dance are taken to be doing something in the initial characterisation of their behaviour. The segmenting of the behaviour into distinct sequences, for example, is by reference to action categories: the painting of faces, the chanting of a song, the building of a hut; these units form the base on which the functionalist explanation is built. But apart from being out of line with functionalist practice, it would be contrary to much empirical evidence to take such behaviour as something less than action. Rituals are taught and are therefore unlike reflexes. Furthermore they are governed by public rules and are performed only under certain specific circumstances. Finally they are associated with what we naturally take as attempts by the performers to tell us what they are doing, what goals they have in mind, and so on. (See G. Lewis 1980, Ch. 3, for the agent's account of ritual.) Such evidence would have to be discounted if we were to refuse to see the behaviour as action. The functionalist therefore will not find a safe recourse from criticism in such a refusal.

There is a second distinctively anthropological approach which, like functionalism, would deny that certain behaviour is to be understood in the ordinary rational way: that is, as the behaviourally rational outcome of beliefs and desires which satisfy in some degree the constraints of attitudinal rationality. This is the approach of the symbolist. Symbolists reject the so-called 'literalist' or 'intellectualist' assumption that the interpreter ought to take strange behaviour, strange utterances or actions, at face value and seek to determine the propositional attitudes underlying it. On this assumption, the behaviour is taken as instrumentally designed, being an attempt to achieve a certain end. Thus it is seen as the product of beliefs about certain connections in the world, connections relevant to the attainment of that end. Different rituals are viewed as reflecting ideas about how disease can be cured, how fertility can be induced, how drought can be ended, and so on. The symbolist dismisses such intellectualism as naive, arguing that the behaviour does not fit the ordinary rational mould. What is thought to be naive in particular is the idea that people might hold such crazy beliefs about connections in the world as those which ritual, if literally interpreted, must be taken to evince. As with functionalism, the motivation to the symbolist approach is the difficulty of applying the principle of humanity in order to make regular sense of the agents in question.

In order to understand the symbolist's positive proposal it may be useful to recall the distinction drawn in the introduction between semantics and pragmatics or, as they are also called, theory of sense and theory of force. Among the sentences of any language we naturally group together sentences which, intuitively, represent the same state of affairs and reflect different attitudes towards it: the belief that it holds, the wish to know whether it holds, the desire that it should be made to hold, or whatever. An example of such a group of English sentences would be: 'There is a lion in the bushes', 'Is there a lion in the bushes?', 'Let there be a lion in the bushes', 'Would that there were a lion in the bushes'. When we discussed the theory of meaning in the introduction, we noted that if the semantic theory for a language gives us the truth condition of each indicative sentence, the pragmatic theory will tell us how other utterances involving that truth condition relate to the assertoric one. The idea is that semantic and pragmatic theory together should be sufficient to enable us to give the meaning of every sentence in the language: the semantic theory will enable us to understand what is said in the assertion of each indicative sentence, the pragmatic will make it possible for us to see what is meant when various non-assertoric relatives of that assertion are uttered. Those non-assertoric relatives may be non-indicative sentences such as 'Is there a lion in the bushes?' or indicative sentences uttered in such a way or in such a context that they take on a non-assertoric force: an example would be 'There is a lion in the bushes?', uttered in an interrogative tone of voice.

By parallel with the case of assertoric and non-assertoric utterance types, the symbolist argues that we should distinguish between literally significant and symbolically significant actions, whether those actions be linguistic or non-linguistic. The theory is that just as an indicative sentence may be used to make an assertion or to ask a question, so a given action type can have a literal, instrumental significance in one context and have a symbolic, expressive significance in another. With respect to a ritual like the Hopi rain dance, the symbolist would suggest that while the actions which the dancers perform may normally be ones for which it is appropriate to seek a regular explanation in terms of beliefs and desires, they do not call for such explanation in the ritualistic context. In that context, so the theory goes, regular rationality is suspended. The activity is not to be explained in terms of what the agents believe and desire, any more than the interrogative utterance of 'There is a lion in the bushes' is to be explained in terms of what the speaker wishes to assert. And what is the symbolic significance of something like a rain dance going to be? There is no general answer to that question, although we can say that the symbolic meaning will presuppose some element of literal meaning. 'A metaphorically or symbolically expressed thought is a thought expressed in a form which normally does have a literal meaning; what makes it symbolic or metaphorical is just that (i) the literal meaning (if any) of the sentence is not the meaning to be understood, and (ii) the literal meaning of the words must be grasped if one is to "decode" the meaning which is to be understood' (Skorupski 1976, p.13).

Before asking after the criticism of the symbolist approach, one important point must be made clear. This is that we understand the approach as saying that the symbolic significance of the behaviour it bears on is not conscious. Were the claim only that some behaviour is performed out of a desire to express certain thoughts symbolically, and that such behaviour ought not to be understood in the straightforward manner which at first appears appropriate, then we could have no objection in principle to it: that claim would not involve a denial of agent rationality; it would merely make a suggestion about the form such rationality sometimes takes, a suggestion borne out by the fact that on occasion people consciously speak or act in a symbolic way. The symbolist approach that we are considering is not concerned with conscious metaphor or ritual but with behaviour which, on the face of it, has no such symbolic design.

The postulation of unconscious symbolic pattern is reminiscent of the procedure of the psychoanalyst in explaining neurotic phenomena. Take the compulsive hand-washer whose hands, as the psychoanalyst argues, are not literally but metaphorically dirty: they are 'stained' by the guilty association with some real or imaginary past misdeed. The psychoanalyst postulates the unconsciously held belief about guilt in explaining the hand-washing and then appeals to the defence mechanism of repression in order to account for why it remains unconscious.[7] In parallel, the symbolist might be said to postulate unconscious beliefs at the root of the behaviour that she takes as symbolic, seeking out later the reasons why the beliefs remain unconscious. Notice that while the psychoanalytic explanation by reference to unconscious belief, and its symbolist counter-part, would represent the behaviour explained as satisfying or functional, it would still not depict it as rational in the sense involved in the principle of humanity. Peter Alexander has pointed out that a condition on rational action is not only that a person act for a reason, act so as to achieve a desirable outcome, but also that the person act for a reason which is her own: that is, be aware of the desirable outcome to which the action is directed (see Alexander 1962).

How persuasive then is the symbolist response to behaviour of which it is difficult to make straightforward rational sense? In general we think that it fails on the same count as the functionalist, for even when the story has been told about the symbolic purposes unconsciously served by the behaviour we are left with the problem which motivated the symbolist response in the first place. The problem is why people should maintain and act on beliefs which to our eyes are manifestly false. Like the functionalist the symbolist does not tackle that problem but merely bypasses it. Unfortunately however the difficulty persists, indicating that we cannot be satisfied with any claim to the effect that rationality is suspended in the behaviour in question.

There is a more specific line of criticism to which the symbolist approach is also open. If it is going to be plausible to say that on certain occasions agent rationality goes on the blink, so to speak, and that the actions performed on those occasions have a symbolic significance rather than their ordinary literal one, then the symbolist should be required to give us some independent means of identifying those occasions. Otherwise the symbolist theory will be capable of being invoked whenever it proves difficult to make regular sense of certain actions; it will serve as a deus ex machina to rescue the interpreter from every difficulty. By parallel, we naturally require in the interplay between semantics and pragmatics that whenever it proves difficult to interpret an utterance as an assertion and the supposition is made that it has some non-assertoric force, there should generally be independent evidence that the non-assertoric construal is a reasonable one. If 'There is a lion in the bushes' is to be taken as a question then in general there should be some sign that it is a question other than the difficulty of taking it as a literal assertion.

The requirement that we should be given an independent criterion of occasions when actions are liable to have a symbolic rather than a literal significance is one which symbolists sometimes fail to meet. Indeed, as Dan Sperber points out, symbolic action is often defined simply as action to which it is difficult to ascribe literal significance. 'I note then as symbolic all activity where the means put into play seem to me to be clearly disproportionate to the explicit or implicit end, whether this end be knowledge, communication or production- that is to say, all activity whose rationale escapes me' (Sperber 1975, p.4). Another commentator makes the same point and notes that the procedure is a suspect way of defining symbolic acts. 'We cannot make sense of them in terms of an intrinsic means-end relationship and so we assume that the action in question stands for something other than it appears to . . . This is surely hazardous as a way to recognise the "essentially expressive" or the "primarily symbolical" element that characterises ritual' (G. Lewis 1980, p.19).

Even when we put aside our general complaint that the symbolist leaves us with our original problem, and the specific criticism that the approach does not always give us a means for recognising symbolic occasions, there are still serious difficulties to be surmounted. In particular, there is the problem of why it is that the expressive goal allegedly pursued in symbolic activity is not approached consciously and directly. Durkheim gives the following explanation of why religious dogma and ritual should not be taken at face value as representing the nature of the cosmos: 'If that were its essential task, we could not understand how it has been able to survive, for, on this side, it is scarcely more than a fabric of errors. Before all, it is a system of ideas with which the individuals represent to themselves the society of which they are members, and the obscure but intimate relations which they have with it' (Durkheim 1915, p.225). This immediately invites the question of why the representation has to be achieved in a indirect fashion, why social relationships cannot be described in a straightforward manner.

One answer which might be given to this question is that if the social relationships were straightforwardly characterised and clearly understood, their binding force would disintegrate. It might be said that the relationships survive because their exact nature is not known to all, or not even to a majority of, the members of the society. Such an answer may well be found unpersuasive because of the overtones of conspiracy theory. However, even if it could be made to seem plausible, the general difficulty mentioned earlier would remain; indeed it would assume a particularly sharp form. We would still have to explain how it is that people can continue maintaining, and acting on, beliefs which may seem to us more or less plainly false or unwarranted: beliefs which as Durkheim himself sees them are 'little more than a fabric of errors'.

In conclusion it must be conceded that the symbolist approach, as indeed the functionalist, comes in so many forms that it is difficult to be sure that some will not escape any very specific criticisms that one formulates. Just to illustrate the variety, the symbolist offshoots of a Durkheimian approach to religion, an approach which also has a functionalist side, may take either of two forms. It may be said that the real reference and extension of the terms used in ritualistic utterances belong, not to the natural, but to the social world, being constituted by the prevailing social relationships. Alternatively, it may be held that while the utterances designate items in the natural world, they serve in some sense to express matters in the social: structural analogies between ritual beliefs and social relations, and the emotional effects of ritual action, might be seen as evidence of such an expressive function. As symbolist approaches diversify in this way, what is needed is detailed study of the different assumptions made; this however cannot be attempted in the present context.

## 5 THE RELATIVISATION OF RATIONALITY

Neither the symbolist nor the functionalist approaches, nor indeed any combination of them, would appear to give promising solutions to interpretative puzzles. Ethnographic evidence supplies us with reasons for believing that ritual actors have a self-understanding which sees their actions in terms of attempts to control and change the environment. Other functions which such actions and beliefs may have are certainly relevant to the anthropologist; but we still need to find explanations of the actions which would reveal the agents' reasons for acting. Another strategy suggests itself: perhaps the notion of 'reason for acting' is not cross-cultural, perhaps the rationality we have thought necessary is one that is variable between cultures. The underlying thought is that we are being unduly culture-centric in our approach to other societies, with the central culture being our own; we are exercising what has been termed 'linguistic imperialism' in operating a principle of humanity across the board (see Hacking 1975, p.149).

There are two ways in which an alien culture may be said to be incomprehensible. (a) The concepts used by them may be held to defy translation: the aliens employ a different categorial scheme, one which parcels up reality in systematically different ways from the way we do. (b) The inferential links between the concepts or sentences may be deemed to be quite different: the aliens may be seen as operating a radically different logic. Before proceeding to examine such possibilities, it will be worthwhile to consider some of the more general pressures towards a relativistic approach. One of the major assumptions usually employed is strikingly close to the principle of holism in semantics. This semantic principle is: 'We can give the meaning of any sentence (or word) only by giving the meaning of every sentence (and word) in the language' (Davidson 1967, p.5; cf. Platts, 1979, p.50). Within the framework of cultural practices, this becomes: 'a symbol only has meaning from (sic) its relation to other symbols in a pattern. The pattern gives the meaning' (Douglas, 1973, p.11). When this is conjoined to the claim that '. . . each symbolic system develops autonomously according to its own rules' (Douglas, loc.cit.), then we are on the way to relativism (which Douglas does not espouse). The philosophical impetus may be provided by some of the work of the later Wittgenstein, particularly as it is deployed by Peter Winch. This work emphasises the diversity of language-games, each such game employing different criteria of adequacy and conforming to a different internal logic.

The relativist thesis threatens to destroy our assumptions. In particular, the principle of humanity is threatened in its function as a way of testing the validity of cross-cultural interpretation. That principle relies on some canons of rationality being universal, so that the plausibility of propositional attitudes and the intelligibility of error can be assessed. Relativism does not allow us to talk of plausibility and intelligibility 'tout court'; in its more radical form, we cannot speak of error 'tout court' either. The plausibility and intelligibility must be relativised to the relevant local conceptions. Weird translation will not, on this account, be evidence of bad translation, as it is just as likely to be the effect of a different conceptual scheme or a different logic. And, the relativist will argue, we cannot say that our scheme or logic is right and theirs wrong, for that again introduces an absolute judgment which has no place in the relativist scheme of things.

Understood in the sense in which it would undermine the application of the principle of humanity relativism is not a compelling doctrine. We may cite two general arguments against it. The first is that if the relativist is to invoke cultural holism as a ground for rejecting the use of an interpretative principle such as that of humanity, the holism in question will have to be made impossibly stringent. Semantic holism is not normally taken to have relativistic consequences because it is assumed that the interpreter can put forward hypotheses about the semantic rules governing part of the language and wait to see later whether these rules will work overall. When the relativist invokes holism, that assumption is not allowed: the holism is taken to mean that any separation of parts from whole essentially disfigures the parts, and that knowledge of the parts in this state is not knowledge of them as they fit within the total structure. Such a holism however cannot be seriously entertained. The relativist thinks that it would make impossible the idea of a culture's being understood from outside and that it shows the necessity of an insider understanding: the sort of understanding attained through being, or going, native. What the relativist does not see is that the holism in question is destructive, not just of understanding from outside, but also of understanding from within. Our contact with our own culture, and with any culture in which we might aspire to go native, is inevitably piecemeal and idiosyncratic; we are never exposed to the totality, only to particular aspects. It follows that if parts could not be properly understood in isolation from whole then we would be condemned to incomprehension.

A second general argument against relativism is that strictly considered it is unintelligible. In order to state the relativist thesis one has to identify the systems of thought the relativity of which is maintained and one has to indicate the respects in which the systems disagree. However, we have already seen in our discussion of charity that disagreements only make sense against a background of consensus, since consensus is at least demanded on those questions relevant to the fixing of the subject matter about which there is a difference of opinion. If we are to disagree with members of an alien society as to whether someone is a witch or not, we must at least agree with them that the individual is a human being, a woman, a person with such and such properties, and so on. Granted that all disagreements presuppose a common background of consensus, relativism cannot be made comprehensible. It wants to recognise systems of thought which on the one hand disagree but on the other have nothing in common, and this is no more sensible than to try to have one's cake and eat it.[8]

Relativism in the sense in which we have been taking it so far is a rather blunt and unpersuasive doctrine. What makes writing of a relativist bent interesting however is that it often contains astute criticisms of anthropological practice and imaginative proposals for anthropological interpretation. To mention one such criticism, we have no wish to deny the validity of the claim that some anthropological writing does an injustice to the complexity of societies by studying an isolated pattern of activity without relating this to the rest of the society. Thus, to take an example used by Winch, looking at magic as it occurs amongst the Azande, and comparing it to 'magic' as it occurs in industrialised Western societies, will be misleading if one forgets the absence of institutionalised science amongst the Azande (see Winch 1964). Our interpretation of magic as practised in the industrialised west will be coloured by the co-presence of science in those societies; the interpretation of magic in Azande society should not be so coloured. If people are exposed to the ways of scientists and still resort to magic, our understanding of them will incline towards deeming them irrational; such a construal of similar activity in a non-scientific culture would be unwarranted. What would need explaining is why an institution (scientific practice) did not appear in that society, not why individuals are irrational.

Criticisms of anthropological practice such as that just mentioned do not necessarily lead to a relativist conclusion, and are often made by thinkers whose relativism is more apparent than real. In this context it is worth mentioning the line of thought adopted by Peter Winch on the basis of the sort of consideration mentioned. This can be presented in five stages, although it does not appear in that form within any of his writings. 1 The evaluation of conduct as being irrational has the normative implication that the agent is behaving incorrectly. 2 Such an evaluation can only take place by reference to some rule or convention which, it is assumed, governs actions of that type. 3 The specification of such rules must be done in such a way that they connect up with the agent's behaviour; i.e. they must form possible reasons for him or her to act in that way. 4 Condition 3 will only be satisfied if the norms via which the behaviour is termed 'incorrect' are those which operate within the society in question. 5 Therefore all evaluations of this nature must be 'internal', relativised to the culture being studied. The line of thought sketched here leads to Winch's criticism of Evans-Pritchard: 'he would have wished to add: and the European is right and the Zande wrong. This addition I regard as illegitimate' (Winch 1964, p. 89). It leads also to an apparently relativist understanding of the alien: 'if *our* concept of rationality is a different one from his, then it makes no sense to say that anything either does or does not appear rational to *him* in *our* sense' (Winch 1964, p.97).

Despite these comments, however, we think that Winch's position is not incompatible with a recognition of the principle of humanity, and with a rejection of relativism understood in the strict sense. The claim under 5 that evaluations must be culture-relative may be given a non-relativist construal: on such a construal, it would say that we should be careful not to ascribe our norms of evaluation, but to ascribe those to which the aliens' circumstances would give rise. Again the comments quoted from Winch may be taken, not as outlawing all cross-cultural comparison, but as criticising specific sorts of comparison made in the literature. That this is the proper way to interpret Winch is indicated by the following passage, where he endorses something like our principle of humanity. 'To say of a society that it has language is also to say that it has a concept of rationality. There need not perhaps be any *word* functioning in its language as "rational" does in ours, but at least there must be features of its members' use of language analogous to those features of *our* use of language which are connected with our use of the word "rational"' (Winch 1964, p.99).

We have been making the point that often what makes relativism interesting is an association with astute anthropological criticism: criticism which need not itself commit one to relativism. What must be added to this is that the relativist disposition has often encouraged imaginative proposals for interpretation in anthropology: proposals, once again, which do not themselves entail the truth of relativism. In illustration of this we would like to turn to one particularly dominant class of proposals, to the effect that in cross-cultural interpretation we should be prepared to discover that our interpretees work with a different logic from that which we follow. This idea is sometimes put forward in such a spirit that strict relativism is entailed: that happens if what is meant by a difference in logic is a discontinuity in thought of a kind that we cannot ever hope to bridge. However the idea may simply be that the logic of the aliens differs in some traceable and contained respect: it may hold out the prospect of a local relativity rather than a global relativism. There is no obvious reason why we should not be able to recognise such a local relativity, so long as the principle of humanity enables us to explain why it should occur.

The relativist, local or global, who proposes that logic is not immutable rejects the common assumption that 'the only explanation that we can have of other cultures will necessarily depend on the rules of logic as we know and use them' (Wilson 1970, p.x). Logic in this context has a narrower sense than that which is often assumed by social scientists; it is concerned primarily with the deductive inferential relations between sentences. It is these relations for example that vary, according to Levy-Bruhl, with the 'primitive mind'. His notion of the prelogical mentality was, quite clearly, not intended to impute to the primitive no logical principle whatsoever. 'Prelogical, applied to primitive mentality, means simply that it does not go out of its way, as we do, to avoid contradiction. It does not have always present the same logical requirements' (Levy-Bruhl quoted in Evans-Pritchard 1965, p.82). The question then arises as to which logical requirements do govern the 'primitive mind' when it perceives logical relations between sentences, or when inferences are drawn. The picture presented is that an alternative logic, different from our own but not therefore inferior, can be extracted from the way in which the alien reasons. Incorporating this logic into our account of the belief set imputed to the agent, the suggestion is that the inconsistencies and absurdities will evaporate and that rationality will be restored.

The claim that there could be such an alternative at work is not one that we can dismiss a priori.[9] It might be comforting to have some kind of transcendental proof of the privileged status of our 'standard logic' (hereafter SL), which would lead us to conclude that there could be no alternatives which would still be deemed 'logical'. However, we do not believe that such a proof is forthcoming: in fact we find alternative logics proposed to deal with difficulties of our own habits of reasoning, so there could hardly be any reason in principle against extending those to others.

A reasonably fully worked out plan for ascribing an alternative logic in cross-cultural interpretation has been provided by David Cooper (see Cooper 1975). SL is characterised by Cooper as embodying a principle of bivalence (p is either true or false). It gives us definitions of the logical constants, 'and', 'either-or', 'not', 'if . . . then', and logical truths such as

(a) Either p or not-p (Excluded middle)
(b) If p, then p (Identity)
(c) Not (p and not-p) (Non-contradiction)

(The rules of inference can be included in the logical truths, but they do not need explicit mention here.) If one abides by the principles given some belief-sets will emerge as illogical. Cooper draws on Evans-Pritchard's 'Nuer Religion' for the following example of such a belief set.

(1) Souls (of humans) only appear with the incisor teeth, therefore very young children do not have souls
(2) The souls of all twins go above at death; therefore all twins have souls
(3) Some children are very young and twins
(4) Therefore these children do and do not have souls

The conclusion flouts the 'law' of non-contradiction so, as it is derivable from the previous beliefs, anybody believing (1), (2) and (3) would be deemed illogical.

Cooper proposes to rectify the situation by ascribing an alternative logic, AL, which was developed by Hans Reichenbach for quantum mechanics. For our purposes we need to know only that AL differs from SL in that it is trivalent; the values propositions can take are true, false, and indeterminate. In SL, if p is true, not-p is false; in AL, p can be indeterminate, in which case not-p will also be indeterminate. This means that the principle of excluded middle is no longer a logical truth: the disjunction of indeterminate p and indeterminate not-p is itself indeterminate. Similarly 'p and not p', a logical falsehood in SL, is not always false in AL: it can be indeterminate. Cooper formalises the beliefs concerning twins and souls in the following way:

(1) Either twins' souls go above or elsewhere
(2) If twins' souls go above, twins have souls
(3) If twins' souls go elsewhere, twins have souls
(4) Some twins, namely very young ones, do not have souls (Cooper 1975, p.245).

The ascription of AL to the believers would remove the apparent contradiction which ensues by treating the disjunction (1) as indeterminate: this would mean that we could not derive a conclusion incompatible with (4), to the effect that all twins have souls.

The motivation behind the proposal to use AL in dealing with quantum mechanical phenomena is that it will eliminate what Reichenbach calls 'causal anomalies' from quantum theory, anomalies produced by the peculiar behaviour caused by what he calls 'inter-phenomena'. The details of this need not concern us. (For a lucid presentation of the two-slit experiment, see Haack 1974, pp. 149-53). What is of interest is whether AL should be invoked to dissolve the contradiction of the thought system under investigation. Is the 'prelogicality' of some alien cultures to be explained by their use of AL instead of SL? The claim is that if we find that certain aliens do not dissent from explicitly contradictory propositions of the form 'p and not-p', then we should interpret them as regarding p, and hence not-p, as indeterminate. Is this reasonable?

Certainly more work needs to be done in order to gain plausibility for the view. The sub-microscopic interactions of quantum mechanics are postulated as interactions required to explain observable phenomena. It is because of the peculiarity of the phenomena that the sub-microscopic processes were held to have very strange properties: the phenomena could not be given a 'normal description' whereby '(1) the laws of nature are the same whether or not the objects are observed, and (2) the state of the objects is the same whether or not the objects are observed' (Haack 1974, p.150). The motivation behind the attribution of AL to the aliens is that their thought-processes would then be rendered less bizarre. However the bizarreness will not be dispelled if the phenomena to which the alien is responding do not warrant the holding of a different logic with respect to those phenomena. The analogy between magico-religious thought and quantum theory will be inadequate unless the phenomena which form the subject matter of the two 'theories' are also analogous.

At a first level the analogy must hold to the extent that we can see the magico-religious theory as descriptive or explanatory; we have to reject symbolist or functionalist accounts of the beliefs in question. Accepting this, we have to determine whether what is being described or explained behaves in the genuinely strange fashion of subatomic particles. Prima facie there is a case against the analogy holding here. It is only at the highly advanced level of theoretical physics that it has been found necessary to experiment with different logics. The objects or events relating to the aliens' beliefs are not of this kind and we might well conclude that they do not call for the same drastic step. Twins are beings for which the law of bivalence would appear to hold. Unfortunately, the issue cannot be dealt with quite that quickly. What kind of thing a twin is taken to be will be dependent on the 'theory' which the community associates with twins. It could well be the case, and seems to be in this example, that twins are taken to be extraordinary, and as such are expected to behave in an 'illogical' manner. The argument must now revolve around the problem of why it is that twins should have this 'peculiar' status in the alien society, why it is that they should be demarcated from other beings in such a way that a different logic is needed to cope with them. If under the guidance of the principle of humanity we can find our way to a convincing explanation of why this should be so, then we may be in a position where we can begin to think of assigning AL to the aliens in their discussion of twins.

We shall not explore further the issue of how likely it is that an anthropologist would be led to ascribe an alternative logic to a foreign society; enough has been said to throw some light on the complex nature of the problem. So far in this section we have looked at the general characterisation and criticism of relativism and we have seen something of the independently interesting contributions often associated with relativist writing: contributions such as the criticism of Evans-Pritchard developed by Peter Winch or the proposal to ascribe an alternative logic which David Cooper elaborates. In the remaining part of the section we turn to a line of approach which is non-relativist insofar as it suggests that differences between cultures need explanation but which is so radical in the differences it is prepared to countenance that it might be mistaken for a relativist theory. The approach in question has been developed fully only in recent years but it was already adumbrated in the writing of Evans-Pritchard. He maintained in discussing the Azande that their intellectual ingenuity is 'conditioned by patterns of ritual behaviour and mystical belief. Within the limits set by those patterns, they show great intelligence but it cannot operate beyond those limits. Or, to put it in another way, they reason excellently in the idiom of their beliefs but they cannot reason outside or against their beliefs, because they have no other idiom in which to express their thoughts' (Evans-Pritchard 1936, p.338).

The view suggested by these remarks has been elaborated most ably by Robin Horton. He sets up a contrast between two predicaments: 'the "closed"- characterised by lack of awareness of alternatives, sacredness of beliefs and anxiety about threats to them; and the "open"- characterised by awareness of alternatives, diminished sacredness of beliefs, and diminished anxiety about threats to them' (Horton 1970, p.155). Horton suggests that whereas we in the contemporary Western world are in the open predicament, people from so-called traditional societies are in the closed. The distinction is drawn on the model of Popper's dichotomy between open and closed societies, the latter being characterised as lacking the scientific attitude which, for Popper, is pre-eminently one of criticism and the search for falsifications. The distinctiveness of the 'closed' attitude to one's beliefs is said to be the 'dogmatic' defence of them when faced with putative counterexamples and this is maintained despite the fact that the idealised picture presented by Popper is blurred by Kuhnian considerations on dogmatism in science (see Kuhn 1970).

One of the consequences of the absence of alternative modes of description is said to be the belief that there is an intimate link between words and reality, such that if one changes the conceptual system, one thereby changes the reality being described.[10] This belief in 'word-magic' is claimed by Horton to be fundamental to magic in general, whereas in a scientifically-oriented culture the existence of alternatives to established modes of thinking renders implausible the belief that there is such an intimate (non-conventional) relation between words and the world. The lack of such alternatives is also held to be responsible for the absence of reflectively held rules of reasoning: 'traditional thought has tended to get on with the work of explanation, without pausing for reflection upon the nature or rules of this work . . . the traditional thinker, because he is unable to imagine possible alternatives to his established theories and classifications can never start to formulate generalised norms of reasoning and knowing. For only where there are alternatives can there be choice, and only where there is choice can there be norms governing "if"' (Horton 1970, p.160).

There are two matters that need to be considered in relation to Horton's claims. The first is whether it is a fact that in some societies alternatives to the established belief set are lacking: the second is why, if that is a fact, there should be a difference between some societies and others in this respect. The first, factual issue is not as close to our concerns as the second but there are two factors worth mentioning, each of which suggests that the matter is more complicated than Horton indicates. The first has to do with how we decide that there are or are not alternatives available to a given theory, if there is a certain degree of theory change than one may have such a loose criterion of identity for the theory that one says that the same theory remains in possession of the field. On the other hand one may tighten the criterion of identity and maintain that a novel theory has ousted the established one. Horton does not make clear what is to count as one theory and since he admits that there is a certain amount of theory change in the closed predicament it is open to an opponent to argue that in that predicament there are therefore theory alternatives. The theory change admitted in the closed situation is that which consists in what Horton calls secondary elaboration: the modification of a theory in order to deal with - in effect, to explain away - unsuccessful predictions.

The second factor which indicates that Horton underestimates the complexity of the factual issue is more empirical. It is disputed, by Goody in particular, whether the situation is really as described by Horton. 'Even in non-literate societies there is no evidence that individuals were prisoners of pre-ordained schemes of primitive classifications, of the structures of myth. Constrained, yes; imprisoned, no. Certain, at least, among them could and did use language in a generative way, elaborating metaphor, inventing songs and "myths", creating Gods, looking for new solutions to recurring puzzles and problems, changing the conceptual universe' (Goody 1977, p.33).

Whatever the outcome of the empirical debate it should be clear that Horton's 'solution' is not going to be thought satisfactory in itself by anybody committed to the principle of humanity. As an explanation it needs completion, or extension, by an account of why the closed predicament occurs. To rely on the anxiety provoked by a threat to the closed belief system would not do the trick: such anxiety is presumably the result of not having an alternative scheme to 'jump to' and cannot thus be held responsible for that lack. The anxiety may reinforce the tendency to cling to an established pattern of thought, but cannot be used to explain how the closed predicament originated. It is also unclear in which direction the explanation of the uncritical attitude should go. Horton suggests that the ignorance of alternative schemes removes one of the preconditions for the development of reflective reasoning but it would be compatible with what evidence there is to claim that the lack of the latter accounts for the former. This line of thought may appear even more at odds with our approach, suggesting the inherent incapacity of members of 'traditional' societies for the exercise of critical thought. If such a view was predicated on the claim that the incapacity was the result of different mentalities at work then it would be diametrically opposed to the principle of humanity, a principle which commits us to the unity of human nature. However if there was an explanation which accounted both for the growth of the scientific attitude in those societies in which it forms a major part and for its absence in traditional societies, then we would have a unifying account of the differences.

Goody has provided the outlines of such an account in suggesting that the basis of the divergent attitudes is the differing modes of communication to be found in the two sorts of society. Briefly, he indicates that the opposition should be one of 'oral' and 'literate' rather than 'traditional' and 'modern' (or 'closed' and 'open') (Goody 1977). A literate society will be able to develop critical attitudes more reflectively and self-consciously insofar as predictions are written down and can be re-examined for error. Texts are available for careful scrutiny so that reading a text is more impersonal and, by implication, more 'objective' than listening to a speaker. One of the features associated with Horton's closed predicament - the tying down of words to occasions - is explained there by the fact that speech is tied to occasions in ways in which a text is not. 'A concern with rules of argument or the grounds for knowledge seems to arise, though less directly, out of the formalisation of communication (and hence of "statement" and "belief") which is intrinsic to writing. Philosophic discourse is a formalisation of just the kind one would expect with literacy. "Traditional" societies are marked not so much by the absence of reflective thinking as by the absence of the proper tools for constructive rumination' (Goody 1977, p.44).[11]

The thesis, then, is that a literate society will have far greater opportunities to develop critical capacities since the decontextualisation and semi-permanence of the written word enables one to check for inconsistencies and contradictions in a manner not easily available to 'oral' communities. Such a solution to the problem of explaining different habits of thought places the source of the difference in material, environmental factors, rather than leaving the explanation at the level of 'ways of thinking'. It is clearly compatible with a principle of interpretation which advises us that, in interpreting a language, we are to attribute to the speakers of that language beliefs and patterns of inference between beliefs as much like our own as possible, the 'as possible' being understood in terms of avoiding inexplicable error. In the context of the present discussion, the advice would be to avoid inexplicable differences in modes of reasoning; such differences constitute prima facie evidence against the theory of interpretation which produces them.

We saw earlier that while accepting the principle of humanity in interpretation one might be led under certain conditions to ascribe an alternative logic to people in an alien society. We see now that equally one might be drawn to the view that those people operate in such a different intellectual environment that they cannot be expected to have our critical habits. In conclusion it is worth noting that confronted with the strange religious beliefs of certain aliens one might refuse to be impressed by the contrast which they make with our contemporary scientific beliefs and focus instead on how they compare with modern religious views (see Skorupski 1976, Ch.13). If one finds the latter views tolerant of contradictions, then one will not be shy of imputing contradictory religious beliefs to the aliens, although one will still be anxious to explain how such inconsistency can be tolerated. It may be that in fastening on the religious-scientific contrast anthropologists have been led to over-emphasise the difference between our culture and more traditional ones, whether that difference be construed in terms of a different logic or a different intellectual predicament.

This thought leads to a nicely ironic reflection. Granted that religious forms of thought co-exist with science in our culture, and granted that scientific forms of thought encourage the development of critical habits of belief assessment, it may turn out that the anthropologist will find the views of contemporary religious believers more difficult to make sense of than she does the views of believers in traditional societies. Those societies lack science, perhaps for reasons related to the absence of writing, and we may well expect therefore that there will not be a tradition of reflecting on the rationality of adopting one belief rather than another. In the absence of such a tradition, contradictory beliefs are more intelligible than they would be in its presence. Thus it may be that the anthropologist, or at least the atheistic anthropologist, will find the sharpest challenge to the assumption of human rationality, not in researches among the alien, but in investigations among her own.

# 2 THE UNDERSTANDING OF INDIVIDUALS: HUMANISM VERSUS SCIENTISM

## 1 INTRODUCTION

In the last chapter we studied some of the issues involved in the interpretation of unfamiliar utterances and actions: this, with particular regard to the project of constructing a finite semantics for a language used by foreigners. More than this, we defended a particular picture of the interpretative procedure, a picture which highlights the need to assume rationality in the people whose self-expressions we are scrutinising. The chapter served as a dramatisation of the semantic enterprise which gives us the viewpoint of our investigation, but it also threw light on one of the traditional topics in philosophy of social science: the understanding of other cultures. In the remaining three chapters of this text we shall take up three other topics in the philosophy of social science, arguably the three central ones, and work out in each case the stance that our semantic viewpoint would counsel.

The first of these topics is the issue, as it is traditionally described, between those who enthuse over a Verstehen way of doing social science and those who aspouse the alternative method of Erklären. The terms are German and they mean respectively 'to understand' and 'to explain'. A Verstehen approach to the study of human beings is any which assumes that the inquiry cannot be modelled on natural science: any 'humanistic' or 'non-scientistic' approach, to use other terms in common employment; an Erklären approach is one which makes the contrary assumption. Nineteenth-century German opponents of scientism often expressed their claim in the assertion that making sense of human beings was a matter of Verstehen, making sense of natural things one of Erklären, and that the two operations were fundamentally distinct.

The Verstehen or humanistic tradition of social science is usually traced to the work of the Italian thinker, Giambattista Vico, 1668-1744. He countered Descartes's emphasis on the certainty available in the natural sciences with his verum factum principle, according to which the true, what we can know for certain, is co-extensive with the made, what we have ourselves created. The idea was that we are in a better position to understand human actions, artifacts and institutions, the products of mind, than we are to grasp material phenomena that are not of our making (see Berlin 1976, Pompa 1975). The insistence on the special scrutability of human as distinct from natural reality was maintained in the writing of Johann Gottfried Herder, 1744-1803, although it is uncertain how far the German romantic was influenced by his Italian precursor (see Berlin 1976). In any case the idea was taken up in the thought of the influential German philosopher, Wilhelm Dilthey, 1833-1911, and through him it passed into various twentieth-century traditions (see Outhwaite 1975 and Rickman 1979). Max Weber gave the idea a central place in interpretative sociology, Martin Heidegger established it in the phenomenological and hermeneutic traditions with which he was associated, and the founders of the Frankfurt School of Marxism made it an essential part of the critical theory which they defended (see Dallmayr and McCarthy 1977).

The claim that human beings are understandable in a way in which natural things are not, and that the study of human beings ought not therefore to be modelled on natural science, has always been strongly challenged. On the grounds that it would undermine the unity of scientific method it has been particularly criticised within the positivistic tradition of thinking about science (see Abel 1948, Nagel 1961). Positivists reacted sharply against the idea that there was a special method of validating hypotheses in human inquiry, such as Vico's 'fantasia' (imagination), Herder's 'Einfühlen' (empathy), or Dilthey's 'Verstehen'. They suggested that while such faculties might play a role in the devising of hypotheses, the testing and confirmation of those hypotheses took exactly the form in the human area that it took in the natural. (Putnam 1978, Lecture 6, attacks the suggestion.) Although positivism has ceased to be the orthodox philosophy of science, the unity of method remains a widely accepted ideal and this has encouraged the survival of scientism even among staunchly anti-positivistic thinkers (see Papineau 1978 and Thomas 1979).

In this chapter we present a case for a humanistic as distinct from a scientistic construal of the understanding available in the study of human beings. The construal defended is within the broad Verstehen tradition although we do not endorse in any detail the views of any of the founders of that tradition. In putting forward our case we shall not address directly the positivistic argument that while human science may be distinguished by our method of devising hypotheses, it is not set apart by our means of vindicating them; that argument will be countered incidentally to our main line of attack. However, our discussion will be marked by one feature that has been distinctive of the positivistic debate. We shall consider the issue between humanism and scientism only in relation to the understanding of individual agents: specifically, in relation to the explanation of the actions which they perform. We have nothing to say here on the matter of whether a special mode of understanding is available, not only in the construal of people's individual doings, but also in the interpretation of collective and institutional phenomena. So far as that topic is explored, it will be treated in the chapter following, when we turn to the understanding of institutions, and the debate between individualism and collectivism.

There are two distinct questions involved in the issue between humanism and scientism. The first has to do with whether the conceptual scheme within which we ordinarily make sense of our own and other people's behaviour is replaceable by a scientifically more respectable framework. Can we seriously envisage giving up our commonsense terms of reference, dispensing with intentions, beliefs, desires and so on, and taking on instead a scientifically fashioned set of concepts, such as those which an advanced neurophysiology might supply? The second question has to do with whether the scheme, be it replaceable or not, is revisable on familiar scientific lines: whether it allows of regimentation, experiment and development in the manner of regular scientific theories. Can we coherently imagine taking the rough and ready concepts with which common sense supplies us, fixing in empirically determinate ways their conditions of application and their mutual connections, and proceeding to test, and perhaps upturn, the convictions by which we are guided in our unreflective use of the concepts?

The humanistic philosopher of social science, the upholder of the Verstehen point of view, denies both the replaceability and the revisability of the conception of human agents which we evince in our everyday explanation of actions. He puts a certain limit on the possibility of scientific progress at the point where people's understanding of themselves is concerned: specifically, their understanding of themselves as intentional agents. Scientific research and theorising may revolutionise our knowledge of ourselves as biological organisms, and it may significantly increase our psychological understanding of ourselves, revealing unsuspected patterns and pressures at work in the formation of our conceptions, memories, images, judgments, beliefs, desires, and so on. But what it cannot be expected to do, according to the humanist, is to prove us mistaken in our general conception of human action as issuing in a certain manner from the states of mind that we invoke in explanation of what we do and say. That conception, established as it is in common sense, in literature, in anthropology and in history, is held to resist any scientistic ambitions for its replacement or revision. Skill may be in place so far as the employment of the scheme goes, for there have always been those who did better than others at making sense of human behaviour; but science, at least when understood in any strict sense, is more or less irrelevant to the exercise: it is not what wisdom is here about.

In what follows we shall take up the replaceability and revisability issues and treat of each in turn. Before we come to the discussion of those matters however it is necessary to look in more detail at what we have spoken of as our everyday conception of human agents. We must see a little more clearly what it is that the humanist prizes, and what it is that his scientistic opponent would be prepared to let go. The framework in question has been implicitly invoked throughout the first chapter but it will be the more perspicuous for a systematic presentation.

## 2 THE ORTHODOX CONCEPTION OF AGENTS

The everyday or orthodox conception of agents is something which each of us picks up in developing competence at accounting for actions, both our own and those of other people. The conception is not appropriated in the way in which we typically learn bits of theory: the initiate is not given a set of axioms about the antecedents of action, nor is he told any particular story about the workings of the mind. What happens rather is that he is introduced to the use of various concepts by means of which action is explained. He learns when it is appropriate to regard a piece of behaviour as an action proper, and not just a reflex, what sorts of questions it is then in order to consider, and how he may make a case for one answer rather than another. In learning these things he picks up concepts such as those of intention, desire, decision, perception, judgment, belief, and a host of associates. The development of skill at applying those concepts, and at using them in the exploration of action, means initiation into the orthodox conception of agents.

But holding by the conception is not just a practical matter of being able to apply certain concepts accurately; it also involves a theoretical component: it means maintaining appropriate beliefs about the agents to whom the concepts are applied. This becomes apparent when we consider that with any of the ideas in question we would not take someone to be competent in its use unless he held by certain corresponding beliefs. Thus we would conclude that someone did not know how to use the concept of intention if he did not recognise that to intend something is normally to perform it, that intending is a state of mind for which it is almost always appropriate to seek reasons, that intending is something which supposes the having of certain beliefs about the alternative actions available in a given circumstance, and so on.

The most important beliefs associated with the adoption of the orthodox conception of agents constitute a theory of persons such as we mentioned in the last chapter and may be summed up in what we described as the assumption of rationality. This assumption breaks down into two generic beliefs: the belief that the normal human agent is behaviourally rational and the belief that, being behaviourally rational, he must also display attitudinal rationality. To take an agent to be behaviourally rational is simply to assume that some of his pieces of behaviour merit the name of 'actions', issuing in appropriate manner from mental states that 'rationalise' them (see Davidson 1963). A mental state rationalises a piece of behaviour described as 'A' if it consists in a pro-attitude of some sort, whether motivated by principle or passion, towards events with a certain property, and a belief that the behaviour, identified as 'A', has that property or stands a good chance of having it. Suppose that 'A' is my drinking a toast to an absent friend. This piece of behaviour is rationalised by the desire publicly to invoke the friend's memory, a desire that may be formally cast as a pro-attitude towards events with the property of being such invocations and a belief that the behaviour described as my drinking an appropriate toast has that property, being a way of publicly invoking the person's memory.

To assume that an agent is behaviourally rational in something he does is to believe that the event should be traced to a rationalising state of mind. It is to hold that the person must have been in such a state of belief and desire that he saw the behaviour as a certain or at least likely way of realising some attractive event, and that he was led on that account to bring it about. This assumption is extremely minimal and it is applied in respect of anything that we take to be properly a human action. When we take a sound as a remark rather than an involuntary cough, when we take a movement as an initiative rather than an automatic reflex, we hold that under some description it appeared to the agent as a desirable prospect, and that its appearing so was responsible for its occurrence.

Behavioural rationality, it should be noted, is not something that comes in degrees: it is possessed fully or not at all. It gives us the sense in which all people are equally rational, so long at least as they are not out of their senses. We should not imagine however that behavioural rationality is a prerogative of human beings in the animal kingdom, for we take other mammals to be moved to action by a similar pressure of belief and desire: the dog runs towards the gate, we assume, because it believes that doing so is a way of getting the ball, something which it manifestly wants (but see Davidson 1975). If there is a distinction to be drawn between human beings and other higher animals it may have to do, not with behavioural rationality as such, but with the wealth of beliefs and desires which supply the resources of such rationality. Lacking an articulated language in which to spell out objects of belief and desire in the indefinite manner of which we are masters, other mammals would seem to have much less scope for the exercise of such rationality as they may possess.

The connection between the assumption of behavioural rationality and the assumption of attitudinal can be spelt out, starting from the following remarks. The beliefs and desires ascribed to an agent when he is taken to be behaviourally rational are what are known as propositional attitudes: states of mind which are identified most naturally by reference to propositions that, in some sense, constitute their objects. Thus the belief that Paris is in France is a state of mind, conscious or unconscious, identified by reference to the proposition appearing in the that-clause, which tells us what in fact is believed: Paris is in France. A parallel story goes for desire. The desire to be in Paris which I may feel is a state of mind identified by reference to a proposition which tells us what I desire: I am in Paris. Alternatively, the desire can be cast as a belief-state which takes as its object a so-called evaluative proposition: it is desirable that I be in Paris. This second representation is more convenient because it removes the operative distinction between beliefs and desires from the obscure realm of the psychological, and it enables us to trace more easily the relations between beliefs and desires: this will appear in a moment. In what follows we shall always understand the propositional correlates of desires to be evaluative, taking the desires to be beliefs which have those propositions as objects.

The propositions which form the objects of descriptive and evaluative beliefs are some of them true, and some of them false, even if not all of them are either. This can be acknowledged on all sides, since no assumption is made about what it is that the truth or falsehood of a proposition consists in: it may be taken in certain cases to be something entirely non-objective (see Ch.4 below). To believe a proposition is to hold it true, to disbelieve it is to hold it false, and to suspend belief is not to hold it to be either (something which may or may not mean holding it to be neither). The connection between believing a proposition and holding it to be true comes out in the incoherence of claiming to believe a proposition which one characterises as not being true. We are interested in the connection because it means that where we ascribe a belief in a proposition to someone, we naturally expect that person to be responsive to anything which tends to show the proposition not to be true. If the person is unconcerned about such matters, if he shows no disposition to worry about the truth of the proposition, we will inevitably wonder whether we got his belief right in the first place.

The assumption that someone who believes a proposition will be disposed to worry about its truth is what we mean by the assumption of attitudinal rationality. We know that a set of propositions cannot be true if it can be confronted with counterexamples or if it generates inconsistencies: such factors are always significant, even if their significance varies as between, say, descriptive and evaluative discourse (see Williams 1973, Chs.11, 12). It follows that to be attitudinally rational is to be disposed at least to change one's beliefs so as to eliminate counterexamples and inconsistencies. This is the core of attitudinal rationality but not the entire substance. To be responsive to counterexamples and inconsistencies might be more or less to stand still, forever improving the profile of a given stock of beliefs. In fact human beings are inevitably involved in the continuous extension and adaptation of their beliefs and we must add that to be attitudinally rational is also to respect the appropriate constraints in this process of development.

At this point it must be admitted that the content of attitudinal rationality becomes woolly, for in neither of the two main forms of belief development are the appropriate constraints salient. The two forms are the theoretical and the practical: the theoretical, in which we seek out the view which it is best to take of some empirical matter; and the practical, in which we try to identify the best action for us to prescribe or perform. Theoretical reasoning is guided by a concern for securing explanatory scope at least cost to empirical support, a concern which pursues the simple and the encompassing, while paying court to the familiar and the economical, the precise and the refutable (see Quine and

Ullian 1978, Chs.5 and 6). Practical reasoning is governed by an urge to find that action in any circumstance which best fits with one's views of what is desirable: desirable not just now but in the future, and not just for oneself but for others too. This reasoning is concerned as much with the development of belief as is theoretical, for to prescribe or perform an action is to stand over the evaluative proposition 'This action is desirable, not just in one respect or another, but *simpliciter*': forming a judgment to this effect, plausibly, is what intending the action consists in (see Davidson 1978).

It appears that as we assume that an agent is behaviourally rational, in construing his behaviour as the issue of rationalising belief states, so we assume at the same stroke that he possesses attitudinal rationality, being disposed to see that his beliefs are true: specifically, being responsive to counterexamples and inconsistencies, and being respectful of the constraints appropriate to theoretical and practical decision-making. Attitudinal rationality is the necessary presupposition of behavioural, being the condition on which it makes sense to construe the attitudes of the agent as beliefs. The two senses of rationality express the important substance of those things which we hold of human beings in applying to them the orthodox conception of agents.

One final comment will be useful before we leave the topic of rationality. This is that whereas behavioural rationality is something that an agent possesses fully or not at all, there is a sense in which attitudinal rationality comes in degrees. All people may be assumed to have the disposition to see that their beliefs are true but, notoriously, the disposition may be more effective in some than in others, being less hindered by such common traits as dimness, laziness, weakness, self-satisfaction, self-deception, and the like. We would resist ascribing beliefs to agents who were entirely unmoved by the presentation of counterexamples and inconsistencies, but our picture of human motivation allows us to understand that many agents will live quite happily in oblivion of such faults in their beliefs. Notice incidentally that while we must require of animals to whom we ascribe beliefs that they are responsive to counterexamples, this is all that we can require of them in the absence of a language by means of which to confront them with inconsistencies: here we see another respect in which any rationality that we assume in other animals is radically more restricted than that which we attribute to human beings.

We have been concerned with spelling out the orthodox conception of agents, the conception implicit in our everyday accounting for our own and other people's behaviour. This conception, we have seen, involves us in applying the usual psychological concepts to agents, and acquiescing in the beliefs that go with these, in particular acquiescing in the assumption that agents are behaviourally and attitudinally rational. The two tasks which we set ourselves in this chapter now come into view: to see whether the orthodox conception of agents is scientifically replaceable or revisable. Before we turn to these however it may be worthwhile looking a little into the sorts of explanation of action which the conception sponsors: the conception is primarily employed in accounting for action 'linguistic or non-linguistic' and we shall not have fully understood it until we see something of the ways in which it serves this function (for a more extended account see Pettit forthcoming).

The most important type of action explanation is provided by a statement which reveals the behavioural rationality of an action described as of type 'A', by reporting that the agent had a pro-attitude towards events describable as 'Bs' and that he believed that the A would certainly or probably be a B, this complex state of mind being responsible for the appearance of the A. Such an account may be characterised as an intentional explanation of the action, for when it is true it enables us to say that the agent performed an action of type A with the intention of performing an action of type B, and that it was intentional of him that he performed an action of type B (see Davidson 1963).[1] The examples of such explanations abound indefinitely. The driver put his arm out of the window with the intention of signalling a turn, the referee blew his whistle in order to penalise the foul play, the teacher used slides as a way of securing the interest of the class. These statements indicate respectively the behavioural rationality of the driver's extending his arm, the referee's blowing his whistle, and the teacher's using slides. They show that in fulfilling the description in question in each case the agent was guided by his attitude towards another description which he thought would be realised by the realisation of the first.

One and the same action may be intentional under many descriptions, and one and the same action may be intentionally explained at many different levels.[2] Why am I forming letters, words and sentences? I am writing. Why am I writing? I am putting a lecture on paper. Why am I putting a lecture on paper? I am preparing it for publication. Why am I preparing it for publication? I am trying to reach a wider audience than my students. And so on, more or less indefinitely. Under each of these descriptions, other than perhaps the first, it is intentional of me that I perform the action: my forming letters, words and sentences may be no more intentional, for all that the example tells us, than my moving muscles in my arm on some pattern that I am not physiologist enough to recognise. Equally, under each of the descriptions other than the first, the action may be explained for an audience which is puzzled as to why, taken under the preceding description, it should have been performed. In each case the description indicates the state of affairs which the agent was intent on realising in bringing about the action as previously described.

The proliferation of intentional characterisations of an action indicates how rich a source of explanations is the assumption of behavioural rationality. Relative to a given action, the exploration of the agent's behavioural rationality may mean revealing level after level of attitudinal states, up to the point where the demand for further explanation is otiose, or can only be met by a different sort of response: some of the different responses available will be mentioned below. It should be noticed that the intentional explanation of an action is often provided in an oblique style which does not reveal clearly the form of the explanation in question. Thus in response to the question 'Why am I putting a lecture on paper?' it could have been said, not that I am preparing it for publication, but more or less equivalently, that I think it should be published, or that the material is publishable, or that there is a journal which publishes that sort of thing, and so on.

It will be useful to offer a picture, however rough and ready, of the different sorts of intentional characterisation that an action may receive and correspondingly of the various kinds of intentional explanation that may be offered in accounting for it. We suggest that an action may be intentionally characterised under any of at least the following three ways of being presented: as performed, being a display of the agent's skill at bringing about things; as preferred, being the chosen member of a set of mutually exclusive options; and as projected in further aspects that it is likely to have.

There are certainly some performative aspects of any action which are not intentional: witness the movement of my arm muscles on a certain pattern when writing. On the other hand some performative aspects definitely are so. The 'basic action' description, to use a term in common employment, is by definition so: it is the intentional description which the agent cannot be said to have made true by realising any other intentional description, and which is not generated from any other such description by the addition of a phrase such as 'in place p' or 'with enthusiasm' or 'late at night' (see Danto 1973, Davidson 1971). The basic action description of my writing, despite the warning entered above, is probably something like 'I form letters, words and sentences', this being the 'bottom' description that I intentionally fulfill. Other performative descriptions that are intentional can be isolated by asking: what descriptions beyond this basic one do I fulfil in order to realise the description that represents the action as preferred to alternatives?

The description that picks out the action as preferred to alternatives is of peculiar importance. We assume that in any case of action the agent was presented with a set of alternatives, if only 'Do this' and 'Decide not to do it'. Were there no alternatives there would be no need to regard the action as issuing from a rationalising attitude on the part of the agent - it would be something that just had to happen - and there would be no reason to see it as an action. The description of an action as preferred depicts it as a member of a set of mutually exclusive options and indicates the primary aspect under which it is presented for the contemplation of the agent. It is only when he comes to think of realising the action under this description that he will have to think of its performative aspect; and it is only when he has conceived of the action under this description that he can begin to trace out the other aspects that it is likely to have. The description represents the action in that profile in which it is, in the most basic sense, the agent's objective. It may be: going swimming rather than taking the dog for a walk or going to a show; deciding to stay on at university for further study rather than entering employment immediately; or writing a paper on the explanation of action rather than writing one on the connection between philosophy and psychology. In every case it points out to us what it is that the agent can be most properly said to have set out to do. (It is misleadingly, if understandably, described as indicating the agent's intention in Pettit 1976 and 1979a.)

Among the effects that an action has, some may not have been anticipated by the agent, as in the case of my offending my friend by something I say, and these will yield non-intentional descriptions of the action. Other effects however will have been foreseen and desired: by effects here we mean effects of making the preferred description true, besides those effects connected with the performative side of the action. These effects will give us the means of further intentional characterisation: in going swimming I also intentionally do something pleasurable, get myself some exercise, and surprise the friends whom I told not to expect me at the pool. Effects of this kind give us intentional descriptions of my action as projected by me, and equally with characterisations of the action as performed and preferred these descriptions may be used in appropriate context to explain what I did. There are other descriptions too which fall into this category and which make further action explanation possible. An effect desired may not have been foreseen for certain, only hoped for, giving us a description such as 'I made contact at the pool with an elusive friend'. And equally an effect desired may not have been actually achieved, giving us something like 'I tried to establish my bathing prowess by going to the pool'. In each of these cases too we are given a further resource for the explanation of the action.[3]

Among the explanations of an action which its intentional characterisation allows there are two that are particularly important, and that are regularly sought in everyday discussion. The one is that which gives us the description of the action as preferred to alternatives and the other that which puts the most persuasive face available on the action: this may coincide with the description of the action as preferred but it is more likely to be a description of it as projected. The first sort of explanation, as we have seen, refers us to what, in the most proper sense, the agent set out to do and its importance is obvious. The second puts what has been called a 'desirability characterisation' on the action, describing it in terms such that no one who understands the language can fail to see why the agent should have been moved to try to realise the description: this, even though the assessor may not approve of the agent's choice (see Anscombe 1963). Typical desirability characterisations represent actions as dutiful, enjoyable, profitable, friendly or, perhaps most commonly, as a mixture of such things. The importance of this sort of explanation is that it cannot in itself cause puzzlement, resting as it does on an accepted model of the sort of things that move normal human agents (see Pettit 1975, section 3).

We have been looking at the explanatory use to which the orthodox conception of agents is put and have been investigating in particular the intentional explanation of action which it underpins. Intentional explanation of action is basic in the sense that other sorts of explanation presuppose it and this may excuse the emphasis which we have put on it. In conclusion to this section however we may mention four other kinds of action explanation which the orthodox conception sponsors. All of them are intended to bolster a given intentional account, explaining further why the desire mentioned in that account should have outweighed other desires that we presume were operative in the agent, or equivalently, why the desirability characteristic in question should have had such a powerful prompting effect. The explanations refer us respectively to a long term policy on the agent's part, to his motivational profile, to his personality or character, and to his social position.

An agent has a policy, such as the policy of keeping promises come what may, when he makes an unconditional judgment in favour of those actions which he sees in future offing for him, that fulfil promises. It is not just that he finds them qua fulfilments of promises attractive or compelling, a state which would leave him free not to perform them, finding them unattractive under other aspects. He selects in all their particularity those actions that he foresees; he decides resolutely for them. Such a policy may be thought to resemble a state of intending something, in this regard (see Davidson 1978). What distinguishes it is that whereas the intending is fulfilled by a single action, however complex, the policy remains intact and directive no matter how many actions have satisfied it.

An agent's motivational profile is constituted by the state of his emotions and drives. Emotions are passing states of feeling which are not associated with any very restricted class of action; fear and anger, shame and joy, despair and sadness, may sensitise agents to any of a number of promptings and may lead to any of a variety of actions. They are associated with characteristic circumstances of arousal and they usually issue in distinctive involuntary expressions. Drives on the other hand are passing states of feeling which are pointed much more definitively towards particular tracks of behaviour: avarice and envy, revenge and ambition, hunger and lust, are primarily identified by the promptings to which they make us responsive and the actions which they lead us to perform. Like emotions they have characteristic circumstances of arousal but they do not have such distinctive involuntary expressions. As states of feeling, emotions and drives have in common the fact that it does not make sense, as it would with a policy, to think of an agent revoking them: they are conceived of as unwilled, if sometimes welcome, visitations.

An agent's character or personality consists in deeply enduring and only partially controllable habits of mind and heart whereby he may be distinguished from other individuals. It is often described by the use of words associated with certain emotions and drives, the implication being that the agent has a susceptibility to those states. Thus we have fearful and joyful, avaricious and envious, people, as well as having the emotions of fear and joy and the drives of avarice and envy. Personality is often characterised too, not by habits of the sensibility, but by habits of thought. When we speak of someone as obsessional or judgmental, or when we characterise his belief patterns as fascist or xenophobic, we are ascribing personality just as much as when we describe his affective dispositions. In either case we are focusing on something in the agent which, like his policies or his motivational profile, may mean that a given prompting occasions a distinctively powerful desire.

Finally, an agent's social position, in a slightly unusual use of the phrase, is the frame constituted by the relationships with other people which constrain his behaviour at any time. The traffic warden seeing children safely across the road, the bank clerk considering a request for credit, the tourist office attendant giving information to visitors: these are examples of people who, so long as they exercise the activities described, are in highly visible social positions. Like the other factors mentioned, position is something on the side of the agent which can mean that a given stimulus to desire is exceptionally potent, and that the desire occasioned has the feature of readily prevailing over competitors.

This may reasonably complete our account of the orthodox conception of agents. We have seen that this conception involves the endorsement of the psychological concepts normally invoked in the explanation of action, and the adoption of the corresponding beliefs, in particular the adoption of beliefs in the behavioural and attitudinal rationality of agents. This conception allows us to follow a number of lines in accounting for the things people do and say. We may pursue the intentional explanation of an action, and this at any of an indefinite number of levels, an action being subject to intentional characterisation as performed, as preferred and as projected. Or we may take the intentional explanation for granted and seek out special reasons why the state of belief and desire mentioned in that account should have been so readily dominant. This other tack would have us look to factors such as a policy on the agent's part, his motivational profile, his personality, or his social position.

## 3 THE REPLACEABILITY ISSUE

The first of the two issues to be resolved in the debate between the humanistic and scientistic points of view is whether the orthodox conception of agents which we have been examining is replaceable by a scientifically more respectable scheme; that is, whether it is possible that such a scheme could displace the orthodox conception in our understanding of ourselves and one another. Is it more or less inevitable that we think of people's actions as the behaviourally rational issue of mental states, and that we take those states themselves to be subject to the constraints of attitudinal rationality? In the last chapter we saw that in attempting to understand even people of a widely removed culture we naturally assume that they are rational and impose on them the orthodox conception of agents. The question is whether all of this might change, were we to have available a scientifically polished alternative to that rough-hewn style of understanding.

The alternative which comes most readily to mind is the behaviouristic scheme of concepts for making sense of human behaviour (see Skinner 1953). This, or indeed any psychologically elaborated view of agents, such as the psychoanalytical theory developed by Freud, would seem to offer a direct challenge to the orthodox conception and would appear to raise the question of replaceability. In fact however we think that there is some doubt as to whether such psychological theorising does put forward alternatives to the accepted scheme. Psychoanalysts, however esoteric some of the constructs they introduce, do not deny that human action is the product of belief and desire, and what they claim may be seen as supplementary to received opinion, rather than subversive of it: we may be scandalised by being told that our desires have unconscious and unseemly springs, but we are not thereby deprived of our rationalistic image of people. Many behaviourists, it is true, do tilt against the mentalistic presuppositions of the orthodox conception but even the theory which they develop can be viewed as an attempt to fill out that reviled scheme: the conditioning invoked in explanation of behaviour may be plausibly interpreted as a mechanism affecting the formation of those beliefs and desires which are the more immediate source of the behaviour (see Goldman 1970, Ch.5 and Ch.1 above, n.7).

In order to be sure that the theory considered does not extend rather than challenge the orthodox conception, we propose to look to neurophysiology as the possible source of a genuinely alternative way of understanding agents. It is not unthinkable that in the decades or centuries to come neurophysiologists will develop a grasp of how the brain functions and how it relates to behaviour, which will enable them to trace pieces of behaviour to brain states in a manner quite independent of their ordinary understanding of that behaviour. Their theory would naturally be spelled out in a language far removed from our psychological vocabulary and it would offer a radically different perspective on agents. It would bear to our orthodox conception something like the relationship between the engineer's understanding of a chess-playing computer and the understanding of the opponent who ponders over the likely strategies and counter-strategies of the machine (see Dennett 1973).

Is it conceivable then that armed with a neurophysiological alternative to the orthodox conception we should give up that conception as being irremediably confused or inadequate? (For an affirmative response see Churchland 1979.) The question is not whether it is practically conceivable that we should do this: it does not ask whether we would be likely to put up with the inconvenience of wearing the scanning equipment that would allow us to play neurophysiologist with one another, nor whether we would be generally willing to go to the trouble of learning the new scheme of explanation and prediction. Assuming that such practical obstacles can be overcome, the issue is whether we can conceive of adopting the neurophysiological theory in place of the old, putting aside the old as a piece of falsehood or only a partial truth. To deny that this is conceivable, it should be noticed, would not be to say that a neurophysiological theory of the kind envisaged could never be developed: that would be an intolerable piece of philosophical legislation. It would be to say only that the theory could not displace the orthodox conception, and that the twin representations would demand to be interpreted in a manner that ensured their compatibility, if not the reducibility of the one to the other.

There are three arguments against the replaceability of the orthodox conception of agents which we shall consider in this section. The first, which we call the argument from introspection, is intuitively appealing but is not in our view sound. The second, the argument from interaction, seems to us to be persuasive but it is unlikely to carry weight with someone of a scientistic bent. The third, the argument from interpretation, makes a case generated by the semantic viewpoint of this text and it seems to us to be irresistible.

The argument from introspection, as the title suggests, makes the point that the truth of the orthodox conception of agents is not a matter for speculation, that it is delivered to us in the awareness which each of us has of the antecedents of his behaviour. (This is presented and criticised in Churchland 1979, section 13.) The idea is that whatever about the uncertainties in our understanding of other people we each know for sure about many of the things that happen within ourselves, and among other things we know that our actions are produced by rationalising beliefs and desires, states which are themselves subject to constraints of attitudinal rationality. It is held to be as certain as anything could ever be that as I write at this moment, the marks which I am making on paper come of a desire on my part to set out certain ideas, my belief being that the marks are an appropriate means of doing this. How, it is asked, could I ever come to doubt such a thing? How could any theory, any exercise in speculation, ever loosen my grip on this quite intuitive certainty?

It must be admitted that in one sense many introspective judgments are intuitively certain and that in this sense they are likely to resist any form of theoretical questioning. They are certain so far as their empirical content goes: certain so far as they mark undoubted features of empirical reality, not mere illusions of theory. When I say that I am hungry or annoyed, for example, we may well feel certain that the state in which I find myself contrasts in some significant fashion with the state in which I would describe myself as satiated or well-tempered. Each judgment marks what we take as a real difference: a difference of which any comprehensive account of my disposition, however novel or revolutionary, ought to take note.

But empirical certainty of the kind illustrated may belong to a judgment without certainty in a second, theoretical sense accompanying it. A judgment such as 'The sun is rising in the sky' is empirically certain, in the sense in question, but is not theoretically so: theoretically, indeed, it is false. Every observational or introspective judgment, even the most lowly, does something more than mark alleged empirical distinctions. It also carries with it the implication that the overall theory or conception in the background of the judgment is reliable. The judgment that the sun is rising is theoretically false in the sense that the non-Copernican astronomy in the background is unsustainable. If the judgment is not misleading in everyday conversation, that is only because the theoretical content is commonly known to be false and the focus of the speaker is naturally assumed to be restricted to the empirical content.

It may seem surprising that every observational or introspective judgment should have a theoretical as well as an empirical content. The thesis can be appreciated by reflecting on the fact that every such judgment applies a predicate and that even a predicate as simple as 'is red' is applied on the assumption that certain general propositions hold. Thus we may be perfectly happy to say that something is red on the basis of perceptual cues, but the judgment will be quickly submitted to questioning, and we may come even not to believe our eyes, if the thing cannot be red consistently with some accepted body of general beliefs, some established theory: say if it is a solution which our chemistry textbook tells us ought to be of some other colour (see Hesse, 1974, Ch.1). By the use of certain devices, we can make it clear that our interest is only in the empirical content of a judgment; we do this for example if we preface the proposition by 'It looks to me as if . . .'. Such formulations, however, are parasitic: they are understood only by those for whom the straightforward judgments are intelligible.

To return now to judgments of introspection, what we wish to say is that while these may be certain in their empirical content, they need not be so in their theoretical. But this means that the argument from introspection does not go through. The argument maintained that the orthodox conception of agents is as certain and irreplaceable as the most certain judgments of introspection in which it is implicated. However what now appears is that these judgments are certain only so far as their empirical content goes, and that such certainty is compatible with the falsehood of the overall theory in the background: that is, the orthodox conception of agents. Judgments to the effect that we are upset, or hungry, or angry, that we see someone on the road, or expect to leave later, that we believe such-and-such, or desire so-and-so: these judgments may often be as empirically certain as we could wish them to be but they do nothing, for all that, to show that the conception of agents implicated in them is incapable of being replaced. For all we can say, the appearance of an alternative scheme might bring about a changed manner of formulating the empirical points made in those judgments and might topple the conception to which we now so tenaciously cling.

The argument from introspection may continue to be found compelling, even when these points have been made, and it may be worthwhile mentioning a possible reason why. This is that even in cases where there are no obvious internal cues, such as the rumbling of an empty stomach or the tension of tired legs, we seem to know certain things about ourselves which others are not in a position to divine. I may know now for example that I intend to play tennis in two hours' time, when this information may not be accessible to others. In such a case, it will be asked, do I not just see the state of mind that I am in; do I not just intuit my intention? If it is thought that I do, then it may seem that introspection is a source of special knowledge, and sufficient testimony to ensure the irreplaceability of our orthodox conception of agents.

But it appears that even such knowledge of our mental states can be represented as something other than pre-theoretical intuition. As a master of the orthodox conception I know that actually playing tennis is sufficient evidence of an intention to play, barring the possibility of sleep-walking or anything of that kind. This means that if I decide that I will play in two hours' time, I have available to me in advance of others the evidence which clinches the matter of what I intend to do. Thus I can announce my intention in perfect confidence, being in a position to make sure that I behave in the way that bears out my self-judgment. This story puts in place of a more or less indubitable insight into my present state of mind the ability to decide in advance what I will do. However this ability, while it is certainly remarkable, is hardly more mysterious than the ability to decide what I will do now: what it requires in addition is the capacity to project myself into the future situation and to go through the anticipated motions of choice. That people have such an ability, plus the related ability to foresee how they are likely to behave under different more or less vaguely characterised circumstances, may explain how they can pronounce on their mental states, even when others are in no position to see into those states, and when the states themselves are not of the kind to be judged by obvious internal cues.

This is enough on the argument from introspection. The second argument for the irreplaceability of the orthodox conception of agents is the argument from interaction. The supposition behind this argument is that if we are to continue to interact with one another in the manner which makes attributions of responsibility sensible, as distinct from adopting towards one another the detached interventionist mentality that we take towards machines, then we must view one another in the fashion prescribed by the orthodox conception of agents. That supposition made, it is argued that the thought of our ceasing to interact with one another in the personal mode is outlandish in one respect or another and that the inevitability of interaction means the irreplaceability of the orthodox scheme.

The validity of the underlying supposition is difficult to question (see Pettit 1978, section 2). In applying the assumption of rationality to an agent, we come to ascribe beliefs and desires to him and we use these as the basis for predicting his future behaviour. But the prediction involved is not of a kind which allows us to foretell for sure the decisions of the agent, for it is uncertain in any circumstances how beliefs and desires may connect with one another or change. Thus there is no reason why the predictive knowledge in question may not be shared with the agent; indeed it will be inevitably shared in part, insofar as he will have known which mental states his actions would lead us to ascribe. The case is different with the predictive knowledge which an exact neurophysiology would give us of someone's future behaviour, for sharing this with the agent would be at best gratuitous and at worst destructive, being likely to interfere with our otherwise reliable forecasts. Thus the knowledge of one another which the orthodox conception gives is capable of being common knowledge, where that which an advanced neurophysiology would provide is best kept in unilateral isolation. However common knowledge is of the essence of interaction, in which the way that we deal with a person is influenced by our picture of what we each make of the other, a picture which we normally take to be shared (see Grice 1957). It appears then that where the orthodox conception of agents would sponsor interaction in any community in which it was dominant, a scheme of a regular scientific stamp would make it impossible. The orthodox conception may not be the only theory imaginable which would allow, and indeed make inevitable, the sharing of much of people's knowledge in respect of one another, but it would certainly score in this regard over a rigorous and comprehensive neurophysiology.

The connection between treating people interactively and applying the orthodox conception to them can be made perhaps more manifest by reflecting on what it is to praise or blame agents, holding them responsible for their actions. The attribution of responsibility in this sense is part of interaction: it is something that we consider uniquely appropriate when we are dealing with agents whose view of us, and of our view of them, is thought to be relevant to how they are treated. But to hold someone responsible for an action is, it appears, to assume that what he did or said was done for a reason, and that it was not the product of some non-rational causality. It is to take it that the action issued from a rationalising set of beliefs and desires, praising or blaming the agent insofar as we think well or ill of his practical reasoning. Where we think that such reasoning had nothing to do with the behaviour, the event being the effect of some other sort of process, we conclude that praise and blame are out of place.

Let us grant that to replace the orthodox conception of agents by an advanced scientific theory would be to undermine the interactive manner in which we treat one another, supplanting it by a kind of treatment which we now reserve for systems that we regard as non-rational: systems which at the extreme may include people who are out of their senses. The argument from interaction claims at this point that we cannot envisage ever giving up the practice of interaction and that equally therefore the scientific replacement of the orthodox conception of agents is inconceivable. But why cannot we envisage ever giving up the practice? One line is to say that the interactive disposition is as deeply and naturally a part of us as is our habit of thinking inductively (see Strawson 1962). Another is to say that the interactive disposition serves a distinctive human interest in communication, an interest which we can hardly help but have (see Habermas 1972, Appendix). This second thought can be glossed nicely by reference to the person who is playing chess with the computer. It is possible for him at any point to give up his chess-playing stance, consult the appropriate engineer and discover which move the computer is electronically determined to make in response to any counter-move from him. It is possible for him to do this but to do it would necessarily be to stop playing chess. The moral is that in the parallel case where we had the option of playing neurophysiologist with someone rather than interacting with him, the adoption of the neurophysiological stance would mean an end to the indefinite number of games by which human exchange is characterised.

Is it likely that the argument from interaction will convince the scientistic thinker that the orthodox conception of agents is after all irreplaceable? We think not, although we regard the case made as a weighty one. Against the claim that there is something deep and natural about the interactive habit our opponent will say that this may be simply the result of tradition and training, and that the habit may yet prove capable of being broken. Against the other claim, that the interactive disposition serves a distinctive interest that would be lost in the adoption of another point of view, he can be equally brief. He will say that the comment is made from a parochial and reactionary point of view and that the progress of knowledge ought not to be held back by an attachment to the satisfactions deriving from older schemes of thought. We would not think much of our forerunners, it will be said, if their attachment to the rhetorical significance of the theory of the four elements had prevented them from espousing the tenets of modern chemistry. By parallel we shall be invited to think little of anyone who would resist the claims of an advanced neurophysiological understanding for the charms of our orthodox conception of agents.

The third argument for the irreplaceability of the orthodox conception of agents is the argument from interpretation. This depends crucially on points which we have tried to establish in the first chapter, for what it claims is that even to assign an interpretation to the noises and marks that people make, to give a meaning to their texts and utterances, is to assume that they are behaviourally and attitudinally rational. The assumption of such rationality, we saw, is a necessary condition for taking noises and marks as worthy of interpretation, and is systematically deployed as we put a construction on those expressions, assigning denotations to names, extensions to predicates, truth-conditions to sentences, and so on. It is as inevitable therefore that we uphold it in respect of the people with whom we are dealing, applying the orthodox conception of agents to them, as it is that we put a construal on their linguistic and other sign-making activities.

Where the second argument tied the orthodox conception to our interactive disposition, this one links it with our interpretative. But just as the last argument had to establish the indispensability of interaction, this must also show that it is necessary for us to try to interpret what people say and write. How can the point be established? It scarcely allows of formal proof but it is powerfully supported by two considerations. The first is that an account of a piece of speech or writing which failed to find any meaning in it, although it systematically traced the physical events involved to neutral antecedents, would miss the most important feature of the matter to be explained, eliminating the difference between that matter and a string of meaningless signs emitted to keep the neurophysiologist busy. To say this is not just to make the parochial point that the neurophysiological account would down play a distinction which the orthodox highlights and which we presently find signficant. We must presume that the most advanced neurophysiologist still sets out his views in linguistic form and the point is that his account of a piece of speech and writing on the part of another would fail to make an appropriate connection with his own habits. For all he knows the events of which he is giving an account may be attempts by a fellow scientist to communicate some important findings or insights.

This takes us to the second consideration in support of the indispensability of the interpretative point of view. It is that no one can fail to adopt that point of view at least in respect of himself. To come to think that everything could be explained according to non-rational patterns, and that the orthodox conception of agents was so much old hat, would be at least to see the words in which one expressed those thoughts as meaningful: it would be to maintain an interpretative disposition vis-à-vis oneself. This means that the consistently scientistic thinker, possessed of an advanced neurophysiology and determined to put it in place of the orthodox conception, would have to put himself out of the world to which he held that such science applied. He would have to see himself as a lone rational ego, uniquely fitted for explanation on the established orthodox lines.

The arguments from interaction and interpretation reinforce one another, for to see the things that someone says or writes as interpretable is intimately connected with representing that person to oneself as a potential partner in interaction. The case from interpretation is the less resistible of the two but because it depends on the points made in the first chapter it may also be the less intuitive. We shall assume on the basis of the arguments that the orthodox conception of agents, while it may not be the compelling datum which the argument from introspection suggested, is a view which it is impossible for us ever to give up. There may indeed be an advanced theory in the offing which will make total neurophysiological sense of people's behaviour, but any such theory must be construed by us in a manner which will render it compatible with the orthodox conception. It cannot, by any stretch of the imagination, displace that conception and reduce us to thinking of ourselves and other people in exclusively neurophysiological terms.

## 4 THE REVISABILITY ISSUE: ACTION EXPLANATION IS NOT NON-INFERENTIAL

To adopt the humanistic or Verstehen point of view is not just to think that the orthodox conception of agents is irreplaceable, it is also to hold that this conception is in an important sense unrevisable. One need not deny that the tenets of the conception may come to be spelled out in a more sophisticated manner, and certainly not that it may be progressively supplemented by scientific research and theorising: the scheme leaves an enormous number of gaps, having but little to say for example on the formation of beliefs and desires, a topic which we assigned to behaviourists and psychoanalysts. What one must deny as a humanist however is that the orthodox conception could be subjected indefinitely to the process of regimentation, experiment and amendment that is characteristic of scientific practice. Such a process could logically lead to a result as dramatic as the replacement of the conception by an advanced neurophysiology and it must be just as subject therefore to the humanistic anathema.

The challenge to the humanist at this point is to show what it is about the orthodox conception of agents which renders it recalcitrant to scientific take-over and development. A first step towards the scientific reformation of the scheme might be held to have been taken with the emergence of decision theory: this represents the desirability of an outcome as its utility, something for which there are strict behavioural indices, and it sets out principles of rational decision-making which sharpen our orthodox convictions. The most famous principle is that according to which the rational agent maximises expected utility: he chooses that alternative the utilities of whose possible outcomes, discounted by the associated probabilities, make the largest sum (see Jeffrey 1965 and Pettit 1980, Ch.12). What the humanistic thinker has to show is that there is some reason why the decision-theoretic version of the orthodox conception, or any other scientific representation of it, cannot progress in the manner which is thought to be universally possible in science.

The attempts to establish this point have been various. We propose to consider three arguments which would support it, the third of which is particularly associated with the viewpoint of the semantic enterprise. The first two arguments, which we shall consider in this section and the following one, do not seem to us to be sound and we rest our case exclusively on the third. They are arguments of which many variants have appeared in the literature but we make no effort to track down such versions or document them. The two arguments are respectively associated with the two major traditions of philosophical thinking over the last hundred years: the Continental and the Anglo-American. The first argues that what makes the orthodox conception unrevisable is the fact that the explanation which it sponsors is non-inferential, the second the fact that the explanation is non-causal. The third argument parallels these in tracing the unrevisability to the fact that orthodox action explanation is non-nomothetic: it does not involve the postulation of a proper 'nomos' or law.

The first argument, roughly individuated, is to be found in the tradition stemming from Vico and Herder to Dilthey and to those in the twentieth century who associate themselves with Dilthey: in particular, members of the hermeneutic and phenomenological schools of philosophy, and adherents of the critical and interpretative varieties of sociology. Our presentation of the argument, broadly speaking, will be a hermeneutic one. It will be in the style of those like Dilthey in the nineteenth century, and Martin Heidegger and Hans Georg Gadamer in the twentieth, who insist on the affinity and parallel between the interpretation of texts and utterances and the understanding of non-linguistic behaviour; this connection is one which we have ourselves emphasised in the preceding chapter. Other presentations of the argument are possible but they seem to us to incur the same objections, or stronger ones. Thus one variant might urge that since the springs of our own action are introspectible, our explanation of such action does not rely in any way on inference: this however would incur the objection that we brought against the argument from introspection in the last section.

The hermeneutic argument to the non-inferential nature of action explanation comes in two versions, neither of which relies on a crude appeal to introspection. The one version we describe as intra-subjectivist, the other as inter-subjectivist. In characterising the intra-subjectivist argument we have relied particularly on the writings of Dilthey (see Hodges 1944, Rickman 1976), in describing the inter-subjectivist one on those of Hans Georg Gadamer and Charles Taylor (see Gadamer 1970, Taylor 1971). Both arguments urge that because we are human beings ourselves, and have the privileged access of insiders, we do not have to rely on any form of inference in putting forward explanations of action. In making sense of what happens in the non-human world, it is suggested, we have to build up a theory conjecturally, starting from careful observation of what goes on, and with this theory in hand we have to try to divine how each event with which we are confronted may be explained. In the process we are outsiders speculating on unknown territory and the explanations which we offer of natural phenomena are ultimately redeemed only by the persuasiveness of our inferential reasonings. The case is said to be otherwise, however, when we seek to find our way about the familiar countryside of human behaviour. Here the explanations that we offer are not secured in an inferential manner and the orthodox conception of agents which they suppose does not have a merely conjectural status.

The intra-subjectivist depiction of how things stand with the explanation of actions can be set out in five propositions. These should be intelligible without further commentary and the only remarks that we shall add will be criticisms designed to show why we do not find the depiction convincing.

1 Being human ourselves we are familiar with the nature of the human mind and this familiarity is an indispensable source of insight both in generating and in corroborating explanations of action.
2 We understand an action of our own, linguistic or non-linguistic, by grasping its relations to our inner experiences and to our other actions: by seeing its place in our subjective life, its personal significance for us.
3 We understand the action of another by detecting its position in a corresponding complex. In the pursuit of this understanding our knowledge of ourselves serves us as guide.
4 In both of these cases the understanding of action is intuitive rather than inferential. Actions, linguistic and non-linguistic, are like spontaneous expressions such as the smile or the frown, serving as manifestations rather than symptoms of the states of mind which give them meaning.
5 The understanding of action is improved in following the familiar hermeneutical circle or spiral, whereby we move to the parts in order better to understand the whole, back to the whole in order better to understand the parts, and so on indefinitely. The whole in relation to which an action has to be understood is the mental life of the agent.

This intra-subjectivist account sets the explanation of action in a broad and compelling context and the points which it makes may be generally taken and applauded. However the crucial matter is whether we are persuaded by the fourth proposition, for it is this which would set action explanation apart in the required manner. Spontaneous expressions might be said non-inferentially to herald the appropriate feelings, to be in this sense manifestations rather than symptoms, insofar as the following conditions are fulfilled: that we scarcely know what the feelings are other than by recognising their expressions, and that we would not necessarily see anything in common between the expressions of a given sort of feeling, say the different smiles in which merriment may be revealed, unless we saw them precisely as such expressions (see Taylor 1978). The idea is that if we do not know what a Y is other than by taking an X as a sign of it, and if we would not recognise an X unless we saw it as a sign of a Y, then an X is scarcely an inferential token of a Y: it does not relate to it in the way in which the broken window relates to the burglary, or the smell of smoke to the basement fire. We have to ask, first, whether this idea is sound, whether expressions are non-inferential tokens of what they express; and second, whether actions resemble expressions in this respect, if indeed the idea is sound. We can be persuaded by the case made for the distinctiveness of action explanation only if our answers to both questions are affirmative.

In fact however we think that both questions should be answered negatively. To take up the first question, the fact that we do not know what a Y is other than by reference to an X does not mean that an X may not be a basis for inferring the presence of a Y: doctors who did not know what the measles virus was other than by seeing its effects confidently inferred the presence of the virus from the perception of the effects. And on the other side the fact that the category of Xs would scarcely be a salient one unless we saw Xs as signs of Ys does not mean either that an X cannot be the basis for inferring to a Y. In the discussion of introspection in the last section, we saw that the terms for describing data, even a simple predicate like 'is red', are often used, and presumably learned, on the assumption of certain theoretical truths. There is no reason then why a term 'X' should not be introduced on the assumption that X-things are evidence of Y-things, where the class of X-things thereby becomes salient for the first time: that is, where the cues by which X-things are observationally identified assume a common property-indicating significance for the first time. And if that did happen, it would not mean that an X-thing could not provide the basis of inference to a Y-one. If we turn again to medicine, we must acknowledge that while certain symptoms might only become a perceptible syndrome when seen as the effects of a common cause, they could yet serve individually as bases on which to infer the presence of the cause.

It appears then that there is no reason to regard the relation whereby a spontaneous expression leads us to a corresponding emotion as a non-inferential one. The happy smile, or at least the expression which looks like a happy smile, leads us to infer that the person is happy. It follows that even if actions parallel expressions in their relation to states of mind, there is no reason not to see the explanation in which we seek out the appropriate states as vindicated intuitively rather than inferentially. But in any case we may add that the answer to our second question above is also negative, and that actions do not display the required resemblance to expressions. Where a given sort of expression such as a merry smile carries us always, cases of deception apart, to the same kind of mental state, a given sort of behaviour, even verbal behaviour, may direct us to any of a number of explanatory states of mind. The reason is that an action, unlike a spontaneous expression, answers to a complex state of belief and desire and that varying combinations of belief and desire may be contrived to fit with it. My hurrying across the road may be explained by a desire not to be run over plus a belief that cars are liable to come by; or by a desire not to get my shoes sticky plus a belief that the tar in the road has begun to melt; or by a desire to avoid evil spirits plus a belief that the road is infested with them. Similarly my saying 'The lake is on fire' may come of a desire to communicate how warm the water is plus a belief that you will take me to be speaking metaphorically; or it may spring from a desire to report a very weird perception plus the belief that you will take my words in the shared literal sense.

These remarks should be sufficient to turn us aside from the intra-subjectivist argument for the distinctiveness and ultimately the unrevisability of orthodox action explanation. The inter-subjectivist counterpart must now be considered and this we can also set out in five propositions.

1 Being human ourselves we are familiar with the ways of our human culture and this familiarity is an indispensable source of insight in generating and in corroborating explanations of actions, whether or not actions which are performed in our own cultural milieu.
2 We understand an action of our own by seeing how best to construe it by the rules of the relevant cultural practice: by seeing where it fits in the matrix of existing customs and conventions.
3 We understand the action of another by setting it in a corresponding pattern. Where the other is from a different culture this understanding may require the extension and even the emendation of our received categories: we may have to create an imaginative third culture to provide an appropriate context.
4 In both of these cases the understanding of action is intuitive rather than inferential. There is no independent evidence from which we can infer how an action may be best placed: we see our way more or less intuitively to the most suitable representation.
5 The understanding of action is improved by following the familiar hermeneutical circle or spiral, whereby we move to the parts in order the better to understand the whole, back to the whole in order better to understand the parts, and so on indefinitely. The whole in relation to which an action has to be understood is the shared cultural context.

This version of the hermeneutic argument retains many of the emphases of the other one, in particular the insistence that explanation is not inferentially based, and, as the presentation suggests, it also has a close structural resemblance to its precursor. The striking difference is that it replaces the earlier psychological focus with a sociological one, depicting action explanation as a matter of exploring the possibilities of cultural representation rather than one of probing the agent's moving states of mind. This change has generated as a corollary an idea which is particularly associated with hermeneutic philosophy today, although it does not appear in our presentation. This is the claim that there is no such thing as the correct interpretation of an action, since interpretation is relative to the cultural categories which it puts into play, and there is no saying that one set of categories is superior to another. The lesson drawn from this claim is that interpretative success is to be measured pragmatically, say by the extent to which the explanation adopted underpins a smooth process of interaction between the agent and his audience. These are very engaging thoughts but unfortunately we do not have the space to investigate them explicitly in this treatment.

Putting aside the matter of its merits in other regards, what we have to ask is whether this second hermeneutic argument does anything to establish the non-inferential nature of action explanation. Again the crucial claim is made in the fourth proposition, where we are told that the process whereby an explanation is divined is not an inferential one, but something more intuitive in nature. The reasoning offered in support of this however is no more compelling than that which was provided in the first case. It is said that we cannot break out of the language of explanation in order to provide an independent characterisation of the cues which guide us towards one account rather than another, and that short of finding such an independent characterisation, we cannot think of the cues as data from which we take an inferential course (see Taylor 1971). The idea, as in the other case, is that the behavioural and circumstantial factors which guide us towards our preferred explanation become salient and mutually reinforcing pieces of evidence only when described in the terms which the explanation would suggest. When we conclude that someone did what he did out of anger, we do so because we see his circumstances as irritating, his expression as exasperated, his style as short-tempered and these factors assemble themselves for our contemplation only when we are already possessed of the idea that anger is the operative motivation. But this idea does not give us reason to regard the relationship between the cues and the explanatory condition that they indicate as non-inferential, any more than the corresponding idea pressed on us the conclusion that expressions do not provide an inferential basis for acknowledging what they express. If one holds on to the assumption that the evidence on which a theory is based must be describable in theory-independent terms one may be led to conclude that the hermeneutic argument, in one or the other form, isolates a distinctive feature of action explanation. However, we have already seen that this assumption is groundless.

This is enough on the first argument for the unrevisability of the orthodox conception of agents. If action explanation were distinctively non-inferential then there might have been a case for arguing that this made the scheme which it engaged, the orthodox conception, resistant to scientific regimentation, experiment and amendment. In neither of its versions however does the hermeneutic argument establish such a non-inferential status: the status ascribed to action explanation is one which we may expect other explanations to exemplify too, at least if we grant that descriptions of data may have theoretical as well as empirical content: that they may be theory-laden. The hermeneutic tradition is a rich and suggestive one and there are many points emphasised within it which one would want to see built into a full understanding of what it is to interpret the doings and sayings of people. But it does not give us the thing we presently require: a reason for arguing that the orthodox conception of agents is not liable to be indefinitely revised in the scientific manner.

## 5 THE REVISABILITY ISSUE: ACTION EXPLANATION IS NOT NON-CAUSAL

The second argument for the unrevisability of the orthodox conception of agents claims that action explanation is distinguished from the explanation of natural events through being non-causal, and that this feature makes the scheme which sponsors the explanation resistant to scientific appropriation and amendment. Where the claim that action explanation is non-inferential was associated with the broad Continental tradition of philosophy, and especially with the hermeneutical, this may reasonably be linked with the Anglo-American tradition, and in particular with the school of philosophical psychology to which Ludwig Wittgenstein's later work gave rise in the 1950s and 1960s. There have been people within each approach who have defended the thesis ascribed to the other, and there have even been individuals like Charles Taylor who have some claim to membership of each tradition. By and large however the non-inferential thesis is distinctive of the Continental tradition, and the non-causal one of the Anglo-American. Those who have been prominent in their defence of the non-causal claim include Elizabeth Anscombe (1963), William Dray (1957), Martin Hollis (1977), Anthony Kenny (1963), A.R. Louch (1967), A.I. Melden (1961), R.S. Peters (1958), Charles Taylor (1964), G.H. Von Wright (1971) and Peter Winch (1958).

The proposition that action explanation is non-causal is, it should be mentioned, logically independent of the proposition that it is non-inferential. One might think that such explanation locates causal antecedents and yet hold by the view that it is essentially intuitive: indeed sometimes it appears that this is what Dilthey himself believed. And on the other side one might regard the explanation as non-causal, taking it to illuminate the action other than by tracing it to generative antecedents, and still look on the enterprise as dependent on straightforward inferential reasoning. There is reason to think that this view may have been assumed by some of the defenders of the Wittgensteinian position.

There are two quite distinct things maintained by someone who argues that what makes action explanation distinctive is that it is non-causal: first, that the explanation of natural events is causal; and second, that action explanation differs in this respect from such regular accounting. With the previous argument there were two corresponding claims but the first, to the effect that regular explanation is inferentially based, seemed so uncontentious that we did not give it much attention. In the present case we must consider both elements in the brief presented, for the first is as open to question as the second. We shall spend some time investigating the nature of explanation in general before we turn to action explanation in particular. What we shall argue is that while the regular explanation of events is indeed causal, there is no reason to maintain that action explanation differs from it in this regard.

Defenders of our second argument for the distinctiveness of action explanation, and the unrevisability of the orthodox conception of agents, have been notoriously taciturn about the assumption that the explanation of natural events is causal. Generally it seems to have been taken that the sense in which such explanations is causal is to be understood by Hume's recommended account of causality: according to this, one event is the cause of a second if events of the first kind regularly precede events of the second and are spatially contiguous with them. Since it is now almost universally admitted that this account is inadequate, we must reconstruct the claim around a different understanding of causality, if we are to give the second argument any chance of winning our assent (on the Humean account see Mackie 1974). Such reconstruction is not particularly paternalistic on our part, since although causality was mostly understood on a Humean model, defenders of the argument tended to hold the strong view that the explanation of natural events is causal in some sense, Humean or not, and that in that sense action explanation is non-causal (see Melden 1961, p.17). In what follows then, we take a general look at the theory of explanation and conduct a line of argument which leads to the conclusion that regular explanation is indeed causal. This conclusion will put us in a position to examine the claim that action explanation is distinguished through being non-causal, for it justifies the presupposition of the claim and it gives us a determinate sense in which to interpret it.

There are two grossly distinguishable accounts of what it is that makes something an explanation, what it is that gives a statement explanatory power. The one would identify an explanatory statement or set of statements, roughly speaking, by its form, and the other by its content and effect: if you like, its force. The standard instance of the first approach is the so-called covering-law theory of explanation which derives from Mill and received its classic formulation in the work of Carl Hempel (see Hempel 1965). According to this account explanation, whether it be the explanation of an event or the explanation of a standing condition, consists in an argument which guarantees or makes probable the truth of a proposition asserting that the event occurs or the condition obtains. The premises of the argument are required by the account to contain a law, universal or probabilistic, and they are also supposed to be true or at least well warranted. Further they are each stipulated to be essential in the sense that the argument would not go through without them.

This covering-law analysis of explanation has one conspicuous merit, which is that it matches our intuition that an explanation should render what is to be explained relatively unsurprising. We call for explanation of things which, although we know them to be so, we think could have been otherwise so far as our background knowledge goes, and the effect of the explanation is to close or at least constrain this possibility: to show that the possibility of things being otherwise is not as open as it had appeared (see Mellor 1976). The covering law account captures this feature of explanation, for the possibility that something be otherwise is eliminated or reduced when we realise that its being as it presently is follows, for certain or probabilistically, from how certain other things are in the context.

The aspiration of the covering law theorist is to provide, mainly in terms of form, a specification of conditions necessary and sufficient for a statement to explain a given event or condition. That goal, we would like to urge, is not capable of being fulfilled and we think that we should therefore go over to an account of explanation from a different angle. The failure of the aim of giving a formal account is seen first of all in the fact that one set of true premises can make a result relatively probable, another lower it. Smith's recovery from his appendectomy is probable granted that most patients survive that operation, but it is rather less than probable granted that he is ninety years of age and that many patients in that age bracket do not survive appendectomies. This fact forces a non-formal amendment on the covering-law theorist, to some effect such as that in statistical explanation the premises must contain all the information available that affects the probability of the event or condition to be explained (see Hempel 1965).

Even with this revision made there is trouble in store for the covering law theory. One source of difficulty is that we can construct arguments satisfying the conditions given which we would not consider for a moment as explanations of the events or conditions recorded in their conclusions. Thus we may argue: water boils under normal conditions when heated to 212 degrees Fahrenheit; this water is under normal conditions and is not boiling; therefore this water has not been heated to 212 degrees Fahrenheit. We have no tendency to regard this as an explanation of the water's not having been heated to the appropriate temperature even though it satisfies the conditions. Again consider: whenever the barometer falls the weather changes; the barometer has fallen; therefore the weather has changed or will change. This would not be taken as an explanation of the weather's changing, for the barometer is only a symptom of the altered atmospheric pressure that gives the true explanation. And a final example:

the sun in the sky is at such and such an elevation; the length of the shadow cast by the flagpole is so-and-so; therefore, granted the physics of light, the height of the flagpole is so-and-so. Where we would be happy to quote the height of the pole in explanation of the length of the shadow, we find absurd the reversal of the relationship involved in this example.

It is an irresistible thought that in these examples the premises fail to explain the events recorded because they do not point us towards causes, but rather towards associated or irrelevant factors. This observation may suggest that the covering law theory should be amended non-formally in the way in which it has been amended to cater for the problem with probabilities mentioned above. Such amendments have been proposed, specifications being entered on the explanatory factors, which are designed to restrict them to the appropriate causal ones. Attempts of the kind promise to be no more successful however than have been attempts to analyse what makes something a cause of another (see Brand 1976, Sosa 1975). Attempts at the analysis of causality usually specify that the cause cannot be later than the effect, and that in the circumstances the cause is necessary and/or sufficient for the effect, but even when these conditions are elucidated and supplemented they fail to distinguish causal connections from certain other relations. Thus the occurrence of a component will satisfy the conditions for being the partial cause of an event even though we would not regard it for a moment as a cause. Where we find such failure we may expect to find attempts at patching up the covering law account also unsuccessful. Just as we would not regard my lacing up my boots as a cause of my dressing, so we would not find an account which mentioned that factor explanatory of why I dressed.

The source of difficulty which we have been probing is the failure of the covering law account to specify that the factors mentioned in an explanation, or at least in the explanation of an event, should be causal. A second source of difficulty is that even where a statement seems not to be offend on the first score, it may fail to count as an explanation because of the way in which it engages with the background knowledge of those seeking enlightenment. Suppose one's dog falls ill. It will be explanatory of the event if one discovers that all dogs eating such and such a new brand of petfood fall ill, and the statement can be cast in the format specified by the covering law theory: all dogs which ate Dog-y-dog fell ill; Rover ate Dog-y-dog; therefore Rover fell ill. However if, with the knowledge about the general effect of Dog-y-dog in the background, one seeks an explanation of Rover's illness, the statement which was earlier found explanatory will prove no longer so, despite the fact that it continues to satisfy the covering law format.

The difficulty here is that whether a statement constitutes an explanation depends on how it engages with the background knowledge of the person seeking explanation. There are ways in which the covering law theorist may try to counter the problem, just as there were strategies available to him for repairing the other flaw. At this point however there is a temptation, and we have no intention of resisting it, to put aside the attempt to characterise explanation by their form, or by their form plus their fulfilment of certain conditions such as that imported to deal with the problem about probabilities. We may well allow ourselves to investigate the other approach to explanation, which highlights the content and effect - the force - of an explanatory statement, rather than its form.

Let us begin the inquiry with the recognition that there are many uses of the word 'explain' and its cognates, and that it would be rash to seek a single analysis of the lot. Since our topic is the explanation of actions, we may restrict our target and concentrate on the explanation of events: the explanation of why one or another event, described as such and such, occurred. When should we say then that a statement will count as explanatory of an event?

One condition that we must acknowledge, consistently with the merit that we admitted in the covering law account, is that the statement must render the event described in such and such a manner, as relatively unsurprising. This means that it must make the event so described seem relatively more probable than it had seemed before and, ideally, that it must make it seem sufficiently probable to be less surprising than its non-occurrence would have been: it must give it a probability of greater than 50 per cent. Some have urged that we sometimes explain an event by revealing it to have had perhaps even lesser probability than had been thought, as when we put the sequence of tails down to chance (see Salmon 1971). We would prefer to say that in such cases we deny that there is any explanation available for the event, properly speaking; it just is a matter of chance (see Mellor 1976). More on this later.

To say that an explanatory statement must render an event relatively unsurprising is not necessarily to go the way of the covering law theory and represent an explanation as an argument or inference. That representation is a distortion, although the popularity of the covering law approach may have obscured the fact. For in explaining an event there is no question of wanting to infer the truth of the proposition giving it expression. Normally the truth of that proposition is taken as granted and the last thing required is to put it on a firm inferential footing. The explanation of an event then may be taken to consist in a statement whose effect is to make the event, described as such and such, seem relatively unexceptional, and not to involve the construction of an argument with that statement in the premises and the proposition that the event occurred in the conclusion (see Mellor 1976 and Salmon 1971).

But what more do we say of the explanation of an event than that it is a statement which renders the event relatively unsurprising? The criticisms we made of the covering law theory can help us here. We noted that the factors mentioned in an explanation have a causal bearing on the event explained and that whether a statement is found explanatory of an event depends on the background knowledge of the person seeking explanation. A statement which explains an event then must give us causal understanding; and the understanding it gives us must be an advance on the cognitive status quo. In a phrase, the explanation of an event must advance us in the search for the event's causes (see Quine and Ullian 1978).

As we have already noted, the analysis of the causal relationship between events is notoriously elusive. Some points however must be mentioned if we are to have a grasp of the ways in which our causal understanding of an event may be advanced. The causal connection between two events C and E, where C is a total cause of E, and not just part of a total cause, is usually thought to involve the following: first, that C is not a later occurrence than E, second, that C is spatio-temporally contiguous to E, or that it is connected by a chain of spatio-temporally contiguous events to E, and third, that C is necessary and/or sufficient in the circumstances for E. The questions lurking here are legion. The temporal clause allows simultaneous causation but in such a case how do we distinguish cause from effect, since the other clauses treat them symmetrically? One answer may be to say that the events are not so much simultaneous as overlapping and that earlier parts of the cause are always responsible for later parts in the effect. The contiguity clause is obscure for the reason that our notions of what is contiguous and what not depend to a good extent on prevailing physical theory. Such a dependence makes the concept of causality more fragile than is generally assumed, although if we learn to tolerate it we may eventually come to cherish it.

The very tricky issue however come up with the third clause. A cause need not be necessary in the circumstances because the effect is overdetermined. But do we really allow that it may not be sufficient: do we admit non-deterministic causation? That is a first question. A second has to do with the basis for the necessity and/or sufficiency mentioned in the clause. An event C, redescribed as 'the event such that it occurs in such and such a position, and at such and such a time, relative to E', will automatically pass as sufficient for E. Clearly the basis sought for sufficiency cannot be the redescriptive one manufactured here and must be something else: the laws of nature. But then we have pressed upon us the unresolved problem of how to distinguish such laws from true accidental generalisations (see Goodman 1973). And there is a third difficulty which also arises with the clause under discussion. There are cases of event pairs which seem to fit all the clauses but which we would not count as causally related, such as: my saying 'Thank' and my saying 'Thank you', my sister's having a baby and my becoming an uncle, my being born in 1900 and my being seventy nine in 1979. With these examples one wants to say that the events are not really distinct but the trouble with the remark is that we lack any agreed criterion for deciding whether apparently different events are one or many.

These comments will remind us of what we know and do not know about causality: the cement, as Hume described it, of our universe. What then may it mean for an explanation to advance us in the search for the causes of an event? Suppose we are presented with an event described as an A-event. We may be advanced in our search for its causes by being directed to a B-event which is its total proximate cause or a part of that cause, supposing the total one to be a combination of the B-event with a C-event - a combination which may or may not be describable as a single complex event. We may be advanced instead, or in addition, by being pointed towards a total or partial non-proximate cause: a proximate cause of the proximate cause, or a proximate cause of the proximate cause of the proximate cause, or whatever. Finally, we may be further advanced by having a hitherto ignored feature of the A-event traced to a feature of a given cause of the A-event, the assumption being that causes pass on certain marks to their effects. These three sorts of advancement in causal understanding, and there may well be others, can be neatly characterised as causal embedding, causal excavation, and causal enrichment. We embed an event causally when we point to its immediate origin; we excavate it when we turn up its remoter springs; and we enrich it when we see how one or another of its features is the legacy of its ancestors. These varieties of understanding will be illustrated shortly by reference to our explanations of action.

We had concluded that the explanation of an event is a statement which renders it relatively unsurprising under its given description and now we have added that it is a statement which advances us in the causal understanding of the event. It is tempting to speculate at this point that the reason why an event explanation reduces surprise is precisely that it advances causal understanding: in that case it would be sufficient to mention just its aspect as causal advancement in specifying what an event explanation is. Is the speculation plausible, then? It is, at least on the condition that causes are assumed to show their effects to have been relatively probable. This condition is fulfilled in the common run of cases and here we can say without hesitation that to explain is simply to advance causal understanding. However there is one special case which requires independent comment and in conclusion we would like to turn to it.

The case is that of an event E for which the cause C is indeterministic and grossly insufficient: C undoubtedly produced E but indeterminism reigns and we believe that only in a small fraction of exactly similar cases would the counterparts of C give rise to counterparts of E. By tracing E to C we may well be advanced in our search for the causes of E, but we are not led to find E described as such, relatively unsurprising; or so it certainly seems. Are we given an explanation of E then by the causal story?

The answer to this question must be that we are not. When E is displayed as the effect of C, in a situation where other events than

E are actually more probable, what happens is not that E is explained but that it is shown to be an inappropriate subject for explanation: it is depicted as an improbable chance happening. Does this mean then that to explain an event is not simply to advance us in our causal understanding of it? Strictly speaking it does, since in the special case considered we can have causal advancement without explanation. What we can say however is that where event explanation is available, i.e. where it is possible to render the event relatively unsurprising, it is achieved by a statement that advances us in our search for the event's causes. This formulation highlights the connection between advancing the causal understanding of an event and rendering it relatively unsurprising, while reminding us of the existence of the special case.

The long discussion of the nature of explanation leaves us with the conclusion that the explanation of natural events is indeed causal, as it is said to be by those who argue that action explanation, in contrast, is a non-causal form of accounting. At this point we are in a position to examine the case made by these thinkers for the non-causal nature of our orthodox understanding of behaviour, but before turning to that topic it may be useful to indicate exactly how action explanation should be taken, if it is to be given a causal rendering. Very briefly, we can say that if an action is causally embedded in the account which indicates the basic description under which it is taken by the agent, it is progressively excavated in the further intentional accounts which show why the agent has a pro-attitude to that description, and to other descriptions short of the one which makes it seem maximally persuasive, casting the action in a desirability characterisation, or in a mix of such characterisations. My pro-attitude to forming letters, words and sentences is explained by my wanting to write plus the belief that this is the way to do so; my pro-attitude to writing by my wanting to put a lecture on paper plus my belief that this is the way to do that; my pro-attitude to setting a lecture on paper by my wanting to prepare it for publication plus my belief that this is the way to prepare it; and so on.

We say that such intentional explanations causally excavate an action, if it is causally embedded in the explanation which mentions the agent's pro-attitude to the basic description. The reason for the conditional form is that it might be held that the proximate cause of an action is the act of intending it, something which is plausibly characterised as an unconditional judgment in favour of the action (see Davidson, 1978). If the intending of the action in this sense is taken as the proximate cause then reference to that intending is what causally embeds the event and reference to the agent's pro-attitude to the basic description is presumably the first step in causal excavation. It does seem that whenever one acts intentionally, one must judge unconditionally in favour of the action and that one must therefore intend it, but consistently with admitting this one might or might not regard the intending as a cause of the action: one might take it as a simultaneous effect, or as something identical with the performance of the action. We do not wish to judge on which of these possibilities is realised, or indeed on whether the same possibility should be assumed to be realised in every case. We also do not wish to rule out the possibility that the intending is a non-proximate cause of the action, having an intermediate place in the sequence of intentional states which lead up to the pro-attitude towards the action's basic description: indeed this seems a more likely story than that which makes it the proximate cause.

So much for the causal embedding and causal excavation of action. But is there anything recognised in our scheme which might correspond with what we have called causal enrichment? We would like to suggest that the further explanation of action which refers us to one of the agent's policies, to his motivational profile, to his personality, or to his social position, can be seen as a way of causally enriching the original event. In the enrichment form of explanation one accounts for a property of the effect by pointing to a property of the cause, the former property being an inherited mark of the latter. The sort of action explanation which refers to policy and such factors does just this, for it makes sense of the property of the action which consists in its being preferred to some attractive alternatives by referring us to a property of the generative state of belief and desire: specifically, the property which is constituted by the fact that this state is realised in someone distinguished by such-and-such a policy, motivational profile, personality or social position. We call for this further explanation without questioning the intelligibility of the line of intentional explanation which refers us ultimately to a persuasive desirability characterisation. What we seek in demanding it is an account of the feature in the action of its being preferred to quite appealing alternatives. The case is parallel to one where, assuming that the noise was made by the drum, we wonder why it was so loud; or, assuming that the recession was caused by the inflation, we wonder why it was so severe.

But let us leave the claim that the regular explanation of events is causal, and the matter of how action explanations might be cast in the causal mould. What we now have to consider is the case made for the claim that action explanation is not after all causal, and that this is what distinguishes it from regular explanation, ensuring that the orthodox conception of agents is not revisable in the scientific manner. The Wittgensteinian thinkers who have defended this thesis suggest that action explanation is of the redescriptive sort that we go in for with unfamiliar objects. 'Why has the box in the corner got a glass front?', someone asks, and 'It's a television set' gives all the explanation that is normally required. The redescription fits the troublesome object into a familiar pattern, representing it as a piece of drawing room furniture which is unexceptional for having a glass front. Similarly, it is said, action explanation takes a piece of behaviour under a description which makes it puzzling, a blot on the social landscape, and redescribes it so as to restore to us a picture of the situation which puts us at ease. We are acquainted with the sort of thing presented in the redescription and do not feel any longer the pressure of puzzlement.

Since one may admit the causal nature of our understanding of action, and acknowledge still that such understanding has the redescriptive effect just emphasised, it is not clear that we shall make any headway by looking more deeply into the positive side of the Wittgensteinian claim. What we shall examine instead is a number of arguments that have appeared in the literature against the possibility that action explanation could be causal. These arguments are to be found scattered in the works of the authors mentioned at the beginning of this section but many of them are summarised in the survey articles by Donnellan (1967), Gustafson (1973) and also in the works by Davidson (1963), Davis (1979) and Nordenfelt (1974). The arguments may be divided into two groups: first, those which claim that intentional explanations lack some feature distinctive of causal accounts, and secondly those which urge that the mental states invoked in intentional explanations cannot in any case be counted as causes of the actions that they help to explain. Many of our responses are derived from Davidson (1963).

To take up the first group, there are at least three different arguments which have appeared in the literature to the effect that intentional explanations are not of the causal variety. They are: that unlike causal accounts these explanations are not always based on the application to an individual case of a generalisation about the factors involved; that unlike such accounts they are not always informative, sometimes offering us nothing better than the explanation parodied by Molière: opium induces sleep because it has a dormitive power; and finally, that unlike causal accounts they often force on us a radical recharacterisation of the event, the piece of behaviour, which they seek to explain. None of these arguments however carries any weight. Action explanations may not indeed be based on known generalisations but that proves nothing since neither in many cases are unquestionably causal accounts of natural events: if I feel a powerful vibration in a room and then see the mirror crack I am quite liable to explain the cracking by the vibration, although I have no generalisation at my disposal about the concomitance of such events. Again, to move to the third case, action explanation may often force us to redescribe the event explained but neither does this establish anything, for causal explanation often has the same effect: once the distant illuminations are explained as due to atmospheric conditions they become simply flashes of lightning.

But what of the second charge, that action explanation is often uninformative, in the manner pilloried by Molière? The thought in this argument is that if what it means for an event to be an action is that it is related appropriately to a rationalising state of mind then to invoke that state of mind in explanation of the action seems to be to make no progress: we are informed of nothing when we are told that someone went for a walk (intentionally) because his state of mind rationalised his doing so. Against this line of reasoning however it is sufficient to point out that for an intentional explanation to count as properly explanatory, it must advance us in our understanding, so that the description under which it represents the agent as desiring the action must not be that under which the action was found in need of explanation in the first place. If we are to explain someone's going for a walk we must refer to his desire to gather his thoughts or to take a break from work. It may be that there is no such further desire to refer to, the walk having seemed attractive just in its own right, but in that case neither is there any further intentional explanation to be given. 'He just wanted to' is not an explanation but an indication that the request for explanation is at this point misplaced.

The second group of arguments against the causal construal of the intentional explanation of actions comprises three arguments to the effect that the mental states invoked in such explanation cannot count as causes of the actions which they help to explain, and that the explanation cannot therefore be causal in nature. Two of these arguments may be dismissed fairly quickly but the third will require more lengthy consideration. The two less weighty ones claim in the one case that the mental states involved in action explanation cannot be causes since they are not events but precisely states, and in the other that the pair formed by a mental state and the action it explains is not an instance of a law in the way in which a cause-effect pair is required to be. Against the first argument the point to make is that even if we grant that causes are always events, what may be regarded as the cause of an intentionally explained action is not the appropriate state of belief and desire itself, but the onset of that state, something which must certainly be regarded as an event.

So far as the second argument is concerned, we may agree that a cause-effect pair must be the instance of a lawlike regularity: that is, that it must be the case that the two events exemplify types such that the first type of event is regularly connected with the second, and we are able to say that had the one sort of event been realised just now the second would also have been brought about, or at least that there would have been a certain independently checkable chance of the second's being brought about. This proposition, sometimes called the principle of the nomological character of causality, is admissible because it would be self-refuting if we claimed that A caused B in a given instance but were not prepared to admit that A-type events had any tendency to cause B-type ones, under any typification of A and B: in that case we would not be prepared to say that there was any general feature of the singular instance which justified our assertion of a causal relation, i.e. we would be representing the assertion as arbitrary (but see Anscombe 1971). The second argument above says that the pair formed by a mental state and the action it explains cannot be a cause-effect pair, since it is not an instance of a lawlike regularity. We have absolutely no reason to be persuaded by this point however since while we may not know of a law connecting the pair of items in question, the conviction that they are causally related is sufficient grounds for thinking that there must be one. Notice that while we classify the items as on the one hand, the belief that p combined with the desire that q, and on the other, the bringing about of r, the typifications under which they are related in a lawlike manner may be quite different: it may even be that they represent the factors in physicalistic terms, the relevant law being a law of physical theory (see Davidson 1970).

We have yet to present the third member of the second group of arguments against the causal construal of the intentional explanation of actions. This is the famous 'logical connection argument' and it can be set out in the following four propositions (cf.Stoutland 1970).

1 Not really distinct events cannot be causally related.
2 Logically connected events are not really distinct.
3 A mental state is logically connected to an action it explains intentionally.
4 Therefore such a mental state cannot be causally related to the corresponding action.

The first of the three premises is uncontentious, for as we have seen, the following event pairs, which intuitively are pairs of not really distinct events, would not count as causally related: my saying 'Thank' and my saying 'Thank you', my sister's having a baby and my becoming an uncle, my being born in 1900 and my being seventy-nine in 1979. Let us grant the truth of this first premise then and concentrate our attention on the second and third.

To say that two events are logically connected is to say that knowledge of the existence of the first allows us to infer the existence of the second, or vice versa: and this, without the invocation of any empirical generalisation about their concomitance; the inference, as we say, is licensed a priori. Is it the case then that logically connected events are not really distinct? Not at all, because on the definition offered, and there is no adequate alternative available, any two events, however really distinct, can be represented as logically connected. Here we can make use of a trick which we also employed in our discussion of causality. Take any two events, C and E, and characterise the first as 'the event such that it occurs in such and such a position, and at such and such a time, relative to E'. From knowledge of the occurrence of the first, described in the recommended way, it will now be possible to infer a priori the occurrence of the second and the events must be regarded as logically connected. It follows therefore that a logical connection between two events is no proof of the lack of a real distinction. Those who think that it is must be guilty of one of two mistaken assumptions. They must fail to recognise that whether a logical connection holds between two events turns on how they are described and that appropriate descriptions can be manufactured at will; that, or they must imagine that some descriptions of an event are 'natural', others 'artificial' concluding that a logical connection obtains only in the case where the natural descriptions of the events license the required a priori inference. The first assumption would be straightforward oversight however, and the second would be extremely difficult to maintain, there being no obvious criterion whereby the natural-artificial distinction can be drawn.

The failure of the second premise means the collapse of the argument but it may be worth commenting briefly on the third: the proposition that a mental state is logically connected to an action it explains intentionally. Such a state will consist in a belief and desire which rationalise the action under a given description A, the desire being a pro-attitude towards events of type B and the belief a conviction that realising A is a likely or certain way of bringing about a B. The idea in the third premise is that under these descriptions the mental state and the action allow an a priori inference, either from the first to the second or from the second to the first. But even this is mistaken, for on the one hand the state could have been realised without engendering the corresponding action: a distraction or another desire might have intervened to prevent the behavioural issue; and on the other the action could have been brought about without the state having occasioned it, for as we have seen an action described in a given way may be rationalised by any of an indefinite number of belief-desire combinations. Thus were we to accept the second assumption mentioned above, taking events to be logically connected only if their 'natural' descriptions allow the required a priori inference, we would not be persuaded by the argument. The descriptions of mental state and action which are employed in an intentional explanation must surely pass as natural descriptions and they do not allow the inference desired (but see note 5 below).

More would require to be said in a full and sympathetic account of the view of action explanation taken by Wittgensteinian writers on philosophical psychology. What we have seen however must be sufficient to convince us that no case has been made out for the conclusion that where the explanation of natural events is causal, action explanation is not so. In any event there is a simple but strong argument with which we can counter such a claim. When we explain an action by reference to a rationalising state of belief and desire, we clearly imply not just that the agent was in that state of mind at the time of acting, but that his being in the state was relevant to the action performed: it was not just a coincidental circumstance. But what sense of relevance can this be, if not causal relevance? What is it that we imply, if not that the state was responsible for bringing about the action performed? These questions will remain rhetorical, and will have the effect of reinforcing the causal construal of action explanation, until the time when the opponents of that construal put forward some alternative suggestions about the matter in hand.

Had the case been made out for a non-causal construal of action explanation then it might have been plausible to claim that the orthodox conception of agents employed in such explanation is not subject to the radical sort of revision characteristic of scientific theory-development. Since there is no more reason to regard that explanation as non-causal than there is to see it as non-inferential, the unrevisability of the orthodox scheme remains something unproven. At this point then we must look further, if we are to vindicate the Verstehen point of view. We must seek out some other reason for thinking that the orthodox scheme is unrevisable. This, we shall argue, is to be found in the failure of intentional action explanation to be, not inferential or causal, but nomothetic.

## 6 THE REVISABILITY ISSUE: ACTION EXPLANATION IS NON-NOMOTHETIC

The third approach to the revisability issue, like the third approach to the issue of replaceability, is associated particularly with the emergence of the semantic viewpoint in recent philosophy. Two key ideas lie at the origin of the approach: one, that in order to interpret utterances and more generally to explain actions it is necessary to assume behavioural and attitudinal rationality and two, that the assumption of rationality in the explanation of actions makes the exercise methodologically distinctive. So far as the lesson for human science is concerned the approach has not been properly explored up to now and we hope that the present contribution will be part of a widely spread investigation (see Davidson 1974b, Pettit 1978 and 1979a).

The precise claim in this third approach is that unlike regular event explanation the intentional explanation of actions is not nomothetic: it does not involve the postulation of a 'nomos' or law. We saw in the last section that a causal explanation may not be guided by a known generalisation about the concomitance of the cause and effect, but that if the explanation is sound the cause-effect pair must be an instance of a causal regularity. Roughly speaking, an explanation of an event is nomothetic if accepting it involves a commitment to a certain sort of formulation of the regularity in question, albeit not necessarily a formulation known in advance and used as an explanatory guide: in this sense it must involve the postulation of a law.

At the beginning of the last section we noted that the claim that action explanation is non-causal was logically independent of the claim that it is non-inferential. It is worth noting here also that the present claim about such explanation is independent of both of the other two. There are eight possible combinations of claims and they are set out perspicuously in the following table.

| | Nomothetic | Causal | Inferential |
|---|---|---|---|
| Case 1 | + | + | + |
| Case 2 | + | + | − |
| Case 3 | + | − | + |
| Case 4 | + | − | − |
| Case 5 | − | − | − |
| Case 6 | − | − | + |
| Case 7 | − | + | − |
| Case 8 | − | + | + |

In the first four combinations action explanation is held to involve laws. The cases differ insofar as the laws are said to be causal or not, and insofar as we are thought to have intuitive access to their truth or are denied such access. Some of the combinations may not be plausible, entailing counterintuitive claims, but none of them is strictly inconsistent. For each we can imagine a state of affairs under which its constituent claims would be simultaneously true. The four combinations in the second half of the list all deny that action explanation involves laws. They differ however on just the grounds that engage the earlier cases, dividing on whether the explanation is nonetheless causal, or nonetheless intuitive. Again, while some of these combinations are fairly implausible, none of them is strictly inconsistent.

To begin then to set out our case for the distinctiveness of action explanation, it is necessary to give a more precise account of when the explanation of an event should be characterised as nomothetic. When someone explains an event E by reference to another event C, we may suppose that he believes that there is something about C-type events which means that E-type events follow or tend to follow: this by acquiescence in the principle of the nomological character of causality. Granted this, we can give two conditions which are jointly sufficient and individually necessary for the explanation to count as nomothetic. The first is a condition which we take to be realised by all event explanations with which we are familiar, including explanations of actions: that the person offering the explanation does not think it wholly misplaced to ascribe to him acceptance of a formulation of the regularity to which he is committed, in the terms 'C' and 'E' that he uses to describe the events. He admits that he is committed to a proposition of something like this form, or a probabilistic variant: 'Whenever a C-type event occurs, an E-type event follows'. We say, something like this form, because we must allow the person offering the explanation to qualify his account of the underlying regularity in response to objections. If it is pointed out that we would not expect an E-type event to follow a C-type one under these or the other circumstances, we cannot prohibit the person from refining the content of his commitment, entering one or another qualifying clause into the proposition given.

The second condition which a nomothetic explanation must fulfil can now be formulated. It is that the proposition to which the person offering the explanation is committed must turn out to be something that is independently falsifiable. It must be the case that we can describe circumstances which if they were realised would give us reason to consider revising or rejecting that proposition, even if in the end we found it more attractive to hold onto the belief and make some other compensating adjustment in our views. In other words, the proposition must have at least putative counterexamples; it must not be immune to rational amendment under presently conceivable circumstances. Without wanting to say that there are truths which could never be rationally denied under the pressure of empirical evidence, we can admit that there are truths which we would not see reason to give up, granted our other beliefs, under any imaginable circumstances: under such conditions the less costly amendment to our views would always be to let some other tenet go. Such truths we may describe as contextually a priori. They are a priori in the context of our other beliefs but not absolutely so, for given a presently undreamt-of alternative to that context, some revolutionary theoretical perspective, it might be that some circumstances would rationally lead us to deny the truths that we now hold so dear (see Pettit 1979b, Putnam 1977, Quine 1951). The second condition required for an explanation to be nomothetic is that the proposition to which the person explaining is committed, the proposition that formulates the regularity in which he believes, must not be one which we would agree in designating as contextually a priori.

On the account described by our two conditions, a nomothetic explanation of an event is one in which a law is postulated that is not itself so deeply espoused as to be held back from the forum of empirical questioning. The explanation is not the application to an individual case of a principle that is so unshakeably entrenched that the only thing up for discussion is the construal of the case itself: in such an exercise, if the explanation miscarries in some way, the principle will not be called into question, only the reading of the case as one where the principle applied. Nomothetic explanation is an exercise in which the implied general proposition is itself at risk. It represents the growing edge of a body of knowledge subject to continuing accumulation and amendment. Non-nomothetic explanation on the other hand engages a fundamentally unquestionable law and represents the application of an established system to a particular case, an application whose success is not seriously in doubt. The one exercise is rightly characterised as a matter of exploring the facts, since the facts are allowed to dictate a revision of the scheme engaged. The other is more a matter of saving the appearances, since the scheme is not itself subject to revision and the only challenge is to find a construal of the facts which will show how it applies.[4]

Our claim is that whereas in general the explanation of natural events is nomothetic, the intentional explanation of action is not. To take the first point about regular explanation, we can check this by constructing examples of accounts that we would spontaneously offer for various phenomena, extricating the principles implied in those accounts, and examining the principles to see whether they are contextually a priori or not. Suppose that I explain the cracking of a jug by my putting boiling water in it. From such an explanation it should be possible to extricate an implied principle, refinements being entered to cater for the objections foreseen: say, a proposition to the effect that whenever glass of the kind in the jug is heated to the temperature to which boiling water would raise it under normal atmospheric pressure the glass cracks. The question then is whether such a principle is one for which we can imagine putative counter-examples. The answer to the question in the instance on hand would certainly be affirmative, for in the case where we failed to crack the glass by realising the conditions mentioned, our natural inclination would be to disbelieve the law in its present form and to look for amendments: it would not be to hold the law fast and look for other reasons for the failure to crack the glass.

The claim that the explanation of natural events is generally nomothetic can only be tested by sustained recourse to such examples and, happily, the exercise must be left to the reader. We should emphasise however that since common sense and scientific bodies of knowledge about nature contain contextually a priori propositions as well as less deeply entrenched ones, there is no reason to hold that the explanation of such natural events is exclusively nomothetic. For examples of such contextually a priori propositions, one might cite a guiding methodological axiom such as: if A, B and C are rigid bodies near at hand and A is longer than B and B than C, then A must be longer than C; or one might give a substantive law, such as the principle of mass-energy conservation. Where principles of this kind are engaged in event explanations, the accounts offered will not count as nomothetic explanations: they will not be genuinely exploratory acts, but exercises in saving the appearances.

But we must turn now to intentional action explanations, and to the claim that these are non-nomothetic in structure. We believe that each one of us in offering such an explanation displays a commitment to a non-probabilistic principle about all normal human beings and that the principle is in every case a contextually a priori proposition. Why should the principle concern all human beings, and not just the individual agent in question? There is no other answer than that it just does. In the action explanations which we offer we bring to bear on individual persons our general view of normal human beings, and not just specific knowledge appertaining to them. And why should the principle be, not just general, but universal: why should it take a non-probabilistic form? Again the answer is, it just does. Suppose that we reveal a commitment to the link between a certain mental state and a corresponding action; that on a given occasion we become persuaded that an agent is in the state in question; and that, to our surprise, the appropriate action does not follow. In such a case we always feel required to explain away the failure of the action to ensue: we got the state of mind wrong in the first place, the agent underwent a sudden mental transformation, the agent is not in normal possession of his senses, or whatever. This shows that we think of the link to which we had originally displayed a commitment as universal rather than probabilistic: the causality involved is deterministic.

The sort of principle to which intentional action explanation reveals a commitment may be extricated by the usual process of forcing the person explaining to construct a formulation which resists the foreseeable lines of objection. Paul Churchland has attempted to work out the form of the principle in question and we may borrow the account which he offers (Churchland 1970). It is particularly suitable that we should base our argument on this account since Churchland is quite scientistic in his commitments, arguing elsewhere that there is no reason to think that an advanced neurophysiology could not displace the orthodox conception of agents (Churchland 1979). The formulation, it should be noticed, is in a form of notation favoured by logicians. At the beginning we find '(X) (ϕ) (A) . . .' and this should be read 'For all X, and for all ϕ (pronounced 'phi'), and for all A . . .'. X is meant here to be any agent, ϕ any desired state of affairs (such as bringing about a desired event, B), and A any action: the point is clear from the overall context.

Here then is Churchland's formulation of the principle implicit in an intentional explanation to the effect than an agent did A because he saw it as a way of realising ϕ, and he wanted ϕ.

(X) (ϕ) (A) (If,
1. X wants ϕ, and
2. X believes that A-ing is a way for him to bring about ϕ under those circumstances, and
3. there is no action believed by X to be a way for him to bring about ϕ,under the circumstances, which X judges to be as preferable to him as, or more preferable to him than A-ing and
4. X has no other want (or set of them) which, under the circumstances, overrides his want ϕ, and
5. X knows how to A, and
6. X is able to A,

then
7. X A-s)(Churchland 1970, pp.221-2).

This frame gives us a form in which to lift out the principle implicit in any intentional explanation, although doing so may often seem a pedantic exercise. Thus if I explain someone's going to a concert by his desire to relax his mind the principle to which I commit myself can be extricated by putting 'go to a concert' in place of 'A' and 'mental relaxation' in place of 'ϕ'. I believe, it transpires, that for any agent, for any case of mental relaxation, and for any action of going to a concert, if the agent wants mental relaxation, believes that going to a concert is a way for him to bring about mental relaxation, believes that there is no equally or more preferable way of bringing about mental relaxation, has no other want which overrides his desire for mental relaxation, knows how to go to a concert, and is able to go to a concert, then he goes to a concert.

If we grant that the Churchland frame gives us at least approximately the sort of principle implicit in intentional action explanation what we have to ask is whether such principles are contextually a priori or not. Our claim is that they are, and that the explanations in which they are engaged are not therefore of the nomothetic variety.[5] The sort of thing maintained in one of these principles is not something of such a kind that we can imagine circumstances which would rationally lead us to reconsider whether it is after all sound. The only doubt which might be raised is whether the principle holds in the case where an agent is visited by moral weakness or some such failure. This doubt however is misplaced for as Churchland himself suggests, moral weakness makes itself felt, not in the link between the conditions described in clauses 1 to 6 and the action described in 7, but rather in the practical reasoning which leads the agent to the state of mind characterised by clauses 3 and 4. Practical reasoning may be taken to issue in an unconditional judgment in favour of the action performed and we may assume that we have such a judgment where we have (clause 3) the formation of the belief that there is no equally or more attractive way of realising the desired state of affairs and (clause 4) the emergence of the desire for that state of affairs as a want which is not overridden by any rivals. Granted the competence conditions of clauses 5 and 6, such a judgment naturally issues in action.[6]

A little reflection will enable us to see both how it is possible, and why it is inevitable, that under no imaginable circumstances would we find reason to reconsider the sort of thing maintained in one of our principles of intentional explanation. The possibility of holding onto a principle under any circumstances is ensured by the fact that in no instance are there firm indices of the fulfilment of clauses 1 to 6 which would assure us that an agent was definitely in the state of mind described by those clauses, independently of seeing whether he performed the appropriate action. If there were such indices available then we could envisage a situation where they were realised but where the action failed to follow, and such a situation would constitute a putative counterexample to the principle. As it is, while there are various behavioural, circumstantial and expressive cues for telling us what state of belief and desire an agent is in, these are not sufficient to persuade us that clauses 1 to 6 of a principle are fulfilled in a case where the action described in 7 fails to ensue. We may hazard a guess in a particular case that the appropriate conditions are realised but our divination will always be sufficiently tentative for us to be able to assume that we got matters wrong in the event of the agent not behaving appropriately: and even if we do not grant that, we may assume that the agent changed his mind between the time of our divination and his action, or that he is not after all a normal human agent (see Pettit 1978, 1979a).

The inevitability of our holding onto one of the principles implied in intentional explanation is copperfastened as firmly as the possibility. It derives from the fact that the principles give specific expression to matters admitted at a general level within the assumption of behavioural rationality: this means that the principles are as irresistible as that assumption itself. When we assume behavioural rationality in an action, we take it that the piece of behaviour in question is the issue of a rationalising state of mind: spelled out in detail, that there are clauses of the form 1 to 6 to which the assertion that the agent performed the action relates as clause 7. Insofar as we take the rationalising state of mind, the state fully characterised in clauses 1 to 6, as the deterministic cause of the action, we commit ourselves to a law-like proposition of a kind which fits the Churchland frame.[7]

It appears then that intentional action explanation is not nomothetic, and that in this respect it contrasts with the general run of explanations of natural events. In the regular explanatory enterprise we put forward more or less tentative hypotheses in the act of explanation, we find reason in one or another difficulty to revise those hypotheses in some respect, we return to the explanatory task equipped with new hypotheses to postulate, and so on in an indefinite itinerary of amendment and advance. In action explanation, it now transpires, we postulate only indubitable explanatory principles and in the exercise there can never be a possibility of revising the principles and recasting the explanations. We approach an individual action, secure in the possession of these principles: they formulate what it is for a piece of behaviour to count as an action, issuing from an appropriate rationalising state of mind. It is no part of our task to look to the accuracy of these propositions; our only problem is to say under which principle the behaviour falls, assuming that it is after all an action. Thus we revolve the piece of behaviour beneath our gaze and we give thought to the agent's background, behavioural record and present circumstances, in the attempt to divine how the behaviour might be most naturally cast as an intentional action: how it might be most smoothly subsumed under one of our contextually a priori principles. Finding an explanation means rationalising the action, in a sense already discussed: it means representing it as the issue of a state of mind in which it is projected as the rational thing to do. But finding an explanation, we can now see, means rationalising the action in another sense too. It means saving the appearance of behavioural rationality by ensuring that the behaviour is suitably construed. To speak of the enterprise as rationalisation in this double sense is somewhat mischievous, for we do not intend to suggest that there is anything slipshod or sinister about the accounting procedure in question. The terminology may be excused however, if it serves to dramatise the remarkable degree of contrast between what goes on here and what goes on in the everyday explanation of natural events.[8]

In reparation for describing intentional explanation as a rationalising process, we may usefully emphasise a point implicit in the account above: that in finding the best explanation for an action we have to satisfy other constraints than that of putting a rational face on the behaviour. To assume behavioural rationality is to ascribe propositional attitudes to an agent and we have already seen that to ascribe such attitudes is to assume that the person is interested in the truth of the beliefs in question: in particular, that he is responsive to any perceived counterexamples or inconsistencies. This assumption of attitudinal rationality means that we will be loath to explain an agent's doing or saying something in a way which means attributing to him beliefs that are inconsistent with beliefs previously ascribed to him or that are blatantly contrary to available evidence. We know that people change their beliefs over time, that in any case they are often unperceptive of inconsistencies in presently held beliefs, and that they are sometimes capable of ignoring the most salient counter-evidence to their assumptions: even so however, the assumption of attitudinal rationality must be an important source of constraints on the explanation which we give of anyone's behaviour. We spoke earlier of giving thought to the agent's background, behavioural record and present circumstances in deciding how best to explain his action. These constraints can mostly be subsumed under what is required by the assumption of attitudinal rationality. The agent's background tells us what relevant beliefs he is liable to have formed in the course of his development, his behavioural record gives us direct evidence of the associated beliefs which he has held in the past, his present circumstances indicate what complex of beliefs he is likely to be in at the time of action: all of this, in a sense in which beliefs include the beliefs about desirability that go proxy for desires.

We have said sufficient in elaboration of the claim that intentional action explanation is not nomothetic and we must now ask whether this feature ensures the unrevisability of the orthodox conception of agents employed in that explanation. Before we turn to that question however it may be just worth remarking that the failure of intentional explanation to be nomothetic in our sense means that in another perhaps more common sense it will also be non-nomothetic. In this sense of the term an explanation is non-nomothetic or ideographic if the enlightenment which it gives us bears on the specific agent under discussion, and not on any significant class to which he belongs. If the principles of action explanation are as we have described them, then they are common knowledge, and the interest of the explanation cannot turn in any way on their promulgation. Thus the information value of the explanation must be wholly constituted by what it tells us of the beliefs and desires of the agent himself or at most of a restricted group of agents who are assumed to be relevantly similar. The body of knowledge in the construction of which the explanation is useful is a corpus which concerns that agent or that group of agents alone; it is not a species-wide theory (Cf. Davidson 1977, McGinn, 1979a).

But finally, and crucially, does the non-nomothetic nature of intentional explanation ensure that the orthodox conception of agents is unrevisable? Does it mean that we cannot expect that conception to be taken up by scientists, and progressively regimented, subjected to experiment, and amended? Very curtly, we can answer that it does. To say that intentional explanation is not nomothetic is to say that the body of principles which it puts into service is not at risk in the explanatory project and that it is not subject to revision in this employment. But that body of principles is nothing other than the orthodox conception of agents writ fine: it is a set of propositions which derive directly from the assumption of behavioural rationality, an assumption which in turn entails the assumption of attitudinal rationality. Thus it appears that there is no way in which scientists could take up the orthodox conception of agents, and the intentional explanation which it sponsors, without treating that conception with a deference which ensures it against radical amendment. Just as it transpired earlier in the chapter that the conception is irreplaceable, so it now turns out to be unrevisable. The twin claims of a humanistic philosophy are vindicated.

## 7 METHODOLOGICAL HUMANISM

To be a humanist in our sense is to hold that there is no possibility that the orthodox conception of agents, and the pattern of action explanation which it sponsors, could be replaced or revised. Replacement is the threat which the conception faces without, revision that which it confronts within. The arguments which the semantic viewpoint has enabled us to generate suggest that the scheme is proof against assault on both fronts. There is no real chance of the conceptions's being replaced, essentially because to replace it would be to lose the ability to assign meanings to the things said and written by people. There is no real chance of its being revised because putting the scheme into explanatory operation involves giving it the status of an unquestionable assumption. The conception is a fortress, impregnable from outside, indestructible from within. Such at any rate is the humanistic credo.

In this final section the question which we want to raise bears on the methodological significance of our stance against scientism. What view should one take as a humanist of the procedures and prospects of the human sciences, especially the social ones? A full investigation of the matter would require a separate volume but we are obliged to give some indication of the line we would defend. The humanist believes that the scheme for explaining human behaviour which we avail ourselves of in everyday life is with us indefinitely, and that there is no hope or fear that the human sciences will dislodge it. In that case there may be room for investigation which does not challenge the central tenets of the scheme, such as the psychological study of the sources of belief and desires, but it is unclear what place there can be for systematic inquiry into human behaviour, such as is practised in social psychology and in the other social sciences that concern themselves, explicitly or implicitly, with individual agents. For the humanist it cannot be a legitimate aim on the part of the social scientist to aspire to a genuinely novel theoretical construal of human action: he is stuck with the orthodox conception that is our common legacy. In that case however what is the point of the inquiry that the social scientist pursues?

We are challenged to find a purpose in social inquiry, specifically in social inquiry bent on the understanding of agents, other than the forbidden one of seeking to develop a revolutionary theoretical scheme with which to make sense of human behaviour. The edge to the problem comes of the fact that as unprofessional everyday theorists of one another's behaviour we seem to do perfectly well in applying the orthodox conception. If that is so, and if the application of that conception is the only path to the understanding of behaviour, then it is unclear what the professional inquirer has to do. It appears that the only job open to him can be the pursuit of a common sense pattern of accounting which amateurs already have well in hand.

In confronting this challenge, our response is to deny that we amateurs do as well as is popularly assumed in the explanation of behaviour. We may get by in the home ground of familiar interactions and initiatives, but our performance is scarcely remarkable in the understanding of people from other backgrounds, be these people from the past generations studied by the social historian, the foreign groups investigated by the social anthropologist, or the sub-cultures on which the social psychologist lavishes attention. As attempts to understand human agents, the disciplines of history, anthropology and psychology may be readily vindicated by the social distance of the agents usually involved. This distance is bewildering to common sense amateurs, and a stimulus to parochial construals which often make the subjects of the explanation come out as barely human. The job of the social scientist is to draw on all the imaginative parallels and other resources within his possession in the attempt to bridge the distance and transcend the limitations of common sense.

It is not incoherent, we should notice, to say at once that social science has no option but to put into operation the orthodox conception of agents implemented in common sense, and that the task of social science is to transcend the limitations of common sense, seeking out more imaginative construals of behaviour. It is one thing to go along with common sense in the acknowledgement of a conceptual scheme for making sense of the things people say and do; it is quite another to go along with common sense in the acceptance of the run of explanations generally proferred for certain forms of behaviour. The social scientist is required on the humanistic view to be a person of common sense in the first matter: he can only be a person of common sense in the second however, at the cost of having nothing significant to say.

The activity of construing human behaviour in social science cannot be modelled on the parallel attempt to account for natural events. In the latter case, as we have seen, the person seeking the explanation is in the business of advancing an overall theory, at least if he does the job systematically. He has to consider, not just how the event on hand can be best subsumed under the laws at his disposal, but whether the law which seems to cover it most adequately is in fact reliable: the case under investigation may show that it is not, and may suggest one or another line of revision. By contrast, the social scientist concerned with making sense of a piece or pattern of behaviour is not required or allowed to turn his attention to the explanatory principles which are put at his disposal by the orthodox conception of agents. His part is to take those principles on faith and to devote himself exclusively to the consideration of how the behaviour can be best subsumed under them.

This task, it should be noticed, is very much more complex than its counterpart in the explanation of natural events. At least in the ideal limit, the laws covering natural events will have exact indices determining where they apply; this is a condition for their being independently falsifiable. But with a law which has firm conditions of application it is possible to tell with a fair degree of certainty whether or not it applies in a given circumstance: what one has to see is whether or not those conditions or indices are fulfilled. Thus the job of finding the law under which a given event should be subsumed is relatively unproblematic in the regular explanatory enterprise. The case is very different with the explanation of actions, for the principles under which an action has to be subsumed do not have firm conditions of application, and the judgment as to which principle covers the case is not guided firmly by the circumstances with which one is presented. Here the person explaining has a discretion unknown in the realms of naturalistic accounting. Any of an indefinite number of principles can be fitted to the action as possible ways of rationalising it and the accountant must decide between them by reference to the numerous and often conflicting constraints deriving from the assumption of attitudinal rationality and from other sources. Intuitively, we feel that there are better and worse ways of satisfying those constraints, and better and worse ways therefore of explaining the action, but the identification of the best account is not anything so automatic and replicable as it is in the explanation of natural events.

Instead of imposing a parallel with the explanation of natural events, we prefer to see the social scientist's explanation of human behaviour on a more artistic model. The exercise can be compared to that of the imaginative writer who succeeds in communicating an insight into the behaviour of his characters which challenges and engages us, offering new ways of viewing ourselves and our acquaintances. Again, it can be compared with the procedure of the sympathetic psychiatrist who searches around for explanations of his patient's actions which will provide a liberation from some present complex, and will make possible a new pattern of relationship to other people. The enterprise, as both these models suggest, is one that requires a very fine skill, even a degree of art; it is not something that could be carried out to order, however detailed the instructions (see Pettit 1978, 1979a, and Putnam 1978).

Social science, insofar as its concern is the explanation of human behaviour, begins to look like a discipline which belongs with the humanities rather than the sciences. Social history, social anthropology, and social psychology, are attempts to do with art what is done crassly by common sense, to apply the orthodox conception of agents with imagination and sympathy in cases where it is more usually applied in a parochial and insensitive manner. Such is the methodological upshot of the humanistic point of view that we have been defending. Before leaving this methodological matter however, and drawing the chapter to a close, it may be worth mentioning that on the humanistic model there is also scope for a social science of behaviour in the familiar territory where common sense seems to reign supreme.

The further scope for social science arises out of the fact that in common sense explanation of one another's behaviour we are not generally disposed to admit what may be called reflexive concerns and this factor combines with other pressures, such as those stemming from the relationship that we may have with the agent under discussion, to render our explanation less imaginative than it might have been. A reflexive concern is not a desire for something relatively straightforward such as wealth or power or status, but a concern to be ascribed one or another straightforward desire by other people. Assuming that agents are rational, and in particular that they are capable of forming beliefs and desires in respect of the explanation which their behaviour will attract from other people, we cannot deny the possibility that their actions will often call for accounting at the reflexive level. However common sense is constitutionally set against explanation of such a kind, and this for a plausible reason (see Pettit 1978, 1979a).

In order to understand the reason, consider what would happen if people began generally to make sense of one another's actions by reference to reflexive desires. As it became less and less exceptional to interpret a given piece of behaviour in terms of a reflexive desire to be taken to have a certain first order desire, it would become less and less plausible that an agent was acting out of the reflexive concern in performing the action in question. Why should he act out of that concern if he is in a position to know that he will not succeed in persuading his audience that he has the first order desire? The result in such a case must be a deep ambiguity about the significance of the action. We must begin generally to assume, as we had done previously, that the sort of action under discussion is the product of the first order desire, or we must press a level further, and ascribe to the agent the higher reflexive concern to have ascribed to him the lower one: a path along which an indefinite regress looms. In either case the habit of explaining a given type of action by a certain sort of reflexive concern is unstable; it cannot become an entrenched pattern. Thus we should not be surprised that common sense accounting is remarkable for its lack of attention to the possibility of reflexive explanations.

This feature gives scope for social science, usually under the name of social psychology or micro-sociology, to invade even those areas where we amateurs feel that our explanations cannot be faulted. The invasion is quite dramatic in the form which it takes within the work of a micro-sociologist such as Erving Goffman. By dint of patient description and painstaking illustration this social scientist has made irresistible the conclusion that in our everyday transactions with one another we devote as much energy to the manufacture and maintenance of satisfying scenarios, scenarios in which we are happy with what is made of us by others, as we do to the accomplishment of the jobs ostensibly on hand (see for example, Goffman 1969). Goffman has revealed a level of significance in avowed actions which common sense would normally overlook, and arguably he has shown that certain 'small behaviours' which are commonly taken as non-intentional are aspects of a well orchestrated performance on the part of reflexively conscious agents.

This must be sufficient on the methodological significance of our humanistic point of view. It should be stressed that there is more to social science than the attempt to understand human behaviour, for it seeks to construe institutional phenomena as much as it tries to make sense of individual. What we have seen however is that even as the attempt to understand persons, social science is not condemned by humanism to disappear into common sense. The orthodox conception of agents may indeed be irreplaceable and unrevisable, but this does not mean that every account of human behaviour is on all fours with the marketplace explanations which that conception fosters. Social science is as likely to transcend common sense, as is sympathy likely to overcome ill will, and imagination to shatter prejudice.

# 3 THE UNDERSTANDING OF INSTITUTIONS: INDIVIDUALISM VERSUS COLLECTIVISM

## 1 THE ANATOMY OF SOCIAL LIFE

The previous chapter directed our attention to what might be called the micro-structure of the social sciences. It resolved our focus on individual people: the agents in whose actions and reactions the patterns of social life are instantiated and maintained. In this chapter we have to turn to the macro-sector of social investigation, lifting our gaze so as to get a view of the large-scale entities which agents constitute, and the large-scale phenomena to which they give rise. What we have to examine is society in its institutional aspect, rather than society as an amalgam of individuals. Social history, social anthropology and social psychology may often look at society from the point of view of individuals, seeking to understand the social by making sense of persons. This is not the only perspective adopted in social science however, or even in these particular disciplines. It is just as common, as for example in sociology and macro-economics, to have society depicted in its institutional guise, as the subject of characteristics and changes which it is difficult even to conceptualise from a micro point of view. In this chapter we are concerned with working out a philosophical account of such an approach to society, as we were concerned in the last with elaborating an analysis of the more individualistic alternative. The account which we offer will parallel the earlier one in incorporating the insights generated by the pursuit of the semantic goal.

Anything that counts as a significant social event can be characterised as involving individuals. This comes of the fact that individuals are the entities out of which society is constituted and that, as a whole does or suffers nothing that is not done or suffered by its parts, so society undergoes no visitation and sustains no activity that is not undergone or sustained by individual people. But what, it may be asked, of a natural catastrophe: is this not a significant social event, although it is not something that intrinsically involves individuals? The answer, we suggest, is that it has social significance only insofar as it bears other descriptions that refer us to individuals, such as a description of it as affecting people's fortunes, opportunities, or attitudes. The cosmic ray that passes through the atmosphere, unnoticed and innocuous, is not a social event, and neither would any happening be that failed of a connection with persons.

The proposition that social events are necessarily personal ones too seems to us unexceptional, but some qualifications may be necessary to parry opposition. Specifically, we must disavow any expressive exhaustiveness or explanatory adequacy that we might be thought to be claiming for it. On the first point: it is not suggested that social life cannot also be represented in non-personal ways, as the systematic fulfilment of certain roles; as the reliable reproduction of certain structures; or whatever. And on the second: it is not implied that the causal explanation of patterns in social life must refer us ultimately to the autonomous agency of people; what are parts of a whole may also be its pawns. Later in this chapter we shall be defending a view that confers a certain causal ultimacy on individual agents but even someone who attacked that depiction of things would have to accept the proposition presented here.

But even if the social is intrinsically personal, it must be recognised that people form groups and that much of what they do and suffer in social life entails the doing and suffering of these other entities: at the limit, of the group which the society itself forms. That people form group alliances is indisputable, for no one will deny the reality of families and villages, gangs and clubs, unions and associations, companies and institutions, or even nations and classes. That these groups are implicated in the fortunes of the individuals who compose them can be borne out by example. The actions of individuals can mean that something is done or undergone by a group of which they are members; if they complain in the group's name, then the group complains too; if they quarrel among themselves then the group suffers the consequence, experiencing crisis or perhaps breaking up. And the things passively borne by individuals can also entail that there is something done or undergone by a group they form: if they each succumb to an appropriate rule of law, this can mean that the group achieves identity or cohesion; if they are each wiped out then, unless it is a case where others can claim to carry it on, the group will be wiped out too.

Groups are extremely important realities on the social stage and to recognise this is to begin to see that even if society is composed of individuals, it is organised by institutions, groups being one sort of institutional entity. In order to see the importance of these supra-personal factors, two points should in particular be noticed. The first is that groups are not equivalent to sets or collections of their members: that, to introduce a useful term of art, they are collectives rather than collections. The set or collection is conceptualised in such a way that A and B are the same set if and only if they have the same members. This means then that a set changes identity if it loses or gains a single member. Such a principle however does not go through with groups, for a family does not become a different entity through the birth or death of a child, a company does not mutate in the turnover of its directors, a nation does not lose its identity as one generation replaces another. The failure of the principle to apply indicates that groups are assigned by us to a different ontological category from that of the collection, an assignment that warrants describing them as collectives. The category in which we place them is that of the whole which, like the physical object, is said to continue identically through time, even when its components are partially or totally replaced (see Mellor forthcoming).

In further elaboration of the point that groups are collectives which may change through time, it is worth mentioning that this makes them concrete and continuant objects. The non-concrete object, on a common way of speaking, is that which does not exist in time, and this condition is one which the set or collection meets. We do not think of the collection as occurring at a time, lasting for a time or enduring through time: unlike the event, or the process, or the continuant, it fails altogether of a temporal connection.

The collective on the other hand does exist in time, specifically in the manner of the temporal continuant. We think of it as enduring through time, despite various changes that may occur in its parts, and enduring in a sense that does not apply to a process or extended event, such as an after-dinner speech or the fall of the Roman Empire. The sense in question is caught in the remark that the collective, like any continuant, exists in toto at every moment of its existence so that to perceive it at any instant is to perceive the whole, and not just a part of the whole in existence then. The after-dinner speech is not a continuant because to hear two minutes of it is not, or at least not usually, to hear the lot; the after-dinner speaker on the other hand is a continuant because to get a glimpse of him is not just to see a second of him: it is to see the whole concrete person.

What we have been saying about groups is that they are wholes composed out of persons as parts, and that they are wholes which exist in time without temporal partition: they exist in toto at any moment. In these respects groups resemble material objects such as tables or trees, mountains or birds, dogs or people. We may notice however that in some features groups are not at all like such objects, and take on the aspect of more artificially delineated entities. The properties which mark them off distinctively are that the people who form their parts are scattered in space and that they are shared simultaneously as parts by different groups (see Quinton 1975-6). With material objects we generally require spatial contiguity of parts and non-sharing of parts by different objects, though as we move away from the objects that form the basic items of reference in scientific theory we begin to find exceptions. We might allow that one and the same forest could be crossed by large tracts of open spaces, thus admitting a scattering of parts. And with two forests which crossed one another, we might say that trees in the overlap belonged to both, thus allowing a sharing of parts. In these respects groups are like forests, rather than the general run of physical things.

We said that there were two points to be noticed if the importance of groups was to be appreciated. The first is that groups are collectives rather than collections, in particular that they are concrete, continuant entities comparable to material objects. The second, which we may now introduce, is that groups often have the character of agents, being specifically comparable to those objects that we describe as organisms and, in the human case, as persons. As a collective which can survive the replacement of particular members, a group may have interests over and beyond the personal interests of its members, interests which people in certain representative positions are committed to pursuing, regardless of their personal feelings. Thus a group may act so as to form commitments which are credible independently of the individual attitudes of its representatives. And, making such commitments, it can incur obligations and enjoy rights over and beyond those that accrue to its members in their individual capacity. In these regards groups, especially formally organised groups such as companies and institutes, mimic individual agents. All that is done in social life may be the responsibility of individuals but their agency is sometimes exercised in their own name and sometimes in the name of group agents that they help to constitute. The bank clerk who cashes your cheque, the city hall secretary who sends the rates bill, the tax official who scrutinises your return of income: these are agents in whom mentality and temperament have been temporarily replaced by official commission; they do not act in their own names, but corporate agents act through them (see Coleman 1974).

On the picture as it has been drawn so far, society is composed of individuals, but these individuals form groups: associations which have the status of concrete, continuant objects and, in many cases, the character of agents; society itself indeed is just such a group. Before we add a further element to the picture a remark on the identification of groups may be in place. Whether a collection of agents is to be regarded as a group depends on how significantly distinctive is the way they treat one another and the way they treat, and are treated by, outsiders; the agents themselves, notice, may be people or groups or a mix of both. It also sometimes depends on how self-conscious agents are of belonging to the collection: for lack of self-consciousness we might want to say that the collection of people over seven feet tall do not form a group, even though they may satisfy the other requirements. Because of the variety of groups it is difficult to formulate more exactly general conditions necessary for a collection to count as a group. Families and nations, clubs and institutes, each have contrasting features that are as salient as what they have in common. And a further complexity is that historical circumstance has an important influence on group formation. Feudal life for example did not require, and therefore did not encourage, the emergence of the limited liability company which became the hallmark of nineteenth century capitalism. In order to parse a society into groups one would need a sense of the circumtances prevailing and the purposes which people are liable to want served.

Groups are one sort of institutional entity that go to make up society. But there is also a second sort of entity on the social scene that deserves of being called institutional. The kind of thing that we have in mind is practices: regularities of behaviour which characterise a society, being taken for granted by nearly everybody and being respected by nearly everybody on the appropriate occasion. The best way to introduce the category may be by example. All the following regularities seem to us to be practices of contemporary British society, albeit not practices of equal importance; those put under the same number are related regularities of such a kind that an action which instantiates the first will in normal circumstances also instantiate the others under that number.

1 Using 'chairs' to denote chairs; speaking English; speaking intelligibly.
2 Smiling as an expression of amusement; responding normally to amusement; using the established facial expressions.
3 Writing only reliable cheques in payment for goods; using banking facilities properly; acquiescing in non-barter exchange.
4 Driving on the left hand side of the road; driving in accordance with the rules of the road; accepting the authority of Parliament.
5 Saying only what one believes to be true; respecting the demands of truth; going along with the received mores.
6 Leaving be what belongs to another; respecting private property; acquiescing in the established mode of allocating goods.

As regularities, practices collect the actions which instantiate them in the way people are collected by groups; more precisely, they may be regarded as entities that have as members or parts pairs which each consist of a circumstance and an associated action. Practices however are no more collections of the items they collect, than are groups collections of agents. Again the reason is that whereas a collection changes identity as it changes members, a practice is something that remains one and the same through the incessant renewal of its membership, as now it is instantiated in this action, now in that. Like a group, a practice has the status of a concrete, continuant object, although it lacks the further character of being an agent. It may seem strange to speak of practices as objects but the characterisation is licensed by deeply ingrained conceptual habits. If we take something like courtesy we see that it is perfectly in order to say that the practice has waxed and waned over a period, that while it has held powerful sway in one place, it has lost its grip in another, and so on through idioms that force us to think of it as an enduring part of the furniture of the temporal world. The designation of 'practice' or 'regularity' may seem to make an abstraction of the thing, but that is a misleading impression. While it counts as a concrete and continuant object, however, it must be admitted that a practice shares with a group the features mentioned earlier:

that its members may be scattered, and that they may be shared among different practices at once. The instantiations of courtesy may be far between, and they may be simultaneously instantiations of any number of other practices, such as greeting when greeted, smiling when smiled upon, and so on. This distinctiveness may console those who worry that by recognising practices as objects we are contaminating the realms of more traditionally established substances.[1]

Neither the term 'practice', nor any other term, is commonly used to pick out the regularities that we have in mind. Words which sometimes come near to doing so are 'customs', 'conventions', 'codes', 'mores', 'norms', and 'rules', but most of these are affected by a systematic ambiguity whereby they may mean either a certain sort of objective regularity, or a regulation prescribing that regularity to people in the society. The ambiguity is parallel to that which we find in the term 'law', as it is used in connection with science. The law that $E = MC^2$ may refer to the objective condition in nature which Einstein thought he had discovered, or to the theoretical proposition in which he sought to give it expression. Similarly the norm of expressing gratitude for the grace or gift of another person may refer either to a regularity in people's behaviour, or to a regulation which they apply in giving assessment and advice.[2]

The fact that the word 'practice' is a term of art, and that no other term is commonly used in quite the same way, puts an onus on us to try to give at least some necessary conditions for a present collection of actions to count as a single practice, and for a temporally extended series of actions each to pass as instances of that regularity. The case is more pressing than it was with groups: since our term 'group' was borrowed from ordinary language, and since people are generally proficient at saying whether a given collection of agents should count as a group or not, we could afford to be vague about the conditions which a collection would have to realise if it were to count as such. Here we do not have the same excuse for tolerating vagueness; we must attempt to spell out the conditions required for a regularity to be a practice.

The first thing to notice is that we do not identify a practice just by picking at random circumstance-action pairs, and presenting them as instantiations of the alleged institution. The individual circumstances and the matched individual actions must represent two types such that we think the regularity law-like or nomic: we think that past evidence that circumstances of the one type were linked with actions of the other supports us in concluding that, other things being equal, if one were to bring about the circumstance one would thereby bring about the action, or at least make it more likely. As is well known, some types allow such projectibility, others do not, and we have little more than our intuition to make the appropriate distinction. Thus, although it is notoriously difficult to say why, we have no faith that the following regularity will continue to be maintained, as it has been in the past: people smile when smiled upon before the year 2000, and smile when frowned upon after that date (see Goodman 1973). Where a regularity fails to be nomic, we can be sure that it is not a practice.

But not all nomic regularities in the behaviour of people within a certain society count as practices. Such a regularity might come about through an accident of similar motivation, or whatever, and in such a case we would not have something that fitted naturally into the list of practices given earlier. Suppose that people all peel potatoes in the same way, drawing the knife towards them and raising the trajectory near the end of the movement. We have here a regularity, and intuitively a nomic one, but we would hardly say that we had a practice. Why so? Well, one crucial feature that is missing is an awareness on the part of those conforming to the regularity that others generally conform too. This condition is realised in all the examples we gave earlier, and it appears to be a necessary condition for a practice.

Let us imagine then that not only do people generally peel potatoes in the same way; they also know that they do so. Would this make the regularity into a practice? We think not. What is missing, it seems, is a connection between the awareness hypothesised and the regularity exhibited: if someone ceased to know that nearly everyone peeled potatoes in the same way, this would hardly affect his own way of peeling them; thus we could expect the regularity to continue to be observed, even in the absence of common knowledge. In the case of the practices given in our earlier list we find that there is at least a weak motivational link between an individual's awareness of general conformity and his thinking conformity desirable. The link may not be indispensable, in the sense that the person would conform even if it were not there; and it may also be unconstraining, in the sense that it may allow him on occasion not to conform. One is tempted to formulate it by saying that the individual's awareness that conformity is general gives him some reason to conform himself but that will not do either because in the cases where free-riding is attractive the awareness may have the contrary effect: knowledge that nearly everyone else will contribute to emergency needs in the community may give me reason not to contribute myself, assuring me that such needs will be met without my help. The formulation to which one is driven is something like the following: that the individual's awareness that conformity is general gives him some reason to want deviance discouraged, including his own deviance if that is the cost of general discouragement. The idea is that the regularity involved in a practice is such that the individual's awareness that it is generally observed gives him some reason to want the regularity protected against deviance, the state of affairs liable to result from deviance being less attractive than general conformity to the regularity. The regularity may not correspond to what the individual would want in an ideal world but conformity to it is more attractive, at least in some respects, than the chaos or other results which deviance would bring (see Pettit 1980, Ch.1).

These reflections enable us to set out a number of informative conditions on when a regularity, specifically a nomic regularity, counts as a practice. The set of necessary conditions must suffice as an account of what a practice is, operating in conjunction with our list of examples to give us the required concept. To state the conditions in schematic form, we can say that a regularity of behaviour, understanding by this a nomic regularity, is a practice in a given society only if:

1 nearly everyone conforms to it;
2 nearly everyone expects nearly everyone else to conform;
3 this expectation gives nearly everyone some reason for wanting deviance discouraged, including his own deviance if that is a necessary cost of general discouragement (see D.Lewis 1969 for a comparable account of conventions, a narrower class than practices).

What we have seen up to now is that while society consists of individual people, and nothing is a social event except insofar as it connects with people, there are also important institutional entities on the social scene: specifically, groups and practices. If society is composed of people, these individuals are organised in such a way that groups and practices are equally part of the social world. An analogy with organisms has suggested itself to many thinkers. If individuals are the atomic or molecular components of the body politic, institutions are the cells or organs. The analogy is not exact, since it may be pressed in one or another direction; and neither is it inviting, since it is often used to beg the question that we shall be discussing. However it has the merit of giving expression to the articulated structure of society in a way in which a mechanical model probably fails to do.

With this rough anatomy of social life, we are in a position to state the problem with which we are concerned in this chapter. The question is whether institutions should be conceived as entities in their own right, over and beyond the individuals who constitute them: this constitution may be in person, as with groups, or in behaviour, as with practices. The question bears on what we shall call the ontological autonomy of institutions vis-à-vis individuals and it allows, grossly, of two possible answers: that institutions have a reality over and beyond the reality of the individuals who compose them, and that they do not. The view which allows autonomy to institutions is known as collectivism or social holism, the opposing view as individualism or social atomism (see O'Neill 1973).

In posing the autonomy question it should be noted that we presuppose the reality of institutions. This is not always done and the question between individualism and collectivism is then represented as the more encompassing one of whether institutions are real and, if so, whether they are autonomous. We also presuppose the reality of individuals in posing the autonomy question and this further assumption is also lifted in some discussions. When neither the reality of institutions nor that of individuals is supposed the question takes its most comprehensive form, asking whether either kind of entity is real and whether, if both are real, there is an autonomy of one vis-à-vis the other (see Quinton 1975-6).

The supposition that individuals are real is incumbent on anyone who takes the orthodox conception of agents for granted, as we certainly do: insofar as we think that this representation of things must be found compatible with any advanced scientific theory, we close the possibility of its ever being established that reality is wrongly depicted in a scheme which countenances persons. But what of the supposition that institutions are real? This is less deeply entrenched, since there is the abstract possibility that the representation of things which has us recognise such entities will someday be entirely displaced in favour of a presently unimaginable alternative. We make the supposition simply because we see no reason to think that the representation will be displaced. We may be forgiven for doing so on the grounds that the assumption is a concession to collectivism, and we shall be arguing ourselves for the individualist doctrine.

The issue between individualism and collectivism offers a parallel from within philosophical sociology to a central question in philosophy of mind or philosophical psychology. In the philosophy of mind, and our discussion in the last chapter belongs to that province, one of the major issues concerns the status of mental phenomena, such as perceiving, imagining, judging, evaluating and deciding, vis-à-vis physical processes in the brain and central nervous system. Here the gross options are dualism and monism, doctrines which each allow of further variations. If whenever mental events occur there are also physical processes, do we take the dualist line that the events are something over and beyond the processes, or do we opt for the monist view that they are nothing more than those processes as they appear to us in our capacity as subjects and interpreters? The question is nicely parallel to that with which we are concerned. Notice that it can also be broadened in a manner which reflects the possibility of radicalising the social issue. We may ask whether mental events are real and, if so, whether they are autonomous; or even more radically, we may ask whether either kind of phenomenon is real and, if both are real, whether there is an autonomy of one vis-à-vis the other. The eliminative materialist denies the reality of mental events, the eliminative mentalist or idealist the reality of physical.

In the two sections following we consider how the issue between individualism and collectivism may be construed, and how it should be judged. Before leaving the matters of this section however we should note that the issue is quite independent of the question between humanism and scientism. There are four possible combinations of views:

1 humanism cum individualism;
2 humanism cum collectivism;
3 scientism cum individualism;
4 scientism cum collectivism.

Each of these combinations can be defended; indeed each has received support within the literature of social philosophy. The first represents the position that we ourselves defend. The second may take any of a number of forms but it can be identified in the idealist view that the mental is not to be understood scientifically and that institutions represent mental entities of a sort, being expressions of the spirit of history, or whatever. The third combination is defended by psychologistic reductionists who think that the science of psychology will displace our orthodox conception of agents and that it will be capable of accounting for what happens at the institutional as well as at the individual level. Finally, the fourth position is the one defended by sociological theorists in the tradition of Comte and Durkheim, who have wanted to say that human beings are as subject as any other objects to scientific understanding, but that the understanding of the social is a different matter from the understanding of the personal, institutions being autonomous vis-à-vis individuals.

## 2 THE EXPRESSIVE AUTONOMY OF INSTITUTIONS

The question as to whether institutions exist in their own right, over and beyond the individuals who constitute them, is scarcely luminous. What we are asked to decide is something formulated in an intrinsically metaphorical way, for the reference to what is 'over and beyond' depends for being understood on a spatial analogy. If we are to settle the matter of the ontological autonomy of institutions, the first thing to be done is to define more exactly the sense of autonomy that is in question. We shall offer two distinct definitions and consider whether groups and practices are autonomous in either sense. The one account we describe as an expressive definition of autonomy, the other as an explanatory one: why we attach these predicates will become clear in context. In this section we ask whether institutions are autonomous in the expressive sense, and in the next whether they are so in the explanatory. We shall argue that they satisfy the expressive demands but not the explanatory ones, and that the explanatory demands are the ones most crucially at issue in individualist-collectivist debates.

The expressive account of autonomy says that one sort of entity X exists over and beyond another sort Y if and only if the following condition is fulfilled: that the addition of terms by means of which we refer to X-type things enables us to give expression to truths that we cannot formulate in a language with terms for referring to Y-type items. The idea is that if we have two sets of referring terms, the one for things of sort X and the other for things of kind Y, we can tell whether the X-terms refer us to things other than Y-things, or to Y-things under a novel aspect, by seeing whether the referring use of X-terms increases our expressive resources. The referring use of X-terms may be explicit, as when we refer to this or that X, or it may be implicit, being supposed in the reference to something else: the reference to an X is implicit, for example, in referring to a so-and-so Y, where what it means for a Y to be a so-and-so is that it has a certain relationship to an X.

The definition in question may be usefully illustrated in other cases before we apply it to institutions and individuals. We may wish to decide whether sets are autonomous vis-à-vis their members, abstract objects vis-à-vis their instantiations, and articulated complexes like sentences vis-à-vis the words they contain. How would the definition guide us in these cases? Are we enabled to give expression to novel truths when we can make referential use of set-theoretical concepts as well as of the concepts appropriate to the members of sets? It would certainly seem so: else we must say that one of the most fundamental mathematical theories is capable of reformulation in less sophisticated terminology. A similar point goes through for sentences and the words which compose them, for to claim that the referential use of concepts for sentences is expressively redundant would be to adopt a very strong thesis in linguistic theory: it would be to say that generative grammar is presently formulated in an unnecessarily rich vocabulary. And what of the case of the abstract object such as a film or play and its instantiations: the performances of the work on different occasions? Here the denial of autonomy cannot be made to seem so preposterous but it is certainly counterintuitive. If we are not allowed to refer to a film such as 'Jules et Jim', this means that we cannot even describe the screenings of the film as screenings of 'Jules et Jim', for to describe them so is implicitly to refer to the abstract object. In that case it does seem extraordinarily unlikely that we can express everything in the more austere language that we were capable of saying in the richer one.

These illustrative applications enable us to see two important points about the expressive definition of autonomy. The first is that while the criterion may allow us to say that X-type entities are not autonomous vis-à-vis Y-type ones, it does not force us as a consequence to say that neither are Y-type things autonomous vis-à-vis X-type ones. This is as we should wish. Suppose we were to decide that sentences were nothing over and beyond words; it would not follow that we thought words were nothing over and beyond sentences. Thus the lack of autonomy in the one direction should not mean necessarily the lack of it in the other. We may be glad then that while reference to sentences may enable us to express no truths that are not expressible just by reference to words, this does not entail that reference to words enables us to express no truths that are not expressible just by reference to sentences.

The other important point which our illustrative applications bring home is that using the expressive definition as a criterion of autonomy means assuming that we can tell when one and the same truth is expressed in different bodies of terminology. There is some difficulty with saying what it is for two sentences S' and S" to express the same truth. We might hypothesise that they do so just in case the one is true whenever the other is true, whether by happy accident or as a matter of necessity. That will not do however because it entails that any two sentences which are true under all circumstances express one and the same truth: '2 + 2 = 4' would have to be held to express the same truth as '6 + 6 = 12', each being true whenever the other is, i.e. always.

In face of the difficulty there are two lines which we might take. The first would be to require that S' and S" must be interpretative or translational equivalents: in the terms of Chapter 1, that either must be capable of being used on the right hand side of a T-sentence on the left hand side of which the other is mentioned, the T-sentence being part of a theory of meaning for the language in which the other sentence occurs. This line would have the effect of demanding that S' and S" are constructed out of non-logical expressions which correspond to one another as synonyms and it points to an alternative way of meeting our difficulty, a second line of response. This second line would be to require, as initially, that S' and S" are true under the same circumstances and then to add that their terms must correspond in the following sense: for every referential or predicative expression in the one there must be a corresponding expression in the other which applies just where the first applies. This criterion of when two sentences express the same truth is easier to satisfy than the interpretative one, for terms may correspond in the sense required when they are not what we would regard as synonyms. Thus on this criterion, but not on the interpretative one, we would take the following sentences to express the same truth: 'The water is at temperature so and so', 'The $H_2O$ has so and so mean kinetic energy'. Which of these criteria are we to adopt? The second one, we think. We shall be arguing that on the expressive criterion institutions exist over and beyond individuals and it is only reasonable that we should choose that understanding of the criterion which makes it the more difficult for us to press our point of view.

Let us turn now to apply our definition of autonomy to the debate between individualism and collectivism. What we have to ask is whether having the terms whereby we can refer to institutions such as groups and practices enables us to express truths that we could not express just by reference to individuals. The answer, unfortunately, is not something on which there is common agreement. Some philosophers have defended an expressive variety of individualism according to which anything that can be said by referring to groups and practices can equally well be said, if only at greater length, by referring to the people who make up those groups and conform to those practices (see

Brodbeck 1958, Quinton 1975-6, Watkins 1952, 1955). Against this others have urged that no amount of paraphrase into the terminology approved by the expressive individualist would allow us to give expression to what we report when we say that the mood of the country is changing, or that the trades unions are regaining confidence, or even that someone cashed a cheque at the bank (see Mandelbaum 1955).

When it is clear that expressive autonomy is to be judged on the criterion described above, it must be granted that on this issue the collectivist is in the right. Traditional discussions of the matter have generally been vitiated by the lack of an agreed account of what it is for two sentences to express the same truth. On our understanding this means that the sentences are true under the same circumstances and have corresponding expressions that apply in the same cases. But if this is what it is to express the same truth then there can hardly be any question but that having the terms to refer to institutions enables us to express truths which we could not express in a language without such referential resources. For many of the sentences formulable in a language with concepts for referring to institutions and individuals, there appear to be no accessible counterparts in the truncated language which is deprived of the means of referring to institutions. In the truncated language we are allowed to refer to individuals, and then only as individuals: we cannot refer to them for example as members of a group, since that would be implicitly to refer to the group. The sentences from the richer language contain expressions with which no expressions from this more austere one can be appropriately aligned.

The point can be brought home if we consider the difficulty of matching individualistic expressions with predicates that we attach to groups. Some group predicates are compounded out of predicates true of individuals and with these we would have little problem: the football team is tall if the players are tall, the company commits itself to X if the directors vote for X, the party is influential if its supporters carry punch in their different walks of life, and so on. But other institutional predicates are not compounded in this manner and it is with these that we must run up against an impassable barrier (see James 1978, Ch.2). The simplest example is the predicate 'has members', or indeed any predicate expressing a relationship between a group and its members, such as 'gains members', 'loses members', 'disbands' or 'regroups'. Other examples are predicates used to express the relationship which something has to the group without being required to have any particular kind of relationship to the members: cases are 'is in the interest of', and 'is inimical to'. Further examples again are temporal predicates of groups, such as 'is one hundred years old', 'is losing its original character', 'is changing for the better'. Finally, when we consider that analogy enables us to generate an indefinite number of predicates for groups, we see an endless source of appropriate examples. Put a group in parallel to a person and we get 'is irrepressible', 'is dispirited', 'is concerned'; in parallel to an organism and we derive 'is robust', 'is diseased' and 'has untapped reserves of strength'; in parallel to a cybernetic mechanism and we construct 'is in equilibrium', 'has good information flow', and is 'self-correcting'; and so on indefinitely, generating predicates that look ever more resistant to an individualistic rendering. (For a qualification on the point argued see the end of section 3 below.)

It will be clear that the lesson which these examples teach might be taught equally by lessons from the case of practices. But however it is supported the lesson must be buttressed against an objection which will certainly be put by the expressive individualist. It will be said that since groups are composed of people, anything that involves a group involves the people who are its members, and that any predicate therefore which attaches to the group must do so only insofar as a corresponding predicate attaches to its members. In that case, it seems, there would have to be an individualistic predicate, however complex, that is the required counterpart of the institutional one.

Against this objection, what has to be pointed out is that while the composition of groups ensures that a group predicate is supervenient on individualistic predicates, it does not follow that there is any available counterpart to the group term. Supervenience means that if the group predicate applies in one case but not in another, there must be some associated individualistic predicates that apply in the first case but not in the second, or vice versa. In other words, it means that there is no group difference without a difference in individuals: specifically, a difference capable of being marked with individualistic predicates. That there is no group difference without a difference in individuals is guaranteed by the fact that a group is a whole of which individuals are the parts, for it is scarcely conceivable that a whole should change without any alteration in its parts. That the difference is capable of individualistic characterisation is supported by the observation that any distinction marked in terms that refer implicitly to institutions, such as the distinction between being a policeman and a probation officer, will not be taken to differentiate two people who are indiscernible in individualistic terms and are in individualistically indiscernible situations.

We may acknowledge that every group predicate is supervenient on individualistic predicates without making the admission demanded in the objection, there is an individualistic counterpart accessible to us for every group predicate, a counterpart which applies in just the cases where that predicate applies. If there were such a counterpart then there would be supervenience, but we may also have supervenience consistently with the following being the case: that the group predicate applies in circumstances characterised by any of an open-ended list of individualistic predicates, or predicate compounds, so that we are not in a position ever to identify a disjunction of such terms which applies just when the group predicate does so. The idea is that in such a case we can effectively say of any given circumstance whether the supervenient term applies there or not; that we may be able to work out after the fact what characterisation in 'subvenient' terms guaranteed the application or non-application of the supervenient one; but that even if we can, we have no reason to believe that only that subvenient characterisation plays such a role, and we have no way of telling, in advance of particular circumstances, experienced or imagined, which subvenient characterisation will engage the supervenient terms and which not. If we had such an experience or imagination that we could determine for every possible subvenient characterisation whether or not it engaged the supervenient term, we might be in a position to formulate a counterpart for that term: a disjunction of subvenient characterisations which applied just when it applied. However this possibility is not considered to be a real one and so the idea is that in the sort of case described a term can be said to be supervenient on terms of another kind without being capable of being aligned with any counterpart framed in these terms (see Kim 1978).

Is the situation with group predicates and individualistic predicates relevantly similar to the case described? Arguably, it is. We apply certain group terms without specific regard to what individualistic predicates are satisfied by the circumstances under consideration. We may be able to say after the fact which such predicates in a given instance guaranteed the application of a group term but generally we do not bother to try. Most important of all, however, we know that many a group term is liable to apply in an indefinite number of individualistically characterised cases and yet we have no way of effectively identifying the individualistic characterisations which will engage that term. These points are borne out by the sorts of examples mentioned above. Our competence in applying to groups such predicates as 'gains members', 'is in the interest of', 'is in equilibrium', and the like, turns in no way on our ability to link the terms to individualistic characterisations of people, even if we can show in particular cases what characterisations of this kind ensured the application of some such group predicate. Further, and this is the crucial point, there seems to be an indefinite number of individualistically describable ways in which any such group predicate may come to be realised. Thus it seems a reasonable claim that though group predicates are always supervenient in individualistic terms, they may often resist alignment with individualistic counterparts: they may prove to be incapable of individualistic rendering.

When we judge that a group term or predicate is resistant to individualistic rendering, what we decide is that it enables us to detect a kind of phenomenon which escapes our conceptual grasp so long as we are restricted to the more austere range of concepts. Take the kind of thing picked out as being in the interest of a certain group. Homogeneous in the group-related respect, this class will certainly be heterogeneous in other ways, and the idea is that without the perspective given us by the notion of what is in the interest of the group we would have no grounds for perceiving it as a unity. This idea is not surprising in itself, and it is plausible insofar as we cannot see our way to mapping the predicate 'is in the interest of the group' on to any individualistic predicate or disjunction of predicates. Those who argue for expressive individualism do so usually because they are committed to the idea that there is a class of canonically observational predicates in terms of which other predicates must allow definition, and to the belief that individualistic predicates serve this function for institutional ones (see Brodbeck 1958, Quinton 1975-6). We see no reason why that idea should be entertained, especially since the distinction between observational and theoretical terms, as we saw in the last chapter, does not have the required sharpness.

It appears to us then that the case for the expressive autonomy of institutions vis-à-vis individuals may reasonably be granted. By having the means of referring to institutions put at our disposal we seem to be enabled to give expression to truths that otherwise would have escaped us, and in this sense we are directed to entities which exist in their own right, over and beyond the individuals who constitute them. But if we rejoice in this result, enjoying the insight which it gives us into the autonomy of institutions, we must also recognise that the status established for groups and practices vis-à-vis individuals is not of a very substantial variety. The collectivist cannot be very heartened, nor need the individualist be very concerned, that institutions are accorded a standing in relation to individual people which sets must equally be granted in respect of their members, and abstractions in respect of their instances. If we consider three objects on my desk and now, enriching our terms, refer to the set which they constitute, we find that there are things which we can then say that could scarcely have been expressed before: such as for example that the set has three members, that it satisfies certain mathematical axioms, and so on. Again if we think about the approximately rectangular table and now refer to the rectangularity in its own right, construing it as an abstract object, it turns out that we also increase our expressive resources: we enable ourselves for the first time to say that the shape is a non-essential property such as metaphysicians discuss, that it is something with unusual geometrical characteristics, that it is not a shape that has launched a thousand ships, and so on. An autonomy that is found as much in sets and shapes as it is in social institutions is not the sort of quality to encourage the collectivist or to confound the individualist. We may reasonably conclude that neither is it the sense of autonomy at deepest issue in our debate.

In a final comment on the sort of autonomy which we have been forced to recognise in institutions, we may note that while we do have to say that groups and practices are not identical with any entities to which we can refer with individualistic resources, this does not necessarily mean the rejection of a monistic point of view.

An institution cannot be identical with an individualistic entity because it is considered as remaining one and the same through a turnover of membership and such an assumption cannot be maintained of any individualistic entity. Thus there is at least one thing true of the institution which is not true of any non-institutional counterpart and so it cannot be identical with any such counterpart. This denial of identity however does not mean the adoption, in the psychological terminology, of a dualistic perspective. We may yet say that whenever one is confronted with an institution all that is there, so to speak, is thoroughly individualistic in nature. The reason we may say this is that while the group is not identical with people, nor the practice with actions, such institutional entities are composed exclusively of people and actions: they are constructions in entirely non-institutional material. The composition of groups and practices means that we are not going to be forced out of a monistic point of view unless we are given to believe that the behaviour and effect of the institutions is in some way independent of their component parts. Such independence is not countenanced in the admission that institutions are expressively autonomous vis-à-vis individuals.

## 3 THE EXPLANATORY NON-AUTONOMY OF INSTITUTIONS

Our second criterion for the autonomy of one sort of entity vis-à vis another is built on the intuitive thought that a whole would be something which existed over and beyond its parts in a very significant sense, if it were possessed of an efficacy that in some way outstripped that of its components. To be somewhat more specific, we would say that the whole was autonomous in more than an expressive sense if it entered into causal interactions and gave rise to causal effects in such a way that we could not describe the interactions, nor explain the effects, just by reference to the parts. In this circumstance it is not only the case that we can express truths which otherwise elude us, by being provided with the conceptual means of referring to the whole as well as the parts. More particularly, and more impressively, having the means of referring to the whole enables us to make causal sense of happenings which must otherwise be left in obscurity.

The explanatory definition of autonomy, which formally mirrors the expressive, says that one sort of entity X exists over and beyond another sort Y if and only if the following condition is fulfilled: that the addition of terms by means of which we refer to X-type things enables us to give explanations of events, taken under certain descriptions, that we cannot account for in a language with terms for referring to Y-type items. It is assumed in this definition that to explain an event is always to explore the causal history of the event, an assumption which we defended in the last chapter. The idea behind the definition is that if we have two sets of referring terms, the one for things of sort X and the other for things of kind Y, we can tell whether the X-terms refer us to things other than Y-things, or to Y-things under a novel aspect, by seeing whether the referring use of X-terms increases our explanatory resources. As in the other case, the referring use of X-terms may be explicit or implicit and, again in parallel to the earlier formula, the definition may deny autonomy in one direction while allowing it in the other: although X-things turn out not to be autonomous vis-à-vis Y-things, it may yet transpire that Y-things have an autonomy in respect of X-things.

In order to illustrate the definition, it may be useful to consider again sets and their members, abstract objects and their instantiations, and sentences and their component words. Although we judged that the higher order entities were expressively autonomous in each of these cases, it is plausible that in no further sense do they exist over and beyond their lower order correlates. It is because of the lack of any such further autonomy that we are naturally inclined to say that the set is nothing apart from its members, the abstract object apart from its instantiations, the sentence apart from its words. Does our explanatory account of autonomy give substance to this intuition: does it elucidate what we may have in mind in denying that there is anything more than expressive autonomy in these cases? We think that it does. It suggests that what we intuitively wish to deny of sets, abstractions and sentences is that they enable us to give causal explanations of events that are inexplicable by reference just to the corresponding members, instantiations and words. More colloquially, it construes our intuition as a rejection of the idea that sets, abstractions and sentences have irreducible causal powers. This construal is not implausible, and it has the further merit that it makes our intuitive view reasonable. What could it mean to be able to explain some occurrence by reference to one of the higher order entities without having the capacity to explain it by reference to the lower counterparts? In none of these cases can we even conceive that the higher entity might exercise an agency which was not also the exercise of an agency on the part of the lower correlates. That being so, the higher substance is autonomous only if the exercise of agency at the lower level is governed from on high, and such an idea seems little short of preposterous.

The question of non-expressive autonomy arises also in more difficult cases. Philosophers would seem to have more than expressive autonomy in mind for example when they ask whether the mental state is anything over and beyond the brain state that is assumed to accompany it, or whether the macro-object is anything over and beyond the micro-particles which are taken to compose it. Here again it is plausible to interpret the inquiry as bearing on the autonomy of mental states and macro-objects in the causal-explanatory sense caught in our definition. The question is whether such states and objects enable us to make sense of certain effects that are in principle inexplicable if we are restricted to referring to the other sorts of entity. Colloquially, it has to do with whether the states and objects have causal powers that are properly their own, causal powers which do not reduce to features of the correlates. But understanding what the inquiry is about in these cases does not mean being able to resolve it. No short argument or appeal to intuition can tell us what the standing of mental states and macro-objects is: here the construal suggested by our second definition of autonomy does not have the further merit that we ascribed to it in adjudicating the question about sets, abstract objects and sentences.[3]

With the explanatory sense of autonomy fixed in our minds, let us now ask whether in this further non-expressive way institutions are autonomous vis-à-vis individuals. Do groups and practices serve to bring about events in such a way that we cannot account for those events just by referring to the people and actions which constitute them? Well, it must certainly be conceded that we do regularly refer to institutions in making causal sense of events in social life, so the question is at least well placed. If signing a cheque explains receiving money it does so only because of the nature of banks; if a slight to a shop steward accounts for an all-out strike it does so only because of the structure of trade unions. Thus in filling out either explanation we refer to the groups in question. Similarly we refer to the law against drunken driving in an explanation which traces imprisonment to an appropriate offence, to the ethic of reliability in an account which quotes a promise as the reason for a particular performance and to the convention establishing the meaning of a gesture in an explanation which relates someone's producing the gesture to another's responding in customary fashion.

The issue before us then is whether such institutional explanations, as we may call them, are indispensable, or whether the events of which we make sense with their help are subject to explanation just by reference to individuals and their actions. It may be mentioned in passing that one of the leading collectivists in sociology, Emile Durkheim, focuses attention on precisely this question, when he defines his allegedly irreducible social realities by the fact that they exercise a directive influence, and do so independently of the influence wielded by people (see Durkheim 1938, Ch. 1). In illustration Durkheim cites the experience of being carried along and directed from outside that one sometimes has in crowds. He might also have quoted the weight and irresistibility of conventional practices, which has been given much attention in recent social psychology. Erving Goffman provides data of just the kind that would have impressed Durkheim when he shows how difficult it is for us to break frame, rejecting the pattern that groups and practices foist upon us (see Goffman 1969). The difficulty is easily exemplified in the resistance every one of us feels to breaking even trivial conventions. Try casually addressing someone in authority by his or her first name, try not making eye-contact in a conversation with a friend or, even more trivially, try to give a bus conductor your fare on the back of your hand (see Milgram 1977).

But to return to our issue, what we have to decide is whether the institutional explanation of social events is indispensable. It might have been that the issue was up for empirical determination, as many think that the issues about macro-objects and mental states are. What we wish to argue however is that accepting the orthodox conception of agents means rejecting the claim that institutions have explanatory autonomy. This proposition amounts to something stronger than an empirical defence of individualism since, being humanists in the sense characterised in the last chapter, we hold that acceptance of the orthodox conception of agents is rationally unavoidable: the conception is one in which we are all reared, and it has the special distinction of being irreplaceable and unrevisable. Our argument from the orthodox conception of agents makes a philosophical as distinct from a regular scientific case against the doctrine that we oppose (see Pettit 1979b).

The first premise in our argument is that any event which institutions might be invoked to explain is of a kind that the orthodox conception of agents would have us explain by reference to the mental attitudes of human beings. The idea is that for any event which the collectivist holds to be inexplicable except by reference to groups or practices, the orthodox conception will suppose that there is a perfectly individualistic explanation by reference to the beliefs and desires of appropriate agents. There are two main varieties of event to be considered. The one is the event which is the occurrence or the outcome of a certain sort of behaviour on people's part. Here the event must be held to be explicable in terms of agent attitudes, so long as the behaviour is taken to be action in the proper sense and not merely the triggering of autonomic responses. The other relevant variety is the event which is described as the occurrence or the outcome of a certain institutional change. Here the event must be held to be attitudinally explicable granted that an institutional predicate applies superveniently on individualistic predicates, so that its applying in a given instance is explained when the application of the subvenient predicates is explained. Such supervenience is guaranteed either through the reducibility of institutional to individualistic predicates or through the obtaining of the weaker relationship described in the last section. It means that the institutional change, or the outcome of such a change, will be attitudinally explicable on this special but entirely natural assumption: that the individualistic predicates on the application of which the ascription of the change supervenes record behaviour; specifically, behaviour which is action proper and not just the triggering of autonomic responses. We can hardly quarrel with the idea that institutional changes occur superveniently on how people behave, as distinct from how they otherwise are, and the behaviour on which we take such changes to supervene can scarcely be regarded as anything less than action, since to regard it as such would be to depict people as regularly going 'on the blink', performing in the mode of autonomic systems rather than agents.

The second premise in our argument is even less controversial than the first. It is that if the explanatory collectivist says that there are some events which can be explained by reference to institutions, but not just by reference to individuals, then he is denying the truth of the orthodox conception of agents. At least with respect to the behaviour involved in those events he is saying that it is not the rational outcome of the agents' beliefs and desires: and this, despite not restricting that behaviour to what might pass as autonomic responses. That he must be saying this is clear from the fact that if the behaviour were the rational outcome of such attitudes, then the events in which it is involved would be explicable by reference to individuals, something which the explanatory collectivist denies. Thus, where our first premise showed us that institutional explanations bear on events which the orthodox conception aspires to cover, the second makes the point that to hold such explanations indispensable in some cases is therefore to deny the claim of the orthodox conception.

The third and final premise in our argument is that the claim of this conception is undeniable, a premise which comes directly from our reflections in the last chapter. It follows immediately that the thesis of the explanatory collectivist must be false, and that there are no events such that having the means of referring to institutions enables us to explain them when otherwise we would be at a loss as to their causal origin. It may be that reference to institutions gives us expressive resources which outstrip those available to us from reference to individuals, but so long as we attach ourselves to the orthodox view of agents we cannot think that it provides us with indispensable resources of explanation.

In order to illustrate the force of this conclusion, the brunt of our explanatory individualism, consider a standard sociological explanation, such as the explanation of the breakdown of the feudal manorial system by the introduction of money into peasant transactions. Here the event explained is an institutional change, the breakdown of a certain sort of group, and the explanation refers among other things to the practice associated with the introduction of money. By our first premise we know that the event explained involves behaviour such as the orthodox conception of agents aspires to encompass. And so it does: the breakdown of the manorial system involves a change in the actions of those traditionally involved in the system, in particular a change in the pattern of peasant behaviour. This event is explained by reference to the introduction of money and the explanatory collectivist might say that it cannot be explained just by reference to individuals, thus denying the ability of orthodox accountants to explain it in terms of the attitudes of the peasants: this denial is what the second premise draws attention to. But, as our third premise assures us, it is manifestly possible to make sense of the behaviour in orthodox terms, and so the claim of the explanatory collectivist must collapse. The introduction of money enabled peasants to attain certain hitherto impossible goals and created conditions within which they came to have desires and make demands that caused the demise of the manorial system. Such a story, and we are simply repeating the received version, trades in precisely the attitudes to which the collectivist would deny explanatory power. We are referred to the individuals involved, their beliefs and their desires, in having explained for us the behaviour that meant the fall of the manor.

The illustration helps to show what is involved in the assertion of explanatory individualism. However it is equally useful in drawing attention to a modified thesis which the collectivist may put forward at this stage. The collectivist, confronted with our argument, may respond by saying that although social events are always explicable by reference to individuals, always involving rationally interpretable behaviour, they are often not fully explicable without reference also to institutions, the institutions being required to explain the occurrence of the attitudes invoked in the individualistic explanation. The idea is that although the fall of the manorial system is explained immediately by reference to the peasants and their changed attitudes, the further explanation of the change of attitudes refers us to something institutional: the introduction of money into peasant exchanges.

What are we to say against this refined brand of collectivism? The idea still is that institutions have irreducible causal powers, but now those powers are said to work via the mental attitudes of people. One variant on the idea might be that institutions held a sort of hypnotic sway over the minds of individuals, and in this case we would be faced with a doctrine as unfetching as the original unmodified claim. But nothing so crude is actually proposed. We are invited to think of people, not as the pawns of institutions, but rather as their prisoners: as agents who form their beliefs and conceive their plans in rational response to their institutional context. The context may not be a coercive ringmaster in the orchestration of social performances but it is a powerful and persuasive factor; and, so the collectivist would say, it is an irreducibly institutional element.

The image of people as the prisoners of institutional context is not in our view an inappropriate one, but the modified collectivism which underpins it errs in suggesting that the picture gives the required sort of causal role to institutions. In characterising and accounting for the attitudes of the peasants in our example there are two ways in which we may seem to be referring to institutions. First of all, in giving the content of the attitudes we almost inevitably use terms for institutions: thus we speak of the peasants' belief that monetary payment was more in their interest than the guarantee of traditional rights, apparently referring to the practice of such payment. But secondly, in giving the origin of the attitudes we often also use terms for institutions: we may say for example that monetary payment occasioned the belief just mentioned, or that it gave rise to the desire for more differentiated goods than were traditionally available. What we wish to suggest however is that neither of these ways of invoking institutions can be used to vindicate even a modified form of explanatory collectivism.

When we speak of institutions in the characterisation of agent attitudes we are not referring in the strict sense to those institutions themselves, but rather to the attitudes; it is more or less incidental that the content of the attitudes cannot be adequately specified without the use of terms for the institutions. We have already seen that a language with institutional terms will be expressively richer than one without and so, if the attitudes of agents in a society are formed in such an enriched vocabulary, it can be no surprise that we have to help ourselves to the vocabulary, or to a translational version of it, in order to characterise the attitudes. But using the terms for institutions in describing the attitudes and then referring to the attitudes in explanation of behaviour does not mean referring to what the terms would denote in non-oblique usage. If I say that an X brought about a such-and-such then I am certainly referring to the entity in question, but if I say that someone's belief that an X is a so-and-so brought about a such-and-such I am only referring to the belief, and not at all to the X. This is brought out by the fact that I may not myself even believe that there are such things as X's: the claim may have been that someone's belief that a ghost was in the attic caused amusement in the company.

The point can be reinforced by the fact that the context of attitudinal ascription is not one that normally creates genuinely referring slots. A slot is taken to be a genuinely referring one if and only if co-referring expressions can be substituted for one another within it without threatening the truth-value of the containing sentence. This test is not satisfied by the major slots within attitudinal contexts. In a sentence of the form, he believes that X is a so-and-so, or he desires that X become a so-and-so, the term 'X' cannot be replaced by a co-referring term, say 'Y', without putting in danger the truth of the overall sentence. I may believe that the secretary of the tennis club is a swindler without believing that my bank manager is a swindler, even though they are one and the same person: this, because I may be unaware that they are just one individual. In most contexts the co-referring expressions 'the secretary of the tennis club' and 'my bank manager' could be submitted for one another salva veritate and this we take as a sign that those contexts create genuinely referring slots. The fact that the expressions cannot be substituted appropriately in attitudinal contexts shows that the slots in question are not genuinely referring ones (see Quine 1960).[4]

But if we do not properly refer to institutions in characterising the content of agent's beliefs and desires, do we have to do so in explaining the origin of some such attitudes? The modified version of explanatory collectivism would say that we must make an ineradicable reference to monetary payment in explaining the beliefs which the peasants in our example came to form about it, and in accounting for the novel desires that it occasioned in them. The idea is that a causal interaction between that practice and the peasants to whom it is introduced accounts for the formation of the peasant attitudes which are held in respect of it and in connection with it. If the notion is sound then it means that if we are deprived of the means of referring to the practice, we shall no longer be able fully to explain the behaviour associated with the fall of the manorial system: we shall be able to trace the behaviour to the appropriate agent attitudes but it will be impossible for us to go further and explain the emergence of the beliefs and desires in question.

Let us admit, to begin with, that there are some objects such that attitudes held in respect of them are often explained as the result of interaction between those objects and the people who hold the attitudes. If the object is perceptually salient, in the sense that consistently with the perceptual cues and circumstances it is inevitable that the percipient identify it in some sense, then we may reasonably say that a causal interaction between that object and the percipient accounts for the attitudes held in respect of it to which the perception gives rise. If I see the water in the pan bubbling and come to believe that it is boiling then it is not unreasonable to say that my belief is occasioned by a causal interaction, specifically the interaction characterising perception, between the water and me. The question then is whether it is plausible to say in similar fashion that when agents come to form attitudes in respect of institutions with which they are presented, the attitudes are formed as a result of a causal interaction between the institutions and the agents.

We think that it is not plausible to say this. Institutions are not perceptually salient objects, for it is not inevitable that they will be identified under certain cues and circumstances: it will always depend on the percipients' having appropriate collateral beliefs, such as the belief that such-and-such treatment is typical of group behaviour, or that such-and-such reasoning is indicative of conformity to a practice. The perceptual interaction therefore that lies at the base of the attitudes which agents form in respect of institutions with which they are presented is not interaction with the institutions themselves but with those items which they take as evidential tokens of the institutions. The items, most plausibly, are individuals and the actions of individuals. It transpires then that we are no more required to refer to institutions in explaining the origin of the attitudes which agents hold about them than we are in characterising the content of those attitudes.

These comments lead us to reject the modified version of explanatory collectivism as well as the original one. Not only do we not have to refer to institutions in order to explain any social events; we do not even have to do so in order to explain such events fully. But in conclusion we would like to mention why we think that the image of individuals as the prisoners of institutions, the image sponsored by the modified version of collectivism, may have some validity in the depiction of social life. The reason is that even though agent attitudes are the driving force of social processes, and even though those attitudes are formed independently of causal interaction between people and institutions, they must ideally reflect how social life is organised, and in particular they must not hold out any prospects or opportunities other than ones which are actually available; otherwise they will cause more frustration than fulfilment. This is to say, more straightforwardly, that the institutional organisation of their society, like the natural structure of their environment, puts constraints on what agents may reasonably think of attempting or achieving. We do not have any direct causal influence here, such as would disturb our explanatory individualism, but we have a sort of determination which on occasion may well motivate the image of agents as the prisoners of institutions. We say 'on occasion', because there is no reason to believe that institutional incarceration is a universally appropriate picture. Institutions create possibilities for agents as well as constraining them, and even in imposing constraints they usually leave sufficient leeway to make the prison image unsuitable. This is an empirical claim which is sometimes contested by sociologists but it seems to us to be borne out by everyday experience. (Elster 1979, Ch. 3, agrees. See also Giddens 1976.)

The picture of individuals and institutions which emerges from the last two sections looks at a first approximation like this. Surveying society from the point of view of a vocabulary for institutions, we notice and give expression to truths that would have escaped us in our individualistic perspective: this, because many of the terms in the vocabulary are supervenient on, but not reducible to, individualistic expressions. Be that as it may, however, no event which we can describe in an institutional vocabulary is incapable of being explained just by reference to individuals. For any such event there will be an individualistic description available, albeit a description to which the institutional one may not reduce: all that is required is that it supervenes on the individualistic description, or on some larger individualistic description of which the given one is part. The event, taken under its institutional description, is explained insofar as it is identified with the event characterised by that individualistic description and the event so characterised is then accounted for by reference to individuals. The picture is similar to one which someone might defend in respect of psychological and neurophysiological phenomena, arguing that psychological vocabulary enables us to describe events in such a way that the descriptions are not reducible to neurophysiological counterparts, although they supervene on such; but that nonetheless every event psychologically described can be explained through being neurophysiologically identified and accounted for. Notice that on both pictures the higher perspective, while not revealing a reality that has explanatory autonomy, does provide a view for which there is no substitute in the lower. It enables us to characterise events which we can explain from the lower perspective but which we would not have identified there.[5]

This sketch is, as we mentioned, a first approximation to the picture emerging from the last two sections. What needs to be added in a final version is that the notion of an individualistic predicate has begun to oscillate between a narrower and a broader sense, the narrower being in question when we assert the expressive autonomy of institutions, and the broader appearing when we deny the corresponding explanatory autonomy. In the previous section, when we argued for expressive autonomy, we took individualistic predicates to be terms which could be understood by someone who had no conception of institutions. In the present one, when we argued for explanatory non-autonomy, we naturally allowed that the individualistic predicates used in non-institutional explanations might include complex attitudinal predicates constructed out of (non-referentially used) terms for institutions: it would be unreasonable to preclude the use of such predicates granted that the individuals are masters of the institutional terms in question and that attitudes formed on the basis of such mastery cannot be formulated in narrowly individualistic terms. What must now be admitted, after recognising the oscillation in the notion of individualistic predicate, is that if individualistic predicates are understood in the broader sense, there is no longer the same reason to believe that reference to institutions enables us to express truths inexpressible by reference just to individuals. The point must be made for clarity's sake, although there is no urgency in the question of whether institutions also enjoy the stronger sort of expressive autonomy: the issue will come up again in section 6. When we refer in what follows to the expressive autonomy of institutions, we should be taken to have the weaker variety of autonomy in mind.

## 4 FUNCTIONALISM AND THE ASSUMPTION OF EXPLANATORY AUTONOMY

The argument so far leads us to say that institutions exist over and beyond the individuals who constitute them in the sense that reference to institutions increases expressive resources, but not in the sense that such reference enriches resources of explanation. At this point however it may be objected that no philosopher or social scientist in his right mind would make the stronger claim, ascribing distinctive causal powers to groups and practices. There is a sense in which we agree with the objection, since we think that to go for the strong collectivistic thesis would be to reject the orthodox conception of agents, a conception which we argued in the last chapter was irreplaceable and unrevisable. However we oppose the complaint if it is meant to suggest that serious and sober thinkers have not maintained that institutions have causal powers which outstrip the powers of individuals, certain institutional events being inexplicable just by reference to people and their actions.

We might delve into idealist thinking about society in the attempt to bear out this claim, for in the notion of the moving spirit of history, and in its various relatives, one can certainly find the idea that institutions lord it causally over individuals. Alternatively we might search out the more extreme formulations of historical materialism in defence of our proposition, since Marx's ideas have often been made to bear a heavy collectivistic interpretation (see James 1978). It is all too likely however that such idealist and materialist schools of thought will be dismissed by our objector as scarcely more worthy opposition than a private straw theory. That being so, we argue in this section that a sort of explanatory autonomy has been credited to institutions by one of the most dominant traditions of sociology in this century: the tradition commonly known as structural-functionalism, or simply functionalism. This school of thinking about society cannot be put aside as exotic or extravagant and if we can show that it involves an assumption that institutions have explanatory autonomy, we shall have made the dialectical efforts of the last section seem worthwhile.

The functionalist tradition goes back to the introduction in the last century of a biological analogy for societies. The analogy was pressed by two of the founders of sociology, the Frenchman Auguste Comte, and the English philosopher Herbert Spencer. What it suggested to both, and in particular to Spencer, was that just as the organs and organ-activities in the body are understood by the function which they serve in maintaining the welfare of the whole, so the various components in a society, and the alterations in those components, can be understood by their purpose in promoting the well-being of society overall. We understand why there is a liver in the human body when we see the various jobs that it does which are essential to the body's health, and the idea is that we understand why there is one or another institutional pattern in a society when we recognise the different beneficial effects of that pattern.

The importance of functional understanding was emphasised by the outstanding French sociologist, Emile Durkheim, although he was careful, at least in theory, about distinguishing it from understanding the cause or origin of the matter in question: this, he took to be a topic for historical inquiry (see Durkheim 1938, Ch. 5). He offered functional accounts of phenomena such as the elementary forms of religion, and the division of labour in advanced society, arguing that they contributed to the integration of the society as a whole (see Durkheim 1915, 1933). Durkheim's functionalism did not have an immediate influence on sociology but it had a large impact on the thinking of two outstanding anthropologists, A.R. Radcliffe-Brown and Bronislaw Malinowski. In the first half of this century these thinkers were responsible for establishing a functionalist mode of analysis as the norm in anthropological theory. They were both unfaithful to Durkheim in one important regard: that they did not think that a functional account of something needed to be complemented by a causal one. Radcliffe-Brown did not otherwise develop the Durkheimian view in any substantial way, preserving even the master's emphasis on the function of social integration (see Radcliffe-Brown 1952). Malinowski was more adventurous, working out inventories of the different sorts of needs which call to be fulfilled in social life, and elaborating schemes of questions which the theorist could pose in respect of any social system (see Malinowski 1944). But whatever their departures from the Durkheimian code, they kept alive the tradition of functionalist thinking during a period when it had little hold among sociologists (see Turner and Maryanski 1979).

Functionalism came fully into its own in sociology in America of the 1940s and 1950s. In 1945 the Davis-Moore hypothesis on stratification was published and this served for many as a paradigm of the new functional style of thinking (Davis and Moore 1945). It conjectured that stratification or the unequal distribution of rewards is a mechanism whereby the functionally important positions in a society are filled with qualified personnel, and the well-being of the society is assured (see Turner and Maryanski 1979). The major functional theorists in the new sociological movement were Robert K. Merton and Talcott Parsons. Merton, whose bent was fundamentally empirical, argued that with a social system one ought to seek out the different consequences, good and bad, of the various parts of the system, in the expectation of isolating fairly concrete patterns of functional adaptation (see Merton 1968). Parsons, like Malinowski, gave a great deal of his attention to the abstract systematisation of the functions which it was required that a social system should fulfill. Thus he argued in one account that in order to achieve what he called equilibrium, the impulses to action stemming from cultural ideas and personal inclinations had to be integrated into a pattern of regular social interaction, and that where some impulses came to disturb the pattern we could expect adjustments which would assure integration and restore equilibrium (Parsons 1951).

So much by way of a brief history of functionalism. We wish to argue that the idea that social patterns are to be explained by reference to their function in promoting social well-being can be justified as a general thesis only on the assumption that the group in which a society consists has explanatory autonomy vis-à-vis individual agents. We claim to find in the infra-structure of the functionalist creed the belief that the institution of society has causal powers which cannot be reduced to the properties of individual people. Thus we think that in putting forward our explanatory brand of individualism we are not tilting at windmills, but pitting ourselves against one of the dominant sociological traditions.

The basic component in a functional explanation of any kind, whether in biology or sociology, is the ascription of a function to the element under consideration. If the element is X and the relevant system is S, we say that the function of X in S is F, or whatever. This can be spelled out on lines such as the following: that the system S has a certain capacity or goal such that the F-ing of X is an essential component in the realisation of that capacity or goal (see Ullman-Margalit 1978). Thus ascribing to the kidneys the function of removing waste products from the blood, we say: the body, S, has the goal of surviving and that the kidneys, X, clear the waste products from the blood, i.e. F, is an essential component in the realisation of that goal. Again, to take an example from the realm of artifacts, in ascribing to the fuse wire the function of melting under a heavy electrical load we say: the electrical installation, S, has the capacity to cut itself off when the load is dangerous and that the fuse wire, X, melts under a heavy load, i.e. Fs, is an essential component in the realisation of that capacity.

In functional explanation we make an ascription of the kind illustrated but we also go further, saying or suggesting that the function ascribed explains both why the item X performs the activity F, and why the item is present in the system S: if not why it came to be there in the first place, at least why it remains a permanent feature of the system. Since the ascription on its own has no explanatory value, this further clause is an indispensable part of the overall explanation. As we might expect from our analysis of explanation in the last chapter, the clause suggests that there is a causal link, however indirect, between on the one hand the role played by the item X in its distinctive activity F and on the other the presence of X and the appearance of F. This link is established in the case of artifacts by intentional design and in the biological case by natural selection. Thus in the fuse wire example, the role which the wire plays connects with its presence, and the appearance of its distinctive activity, via the intention of the designer: wanting the role to be fulfilled the designer puts the fuse wire in place and ensures that it melts under appropriate conditions. The biological case is more complex. The cause of the kidney's being present and serving to remove waste products from the blood, is that the body is genetically coded in a certain manner. The connection with the role of the kidneys however is that in view of that role human bodies in which the cause operates have been naturally selected for under evolutionary pressures: mutations in which the genetic coding does not produce suitable kidneys are destined not to survive (see Woodfield 1976).

With these points made about functional explanation, we may turn now to the question of when it is appropriate to offer such explanation in social theory. It is relatively easy in many instances to identify the socially beneficial effects of parts of the overall system and the question bears crucially on when it is appropriate to say that the identification of such effects is explanatory. Specifically, what we want to know is when it is possible to trace a causal link between on the one hand the social function served by a component of the social system and on the other the presence of that component, and the appearance of its proper activity.

The most straightforward case where functional explanation is appropriate is that in which the members of the society are in intentional control of the component that produces the beneficial effects and maintain the component out of a desire for those effects. This sort of explanation has not been much favoured by sociologists, probably because where it applies it is often not in need of being spelled out: it is as obvious as the explanation of why the electrical device has a fuse wire. The intentional planning in question may be common and barely conscious, as when we say that people in war-time evolve certain patterns of fraternisation in order to keep morals up, or that people go to church in order to reinforce their membership in the community and their status relative to others. On the other hand the planning may be deputed to a small group which carries it out in a conscious and calculated way, as when we say that the Government monitors the educational system in order to ensure that a supply of appropriately trained professional personnel is maintained.

A second relatively straightforward case where functional explanation is appropriate in social science is one in which there is intentional selection of a pattern that produces a certain social benefit. An example that has been quoted to illustrate this is the explanation by reference to their military relevance, of why certain scientific projects proliferate. It is not that the scientists themselves are interested in furthering military goals: we may presume that individual investigators each have their own reasons for pursuing the research they have on hand. Rather, the explanation is that one of the main funding agencies, the Department of Defence, selects in favour of those projects that happen to promise some military application (see Elster 1979, Ch.1). This sort of explanation is of considerable interest but obviously it applies only in a severely limited number of cases. Unsurprisingly, it has not been much pursued within the social sciences.

A third instance where functional explanation will work in the social area is one in which a mechanism of social selection operates at the level of institutions. The prime example here, and it is conspicuous for the special features involved, is the explanation of why firms follow certain rules of decision-making by reference to the profit-maximising effect of those rules. It is not supposed that the firms are capable of the very complex calculation required to see the connection between their procedures and their profits: the functional mechanism is not intentional design. Rather, what is said is that the market selects in favour of firms which follow the appropriate rules: such firms survive where others do not, and their procedures are propagated through imitation and incorporation (see Elster 1979, Ch. 1). This variety of functional explanation is clearly economical and attractive and we suspect that it is the sort of account which functionalists would applaud most generally. Unfortunately, there is little room for it in most of the areas covered by social scientists, since we do not generally find such clear notions of fitness, survival and propagation. Indeed, the claim has even been made that the economic example of such explanation is the only convincing one available in the corpus of sociological literature (Elster 1979, Ch.1).

We believe that intentional design, intentional selection and social selection are the only mechanisms discernible on the social scene which can be legitimately invoked in functional explanation (see Stinchcombe 1968, Ch.3). This does not augur well for functionalist social science since, as we have indicated, the mechanisms have only limited application. The poor outlook has often been obscured by the cultivation of vagueness in functionalist annals, particularly in the oft mooted suggestion that evolutionary theory can be used to underpin functional explanations. It is worth saying, as against this suggestion, that the natural selection of individuals with certain dispositions can only be plausibly used to explain the existence of socially useful patterns which are common to most societies: this, because of the time scale required for biological selection, and the massive mixing of human races. Thus natural selection at the individual level has been postulated as the mechanism which accounts for people's generally maintaining deferential patterns of interaction, patterns which are certainly of benefit to social life (see Milgram 1974). The fact that the patterns explained by biological evolution must be socially widespread means that the natural selection of individuals cannot be invoked to underpin the very specific functional explanations which social scientists are wont to pursue.

Finally then to the dénouement of our tale. We suggest that in most cases where functional explanations have been defended in social science there is no mechanism discernible which would underpin the causal link between the fulfilment of the function described and the maintenance of the factor which ensures that fulfilment. The point applies to Durkheim's explanation of the division of labour, to the account which Davis and Moore give of stratification, and to the vast majority of analyses that have appeared in the functionalist literature over the past quarter century. If such explanation is to be maintained, it can only be on the assumption that there is some further hidden mechanism which operates in every society to ensure that socially beneficial effects are systematically realised. To make this assumption is precisely to assume that the institution of society has distinctive causal powers of its own, that it has an explanatory autonomy vis-à-vis individuals.

This conclusion rescues our efforts to establish explanatory individualism from the charge that we are attacking a position which has not been occupied by any sober or serious thinkers. Functionalist social scientists are as sober and as serious as one could wish one's opponents to be, yet they are clearly committed to the thesis which we have railed against: they are clearly forced to say, in defiance of the orthodox conception of agents, that certain social events can be explained by reference to institutions, specifically to the self-regulating mechanism of society, which are inexplicable just by reference to individuals. This interpretation of functionalist commitments, we may note in conclusion, is not an idiosyncratic one: it is fundamentally in line with that of Elster 1979, and Turner and Maryanski 1979. Thus, to quote Elster: 'A large body of sociological literature seems to rest upon an implicit regulative idea that if you can demonstrate that a given pattern has unintended, unrecognised and beneficial effects, then you have also explained why it exists and persists. I believe that if you open at random any book on deviation, crime or conflict, you will find statements that support this interpretation' (Elster 1979, p.32).

## 5 THE SOCIAL NATURE OF PEOPLE'S ATTITUDES

We have argued in this chapter that individuals and institutions are both real entities on the social scene, and that institutions are autonomous relative to individuals in an expressive sense only: reference to them enables us to express truths which would otherwise have eluded us but it does not make it possible to explain events which would otherwise have been inexplicable. We are collectivists then on the expressive issue and individualists on the explanatory one. The title of individualists is not one which we cherish however, for individualism in social philosophy has had many associations with which we would not wish to be burdened. In this section we do something to put the associations right, arguing that while people's attitudes are the moving forces of social life, as our explanatory individualism has it, those attitudes cannot be understood as the private property of particular individuals: they are intrinsically social, and in more ways than one.

A form of individualism which would cast beliefs and desires in a distinctively non-social mould has been called the theory of the abstract individual (see Lukes 1973). The theory is a doctrine pilloried in the works of thinkers as various as Marx and Durkheim, F.H. Bradley and G.H. Mead. It supposes, so far as it allows of exact formulation, that the significant characteristics of human beings are determined independently of social initiation and experience. In its classic form, it depicts people as rational egoists whose selfish ends are the product of common inclination and whose strategies for satisfying those ends are the output of native cunning. The view is often thought to be implicated in Hobbes's model of the contract that inaugurates political society and in the more mundane models which economists use to explain and predict market phenomena. What it suggests is that individuals derive their goals from a psychological rather than a sociological source, and that we may expect to find substantively common patterns of motivation and reasoning across very different cultural contexts. Such contexts do not deeply touch people, they merely provide them with different theatres of action.

Against any such doctrine as the theory of the abstract individual, we want to suggest that although the orthodox conception of agents must be assumed to apply across any cultures which we aspire to understand, there is something deeply culture-specific about the psychological qualities of human beings, and in particular about their beliefs and desires. We want to say that people's beliefs and desires are not formed in the socially independent manner envisaged in the theory of the abstract individual, and that there is no saying how an individual will view or value things until a great deal is known of the society of which he is a member. We shall develop our point of view by elaborating on three respects in which people's attitudes can be seen to be social.

The first respect is this: that people are indebted to the cultural habits of their society for the resources of expression at their disposal and these resources establish what individuals are capable of coming to believe and desire. The first part of this proposition is uncontentious, for the extent to which any individual can invent and improvise linguistic and symbolic means of expression is extremely limited. There are new departures and breakthroughs in the area but even these are usually the work of a number of individuals in interaction and mutual reinforcement. The second part of the proposition is borne out by these facts: that people cannot believe or desire something which they are incapable of representing to themselves and that the most powerful means which they have of representing potential objects of belief and desire are the expressive resources at their disposal.

We hinted at this first respect in which people's attitudes are social when we said in the section before last that if the members of a society are possessed of concepts for institutions it cannot be surprising that we have to use such concepts in giving the content of many of their beliefs and desires. The introduction of institutional concepts naturally expands the vision and the ambition of beneficiaries: it gives them new sorts of things to believe about their social world and it offers the possibility of their conceiving new desires in regard to that world. Thus we said it was impossible to represent what those individuals think, or what they aspire after, without access to concepts which offer equally broad horizons.

It is a very powerful claim to say that people's possibilities of attitude-formation are determined by social context. And yet it is also impossible to resist. If we think of the various political concepts which have served to enliven human imagination over the past couple of hundred years we begin to appreciate that what agents believe and desire is not just a function of individual insight or intelligence, but something shaped by their social form of life. The patriot, the freedom fighter and the socialist are not possible in any social world deprived of appropriate conceptual resources. There is no patriot who lacks the concept of nation, tradition and independence, no freedom fighter who is without the ideas of liberty, oppression and respect, no socialist who is unfamiliar with the notions of class, exploitation and equality.

And yet the concepts required for the fashioning of the corresponding beliefs and desires come to individuals only by grace of the community to which they belong. Thus there is a quite exact sense in which political figures such as we have described are made possible by their time and place.

So much for what we might call the social 'capacitation' of attitudes. The second respect in which attitudes are social takes us to the familiar topic of ideological formation: the process in which individuals undergo indoctrination in cultural beliefs and inculcation of cultural values. Here we are concerned with social context in a coercive guise, rather than in the guise of a capacitating factor. What we are shown is a respect in which the individual is forced by his fellows into having one or another pattern of beliefs and desires. We see now that socialisation is a two-edged sword. On the one hand it means that individuals are indebted to their context for the different modes of vision and aspiration which are put at their disposal. On the other it means that they are put under contextual pressure to adopt a particular mode, thinking the thoughts and dreaming the dreams that are appropriate to their station.

We need say but little on the coercive aspect of socialisation, since it is a familiar phenomenon. In any social group certain views and values are bound to become established, if only because harmonious association is scarcely possible without substantive attitudinal agreement. As someone is raised and educated within the group it is inevitable that he will be introduced to this pattern of thought and evaluation: this ideology. And as he matures it will naturally be difficult for him to break from the received frame and begin to find his own way. Unorthodox opinions attract the sanctions of misunderstanding, scorn and ostracisation and few people have the wherewithal to brave such a storm. Thus it will be a rare individual who kicks the habit of his native ideology, finding a path towards beliefs and desires which fail of legitimation among his fellows.

The first two respects in which people's attitudes are social can be summed up by saying that people are socialised into the things which they believe and desire: the possibilities of belief and desire are socially established for them, and the precise patterns which they adopt are often socially imposed. Where socialisation in both of these respects is something which is generally acknowledged among social theorists, the third respect in which people's attitudes are social takes us into relatively unknown territory. Here we are not restating points that are commonly urged; rather, we are struggling against the current of the received views. The respect in question is this: that in a figurative but perfectly intelligible sense, the subject of belief and desires is not the individual human agent, but the community to which the individual belongs (see Taylor 1971); or more prosaically, that in order to ascribe beliefs and desires to an individual agent, one needs to have regard to his community, since the same pattern of individual behaviour can attract different ascriptions in different communal contexts (see Introduction above).

In its prosaic form, the claim can be generated from within the semantic point of view that we have adopted in this study. It is supported by the following argument, which we borrow from Tylor Burge (Burge 1979). The argument begins by asking us to agree that a situation can be envisaged in which our natural habits of interpretation would dictate the following story: a particular individual believes that arthritis is a disease manifested in various rheumatoid pains; he believes that he himself has this disease, a view corroborated over the years by the reports of his doctor; he fears arthritis, desires the be rid of it, hopes that it will not spread, and so on through various emotive attitudes; and finally, he forms the view on the basis of new pains that his arthritis has spread to his thigh: wrongly, since arthritis is a disease of the joints. We would tell such a story, in our language of interpretation, on the basis of finding the person disposed to behave in certain ways, making appropriate expressions of pain, taking suitable steps for improving his condition, using the word 'arthritis' in appropriate avowals, and so on.

The second stage in Burge's argument asks us to imagine what we would now say in interpretation of our patient's attitudes, if we discovered that in the community to which he belongs the word 'arthritis' is not used for the disease we recognise but for any sort of rheumatoid complaint, be it in the joints or elsewhere. It is clear, for a start, that we would not say any longer that he believes wrongly that his disease has spread to his thigh: this belief is not mistaken, because what he feels in his thigh is a sort of rheumatoid complaint. But once we grant this we realise that it would be inappropriate in the situation now imagined to attribute to the person any attitudes in respect of arthritis, as we understand it. His belief about symptoms, his belief about his own condition, his fears, desires, and hopes: these are not the attitudes that we thought they were before; they are not attitudes held in regard to arthritis, but mental states with a different content and of a different kind.

If we agree that our interpretative practice in the two situations would be as described, then we must admit that just by varying an individual's communal context, we can force a variation in the pattern of attitudes that is properly ascribed to him. As between the first and the second situation, we can imagine that there is no difference other than the variation in the communal usage of the word 'arthritis'. The individual's own usage up to the time in question and his exposure to the usage of others can be imagined to be the same, as indeed can everything about the way he physically is, and the way he feels. Thus it transpires that communal context is crucially relevant to the interpretation of an agent's attitudes: that we must keep the community as much as the individual in view in working out what those attitudes are.

There are a number of objections that may be brought against this argument but we do not have the scope for reviewing them here; in any case they are extensively treated by Burge. One objection however is worth considering because it shows up an important aspect of the claim which we are defending. It is that in the original situation, the fact that the patient believed that arthritis had spread to his thigh shows that we should take him not to know what arthritis is, and that we should ascribe to him more or less the attitudes which would be ascribed in the second situation: that is to say, attitudes which bear on something other than arthritis proper - say, tharthritis, where that is taken to be a rheumatoid disease which is found not only in joints but also in the thigh. The objection would undermine our argument, since it would have us interpret the person's attitudes in the same way in both situations.

We think it is clear that our natural interpretative practice would not counsel us to follow the line prescribed in the objection. However we also think that the pattern in question is one which meets less well the constraints on interpretation that we discussed in Chapter 1 than the construal originally proposed. In particular, it makes less good sense of the general behaviour which we would expect of our patient, casting him as unlikely for example to argue with anyone who holds different beliefs about what is described as 'arthritis': since his own beliefs are said to be about only what would make them true - tharthritis, in our example - there will not be the usual point in such argument. One particularly striking way of showing the poverty of the objector's construal is to point out that it would support the following prediction: that if the patient comes to be persuaded that what is generally called 'arthritis' does not occur in the thigh, he may revise his own use of the term, but he will not consider that his earlier belief about the disease in his thigh was mistaken, nor will he feel any relief that his arthritis is not spreading. This prediction is quite outlandish and what it shows is that the objector's interpretation does not correspond with the pattern of the agent's self-interpretation. The agent 'aims' at having beliefs about that disease which is known in his community as 'arthritis', not at having beliefs about whatever will make them true. Thus the interpretation originally offered, according to which he believes falsely that he has arthritis in his thigh, is that to which he will himself subscribe if he is persuaded that what is known as 'arthritis' only occurs in joints.

What is the upshot of admitting the third respect in which people's attitudes are social? So far as social science is concerned, it is that in order to understand social events, tracing the behaviour involved to the beliefs and desires of individuals, we must look to the community as a whole, and not just to the individuals in isolation. In the metaphor adopted earlier, the community is the subject of interpretation, as much as the persons who make it up. Here perhaps we have the key to the understanding of that Hegelian, and indeed hermeneutic, tradition according to which it is individualistic prejudice to look exclusively at the ideas of particular people and to ignore the attitudes incorporated in a society considered as a whole.

The methodological significance of the lesson is emphasised by Charles Taylor (Taylor 1971). It is that we cannot expect to be able to fix those attitudes of individuals which are relevant to a given social event just by a procedure of interviewing individual subjects, sifting out their subjective and often quite personal reactions to the objective phenomenon in question. In order to identify the appropriate beliefs and desires one must first resolve the focus of inquiry at a higher level, isolating the communally established terms that form the grid on which individual attitudes have to be mapped. In Taylor's terminology one must seek out the patterns of intersubjective and common meaning before one can hope to understand how individual agents in the community view things and value them.

A brief example may help to bring out the point. In Paris during May 1968 one might have sought out the subjective reactions of individual students and workers to the events of the time, describing those events in neutral, even clinical, terms. But it is certain that one would have missed the real significance of what was going on by focussing one's inquiry in this way. In order to extricate that significance one would have needed to establish the general usage of the terms commonly used to describe contemporary happenings: 'les évènements' and the like. Only with that done could one have hoped to uncover the attitudes of those who participated in 'les évènements' and those who opposed them. The important point is that in the inquiry one would have had to move back and forth between individuals and community in fixing the significance of what took place; one could not have rested content with the usual interviewing technique.

In this section we have seen three respects in which the belief and desires of individual agents are social. Such attitudes are limited by the concepts made available to individuals by their society; they are formed under the pressures associated with the orthodoxies of social life; and they are ascribed on the basis of community practice as well as individual performance. The social nature of the attitudes makes it possible for us to claim that they are the moving forces of social life, without supporting the theory of the abstract individual that we discussed earlier. It shows that in espousing explanatory individualism we are guiltless of the crudities often alleged undiscriminatingly of doctrines which bear the individualist name.

## 6 METHODOLOGICAL INDIVIDUALISM

The individualism which we have been discussing in this chapter is an ontological variety of the doctrine: it raises questions of existential status, in particular questions of relative status between individuals and institutions. In this final section we turn from such matters to more pressing methodological ones, seeking out the significance of the position which we have adopted for the pursuit of social inquiry. On the expressive criterion of autonomy, we have argued that institutions do exist in their own right over and beyond individuals; on the explanatory, we have argued that they do not. The issue before us now bears on where this line of argument puts us in the debate that has raged in philosophy of social science since F.A. Hayek and Karl Popper put forward their individualistic manifestoes in the 1940s and 1950s (see Hayek 1942-3, Popper 1957; also O'Neill 1973).

Methodological individualism has been associated with two claims: first, that there are no autonomous social facts, and second that there are no irreducible social laws. The first claim is difficult to interpret in view of the obscurity of the notion of a fact, but on any interpretation it would appear that our expressive collectivism must force us to reject it. A fact is usually said to correspond to a proposition: it is an entity of such a kind that it obtains if the proposition is true, and does not obtain if the proposition is false. Social facts may reasonably be taken as the facts answering to propositions which refer explicitly or implicitly to institutions and in that case their autonomy is assured. Since such propositions express truths that cannot be expressed just by reference to individuals it seems that they must be said to have facts corresponding with them which are distinctively social.

The more important claim made by methodological individualists is that not only are there no autonomous social facts, there are no irreducible social laws. Again this claim is obscure and we must put an interpretation on it before we pursue our discussion; the discussion will take up most of this section. It is necessary to be explicit first of all on the sense of 'law' in question: whether it means objective regularity, or theoretical generalisation. We construe it in the first sense, taking methodological individualism to raise the question of whether there are regularities in social life which are in a certain sense irreducible. The regularities at issue are nomic ones: that is to say, regularities such that we take evidence that they have obtained in a given number of instances to indicate that they obtain generally, even if only probabilistically. Put otherwise, the regularities in question support counterfactuals: if one of them bears on the succession of B on A it licenses the counterfactual conditional, if A had been brought about now, B would have followed, or at least have been made more likely (see Goodman 1973). The reason the regularities must be nomic is that it makes no sense to say that a non-nomic regularity is reducible or irreducible. To reduce is always in some sense to explain, and there is nothing to be explained about such a regularity: to say that it is non-nomic is to say that it is a coincidence which requires no special explanation.

The question of whether there are irreducible regularities in social life is usually understood as a question that concerns inter-theoretical reduction. One theory T' is reduced to another T" if and only if two conditions are fulfilled. First there is the connectability condition, that the propositions of T' can be matched satisfactorily with propositions framed in the language of T": if they are not translated by their counterparts, at least the terms in which they are cast apply just in the instances where corresponding terms or expressions in the counterparts apply. Secondly there is the derivability condition, that the counterpart propositions framed in the language of T' must be capable of being derived within T": they may not have the same importance within the reducing theory as they had in T' but they must at least come out as corollaries of it (see Churchland 1979, Section II; James 1978, Ch. I). If the debate between methodological individualism and collectivism is understood as a debate about inter-theoretical reduction, the question between them is whether social science, assuming that it formulates distinctively social regularities, is reducible to our theory of individual human beings, be that theory taken to consist in a formal psychology, or the orthodox conception of agents.

We do not think that the methodological debate is properly cast as a debate about inter-theoretical reduction; indeed such a construal we regard as mischievous, since it suggests that the individualist assimilates sociology to psychology. The reason for rejecting the construal is that in the case before us we are not presented with two theories, two bodies of laws, such as inter-theoretical reduction supposes. By our account we have on the one hand a framework of beliefs which guides us in the explanation of what human beings do: the orthodox conception of agents; and on the other an ongoing set of inquiries which aim at detecting nomic regularities in social life: the social sciences, in particular the social sciences concerned with macro-patterns. Neither of these enterprises counts as a theory in the sense which would be required if we were to raise the question of inter-theoretical reduction in their regard.

On our formulation of the methodological debate we are concerned with a single comprehensive mode of analysing social life, a mode of analysis which allows us to refer both to individuals and institutions, and the question is whether there are any regularities to be discovered in social life which are not capable of being explained just by reference to individuals, albeit to individuals with the social attitudes discussed in the last section. Like an individual event, a regularity is explained by a statement which advances us in our causal understanding of it, the adequacy of the explanation being judged by whether the advance is sufficient for our purposes. If the regularity is that A-type events are followed by B-type events, what is required is a grasp of causal mechanisms and connections which will at least make likely the succession of an event with the property B on an event with the property A. The question before us then is whether we should expect to find regularities in social life that do not allow of being traced causally to the attitudes of agents, those agents being understood according to the orthodox conception.[6]

It may be useful to make a further comment on this question before we take up the discussion of it. Granted our admission that institutional predicates may supervene on individualistic ones without being reducible to them, it appears that we might acknowledge a nomic regularity in the succession of B-type events on A-type events, where the predicates by which those types are identified are institutional ones of a kind that are irreducible to individualistic expressions. In that case, while each particular A-B succession might be explicable just by reference to individuals, there would be no individualistic explanation of the succession taken as a nomic regularity: this, because there would be no unified individualistic way of characterising the regularity, each A-B succession being liable to bear any of an indefinite number of individualistic descriptions. The methodological individualist denies that there are any such regularities to be discovered and thus he closes a possibility that is left open by our admission in respect of the supervenience of institutional predicates. What he claims, by implication, is that any institutional predicates used in the formulation of nomic regularities must be predicates that reduce to individualistic counterparts. This claim however is not so striking as it may seem, for it will be sufficient for the methodological individualist if the counterpart terms are individualistic only in the broad sense distinguished at the end of section 3. But to return now to the main line of inquiry, we have to determine whether there are any nomic regularities in social life which are inexplicable just by reference to individuals.

We may approach the investigation by asking whether there is any likely scenario under which a social scientist ought to countenance such a regularity. On any scenario we must suppose that the scientist has been presented with empirical evidence of a regularity, say a regularity in the succession of B-type events on A-type ones: that is, he must have found a number of cases of the succession. Similarly on any scenario we must take it that the scientist sees no way of explaining the existence of a nomic connection between these two types of event by reference to individuals. What we have to ask then is whether the empirical evidence should ever persuade him to refuse to dismiss the regularity as a coincidence, and to take it as something nomic, something allowing confident prediction that A-type events, whether universally or with a certain probability, will be followed by B-type ones.

There are two circumstances under either of which we think that the inquirer should recognise a discovered regularity as nomic: one is where the regularity has empirical salience, the other where it has theoretical support. The first case would arise with any regularity which was formulated in appropriate predicates, the event-types allowing projectibility, and which was subject to corroboration in an indefinite number of tests or observations. The indefinitely replicable succession of appropriately characterised events on each other should persuade any scientist that he was dealing with a nomic regularity, even if he could not explain the regularity within received theory.

Is it likely that empirical salience will generate recognition of individualistically inexplicable social regularities? We think not. The reason, and admittedly it is a highly contingent consideration, is that the social sciences are not in the habit of presenting empirically salient regularities of any kind, individualistically explicable or not. For any hypothesis such as that which links A-type and B-type events there will be a limited number of observations and, social life not being subject to laboratory experiment, it will not be possible to test the hypothesis in an indefinite number of instances. Other factors too contribute to the lack of empirical salience in alleged regularities of social life. One is that most observed social regularities are probabilistic rather than universal, and even when indefinite replication is possible probabilistic regularities are difficult to make salient: it will rarely be impossible to dismiss them as coincidences. And a second additional factor which helps to deprive observed social regularities of empirical salience is that their characterisation is rather more easily contested than is the formulation of regularities observed in the natural realm, so that a sceptic can always argue that the facts are forced improperly into common categories of description. The difficulty with characterisation arises from the variety of human cultures, and the role played in those cultures of the concepts used by natives: a generalisation about religions may be challenged on the grounds that our concept of religion does not apply irresistibly to the practices in other societies which we use it to describe.

The other circumstance under which an inquirer ought to recognise a discovered regularity as nomic, even if the regularity is not empirically salient, is where it has theoretical support. A regularity has such support when some accepted body of theory gives us reason to expect that it should obtain. On the basis of such support it is methodologically reasonable to countenance the regularity, taking the evidence available more seriously than it might otherwise have been taken. Is it likely then that theoretical support will generate recognition of individualistically inexplicable social regularities? The question, if we hold by explanatory individualism, must be answered with a firm negative. Individuals and institutions are the only obvious forces in the social arena and if we say that nothing is causally explicable by reference to institutions that is not explicable by reference to individuals, we suggest that nothing on the social front is explicable in any way if it is not capable of being individualistically explained. But this is to say, with particular reference to the case on hand, that a social regularity is not explicable in any fashion, if it is not capable of being individualistically explained; and, not being explicable in any fashion, that it cannot have theoretical support, such support being a form of explanation. A doctrine such as sociological functionalism might have been introduced as a way of providing support for an alleged regularity that is not individualistically intelligible. Our explanatory individualism has the effect of denying that any such doctrine is available for this purpose: it means that the only theoretical support on the basis of which a social inquirer might be led to take evidence of a regularity seriously is the support provided when we see that the obtaining of the regularity can be plausibly explained by reference to individuals.

The considerations in respect of empirical salience and theoretical support suggest that a social inquirer is not likely to be compelled by the evidence before him to recognise as nomic any regularities which are individualistically unintelligible. More strongly however, we may also urge that it would be methodologically unreasonable of him to countenance such regularities. The reason is that he would have to depict the regularities as isolated features of the world, causally unconnected with what we know about the individuals and institutions that make up society; he would have to present them as anomalies or miracles. This sort of judgment is not recommended on any account of the principles of scientific method and we think that the social scientist would do better to avoid it, availing himself of the option which the lack of empirical salience and theoretical support keeps open: that of dismissing the regularity as a coincidence.[7]

We may conclude that any regularity likely to be discovered by a social scientist will always be better put aside as a coincidence than held up as an individualistically inexplicable but still nomic pattern. The conclusion means that we espouse, not just the explanatory version of ontological individualism, but also individualism in the methodological sense. We say that it is unlikely, although not altogether inconceivable, that there are irreducible social laws: nomic regularities of social life that fail of being explained by reference to individuals, and that fail in particular of being explained in terms of the orthodox conception of agents.

This methodological individualism offers a constraint which is a useful guide to the practising social scientist. It suggests that the social inquirer ought not to give credence to any regularities which would not be individualistically intelligible. The constraint is a loose one, since it will often not enable us to discriminate between rival accounts of the regularity in question: each account may satisfy the test, describing a pattern which it is possible to conceive of explaining by reference to individuals. Even though it is loose however the constraint is not entirely vacuous. It would preclude the recognition of many of the regularities which anthropologists and sociologists hailed under the bewitching illusions of functionalist dogma. Methodological individualism is an outlook opposed to the dispositions associated with functionalism and other theories that confer explanatory autonomy on institutions.

We may mention in passing that there are other versions of methodological individualism which would impose tighter constraints on the practising social inquirer. One, the psychologistic version, would say that any regularity countenanced must be explicable, not just by reference to individuals, but to individuals as they might have been, in the absence of interaction and socialisation. (see Nozick 1977 for a characterisation). Another, non-psychologistic but rationalistic, would say that any such regularity must be capable of being explained, not just by reference to individuals, but to individuals whose relevant attitudes are rationally justified (see Miller 1978 for an account). The psychologistic version seems to us unworkable, first, because it is hard to see how we are supposed to know about the attitudes of unsocialised individuals, and secondly, because the prescribed approach would systematically miss the effect of those attitudes whose content requires the use of concepts for institutions. The rationalistic version seems to us excessively restrictive: it would allow us to invoke beliefs which were well supported by evidential factors, but it would gratuitously deny us access to beliefs in whose formation non-avowable factors such as self-righteousness played a decisive role.[8]

We have been concerned in this chapter with social science as a form of macro-investigation. The lesson we draw is that macro-theory cannot proceed in neglect of micro-understanding, an understanding which we take to fit the humanist's charter: this, by the argument of the last chapter. In conclusion it is worth mentioning that our methodological humanism does not commit us to the view that in doing social science we should always take our starting point from individual motives and actions. Such a view, which derives a strategy as well as a constraint from ontological individualism, recommends to the social scientist that in investigating macro-phenomena he take the point of view of the individual agents involved, approaching the phenomena either in the manner adopted by the economist, or in that often associated with the historian. On the economic way of doing things we reconstruct provisionally the beliefs and desires of typical agents in a given sort of circumstance, usually putting severe egoistic constraints on the motivation allowed, and we work out, first, what the agents would rationally have done in that situation, and, secondly, what the outcome would have been of such individual actions. Where the predictions come out right we assume that our motivational and other premisses give us the explanation of the phenomenon in question; where they are not fulfilled, we go back and amend the premisses, subject to various standards of plausibility, until we succeed in getting the correct results. The historical approach is a variant on this which is appropriate when we have independent access to the people involved in the events we wish to explain and can help ourselves to collateral information on their motivation and understanding. Here we again assume that the agents acted rationally and this assumption together with the collateral information on their beliefs and desires enables us to reconstruct what they would do in the circumstance under discussion, and what such action would lead to at the aggregate level. This reconstruction is then tested, as it was in the other case, by whether it represents the events to be explained as an intelligible outcome. Where it does, we may rest content; where it does not, we must go back to the drawing board.

We think that the economic and historical patterns of macro-explanation are ones which the methodological individualist must always applaud: after all, what they do is to render social events individualistically intelligible, thus vindicating the doctrine of explanatory individualism. However we do not believe that the methodological individualist has to recommend the pursuit of such explanations as the first aim of social inquiry. He may equally well approve of a procedure which resolves the focus of scrutiny at a level where individuals are barely taken into account, for such a procedure is quite likely to reveal patterns and correlations that would have been overlooked in the other approach: they must be explicable by reference to individuals, but they may not command attention on a strategy which keeps individuals in view. He can argue that on the old counsel of seeing the wood, not the trees, we should be prepared to explore society at that level where our gaze is fixed on large-scale entities and phenomena: nations and classes, cultures and economies, migrations and wars. It may well be that within such a perspective we shall detect regularities, albeit regularities that call for individualistic explanation, which would have eluded us had we kept our attention focussed on individual actors. It is doubtful for example whether the regularity connecting the introduction of money to peasants with the decline of the manorial system would have been visible to someone following strictly the alternative approach.

This completes our reflections on the nature of macro-inquiry in social science, and in particular on the debate between individualism and collectivism. As we are humanists on questions pertaining to micro-inquiry, so it turns out that we are individualists on the matters discussed in this chapter. The commitments are not unconnected, for it is our humanism which forces us to reject the idea that institutions have explanatory autonomy. If we are individualists however, we are individualists with a difference. While we believe that institutions do not have an explanatory autonomy, we hold that they are autonomous in an expressive way. And while we think that social science should not countenance regularities that are individualistically inexplicable, we say that it may well seek out and systematise regularities in neglect of the matter of their individualistic explanation. But finally, and most important of all, what it means for us to explain an event by reference to individuals is not itself distinctively individualistic. For as we emphasised in the last section, our individuals are people with deeply social attitudes, not figments of an atomistic imagination. Our individualism denies that agents are institutional puppets but it allows that they are the products of social life.

# 4 TRUTH AND VALUE

## 1 ALLEGATIONS OF VALUE-LADENNESS

The question concerning the nature of the relationship between truth and value in social scientific theories is one that has provoked an enormous amount of debate amongst both philosophers and practitioners of the social sciences. An assumption shared by most of the participants to the dispute, and shared by us, is that the natural sciences, by contrast with the social, do not have a 'value-problem'. Individual natural scientists may be influenced by moral or political commitments in their choice of theory, their experimental technique or observational judgement. However such influence is not unavoidable and where it is likely to have an effect, the scientist can take steps to inhibit it. Not being unavoidable, influence of the kind in question may be condemned or condoned, depending on the point of view of the assessor. The natural sciences do not have a 'value-problem' in the sense of being inextricably bound up with any evaluative commitments.

This background assumption is challenged but not undermined by considerations raised in the work of the historian and philosopher of science, Thomas Kuhn (see Kuhn 1970). Kuhn makes a case against the 'critical' view of the selection of scientific theories sponsored by Sir Karl Popper and in order to understand his claims we must look briefly at that view. Popper's methodology is purportedly anti-inductive, the justification of theories via a (probabilistic) measure of their evidential support being deemed to be both impossible and undesirable. The impossibility thesis need not concern us, the undesirability claim, which does, is based on the supposed affinity of 'inductivism' to dogmatism.[1] 'Inductivists' are indicted by Popper from their ability to sustain the credibility of 'bad' theories by looking for, and finding, confirmation of those theories. The apparent ease with which theories can be inductively 'confirmed' allows the inductivist, allegedly, to maintain support for a theory which, on Popperian grounds, should be rejected.

As an alternative to what he takes to be the inductivists' criterion of good theory (high degree of confirmation), Popper proposes that theories should be assessed by their degree of corroboration.[2] Essential to this alternative is the central claim that although we can never tell if a theory is true, we can tell if it is false:

it is false, so Popper says, if it has a false consequence. Two lessons are derived by Popper from the claim. The first is that the scientific status of a theory is determined by its being falsifiable (and its degree of 'scientificity' by its degree of falsifiability), and the second, a methodological precept, is that scientists ought to adopt a critical stance with respect to the investigated theories, looking for falsification, rather than confirmation of those theories. When Popper recommends that theories should be assessed by degree of corroboration, he takes corroboration to turn on the failure of the theory to be falsified, despite the best efforts of scientists to find consequences that show it to be false.

Kuhn criticises Popper on the grounds that the adoption of the critical methodology recommended by Popper would cause chaos in science, rather than progress. Many of the most fertile scientific theories, he says, were 'born refuted': they were such that in their early days a critical methodology would have counselled their rejection. This state of affairs is explained by Kuhn as follows. When we are presented with a new theory, we are more inclined to believe that its consequences are false than we would be with a more established theory. The reason is that the consequences are likely to jar with our overall view of the world, this view being the product of traditional theories. Since it takes time for us then to get used to the idea that certain consequences of a novel theory might be true, Kuhn says that we should beware of passing summary judgment on whether they are realised and on whether the theory which sponsors them is reliable.[3]

On the positive side what Kuhn recommends is that we should give a fledgling theory time to get airborne before we adopt the stern disposition of the critic. In particular, we should pay attention to what it can explain, ignoring for the moment the difficulties on which the critic would focus. The rationale behind the procedure is that by taking this line we may find ourselves drawn into the perspective of the novel theory to the point of no longer being overwhelmed by difficulties that at first looked definitive. It may be that those difficulties will begin to vanish as we learn to see the world in the fashion of the new system. In defending tolerance towards novel theories, Kuhn takes himself to be opposing Popper's equation of the rational with the critical. By contrast he argues that in the advancing new departures in science it may be rational, not to be critical, but rather to be dogmatic. Some of the best theories were given the necessary opportunity to get into the air, he says, only because of an 'irrational' dogmatism on the part of their supporters, a dogmatism which made it possible to ignore apparent refutations of the theories.

The dogmatism counselled by Kuhn may have one perfectly praiseworthy source: a conviction that if the new theory is given a chance, we shall learn to see the world in such a way that objections to it will wither. However other factors may also underlie the dogmatism, factors unconnected with the likelihood that the theory will win us over to its way of depicting the world. Metaphysical dogma, religious belief or evaluative commitment may also underpin a determination to hold onto a new theory which, assessed by critical canons, ought not to be retained. The radicalism of Kuhn's view lies in the suggestion that far from being an aid to correct science, the attempt to remove such warping influences would be positively dysfunctional. He does not say that those who come eventually to accept the theory should also have to endorse the biassing tenets but he thinks that criticism of the tenets may lead to premature dismissal of the theory.

We said at the beginning of this section that the considerations raised in Kuhn's work challenge but do not undermine our assumption that the natural sciences do not have a value problem. We can now appreciate why this is so. Extra-scientific views and values may play a role in the fixing of the beliefs of individual scientists, and it may even be dysfunctional on a scientist's part to try to neutralise those influences on her theorising. It remains the case however that scientists do not have to endorse any such views or values in coming to accept a theory which such tenets sustain. It may be important that the early supporters of a theory are dogmatic in their commitment to it but the source of that dogmatism does not matter and may be rejected by later adherents. Thus those convinced by the Copernican world-view did not need to hold by the perfection of circular movement and those who followed Kepler did not have to believe in the harmony of the spheres.

Assuming that the natural sciences do not have a problem with values, our task in this section is to see whether the social sciences do. We shall be interested only in alleged value commitments in social science which are not paralleled by similar commitments in natural; what we are looking for are respects in which the social disciplines can be said to be distinctively bound up with values. In our discussion we take it to be more or less intuitively clear what is and is not a value commitment. Keeping off controversial matters of analysis we may say that such a commitment is involved in any opinion as to the desirability or undesirability, or the rightness or wrongness, of something; it is also involved in any felt desire or aversion but these do not need explicit mention since they lead respectively to opinions about what is desirable and what undesirable. Value commitments may be expressed in the form of prescriptions about what should or should not be, in the form of assertions using such terms as 'desirable', 'good', 'right', 'ought' and so on, or in the form of assertions using less formally evaluative expressions: for example, 'generous', 'charming', 'cruel' and 'boring'. They are marked by the close connection they bear to action, for we take each value commitment to give an agent a reason, whether or not conclusive, for performing or not performing certain actions. The exact nature of that connection is something which we would prefer to leave unanalysed since the matter is disputed and for our purposes we do not need to have an opinion about it.

Turning then to the alleged value-ladenness of social science, it will be useful first to set aside some irrelevant claims that are often raised in discussions on the topic. It is sometimes said that social scientists are evaluatively committed insofar as they have to value truth, and the honesty required by the pursuit of truth, but this is beside the point so far as we are concerned since the commitments in question do not mark a contrast between the social and the natural sciences. Again it is often pointed out that social scientists display evaluative opinions on the relative importance of various issues in delineating their area of inquiry. However such commitments are also of no concern to us since they are equally involved in the enterprise of natural scientists. Finally, it is maintained that the social sciences are enmeshed in evaluative issues to the extent that their methods raise ethical problems about experimenting with human beings and to the extent that their results are used in the formation of social policies. The issues in question are important for any discussion of the acquisition and application of knowledge but they are also issues for the natural sciences and we may therefore leave them.

It may seem too short a way with alleged value commitments to dismiss them on the grounds that they arise also in the natural sciences. What may be added in justification of the procedure is that none of the evaluative commitments mentioned raises what we describe in a later section as the problem of value-ladenness. To anticipate, and simplify, we may say that value commitments raise a problem when they are likely to lead different inquirers to different results. The commitment to truth and honesty is not liable to have this effect since it is assumed to be universal. And neither are commitments about the importance of certain topics, or about the propriety of certain methods or policies. Such commitments may vary as between people but they determine the inquiries made by researchers, not - or at least not necessarily - the results reached in those inquiries.

There are three arguments for the value-ladenness of social science which we shall consider. The first two, both of which can be found in many different forms in the literature, do not seem to us to be conclusive but they are nonetheless worth considering. The third is an argument based on premises which will be familiar from our discussion of the semantic enterprise and we think that it is the one most deserving of examination. We shall come to it in the last part of this section but our main discussion of it will be postponed until the next.

The first argument for value-ladenness is based on the fact that social scientists are also social actors and that social actors necessarily occupy a particular social position, a position which gives them distinctive interests and biases. The claim is that inevitably social scientists will import those evaluative dispositions into their work and that their researches will be warped to yield congenial conclusions. The charge may be brought in many forms but it will be most familiar in its Marxist shape. There it becomes castigation of 'bourgeois' social science, the idea being that the bourgeois position of regular social scientists ensures that they will bias their theories so as to give only a partial and class-serving perspective on social reality.[4]

What are we to say to this claim? One point to note is that there are bourgeois social scientists who do not subscribe to what would be described as bourgeois theories and that the process of ideological distortion cannot therefore be deemed a necessary consequence of class position. The threat of bias may be present but bias cannot be said by the Marxist to be inescapable; science, in particular social science, must be allowed a certain autonomy vis-à-vis the forces and relations of production.[5] More generally, the accusation of socially motivated bias is premissed on the possibility of viewing things correctly: the possibility of viewing them without the distorting focus of ideology; it does not matter whether this possibility is thought to be realised by the enlightened bourgeois scientist or by the scientist who is representative of the universal, working class. That ideological views presuppose a non-ideological one is recognised by the French Marxist, Louis Althusser: 'while admitting that they do not correspond to reality, i.e. that they constitute an illusion, we admit that they do make allusion to reality, and that they need only be "interpreted" to discover the reality of the world behind their imaginary representation of that world' (Althusser 1977, p.153).

Although the first line of argument for the value-ladenness of social science does not seem to us to be persuasive, it is based on an important observation. The Marxist claim suggests, and the suggestion is surely plausible, that if the preponderance of social scientists come from an oppressor class, or are hired by members of that class, the view of social reality which they peddle will be systematically skewed in favour of the interests of that class. The suggestion might be borne out by reference to the normal self-protective dispositions of human beings but another reason for supporting it is the unlikelihood that social scientists who represent an oppressor class will be able to perceive correctly the opinions and the sentiments of people in the oppressed. Such representatives may be in the worst situation to penetrate the appearance and discern the resentment behind the smiling face. Thus it may be that a non-repressive society is required for the generally satisfactory pursuit of social science (contra Lessnoff 1974, Ch.6).[6]

The Marxist emphasis is important because it is commonly, if not convincingly, maintained that although social theories are biassed, the conflict between biassed theories will enable us eventually to see how things really are. This is the 'rinsing' approach to distortion: pummel conflicting theories hard enough and the bias will drip out. Ernest Nagel writes as follows:

> Modern science encourages the invention, the mutual exchange, and the free but responsible criticsm of ideas; it welcomes competition in the quest for knowledge between independent investi-

> gators even when their intellectual orientations are different; and it progressively diminishes the effects of bias by retaining only those proposed conclusions of its inquiries that survive critical examination by an indefinitely large community of students, whatever be their value preferences or doctrinal commitments (Nagel 1961, pp.489-90).

The weakness in the case made by Nagel, so far at least as social science is concerned, is that the community of students he mentions is not indefinitely large in the appropriate sense; it may well be populated by the representatives of only one class. Sir Karl Popper, who also defends a rinsing approach, shows a keener appreciation of the relationship between science and social structure.

> The objectivity of science is not a matter of the individual scientists but rather the social result of their mutual criticism, of the friendly-hostile division of labour among the scientists, of their co-operation and also of their competition. For this reason, it depends, in part, upon a number of social and political circumstances which make this criticism possible (Popper 1976, p.95).

Insofar as objectivity is dependent on such political circumstances, and Popper mentions the power of the state as being especially relevant, it would appear that he is not far off from agreement with a Marxist like Adorno, who claims that 'the idea of scientific truth cannot be split off from that of a true society' (Adorno 1976, p.27). Where they differ is in deciding where and when that true society exists. For Popper, free competition in the market-place of ideas ensures objectivity, and that market-place is to be found in the liberal democracies of western capitalist societies. For Adorno, market success is not an indicator of truth; it does not testify to the qualities of an object, even if that object is an intellectual theory.

A second line of argument for the value-ladenness of social science is suggested by Marx's critique of bourgeois political economy. Marx claims that bourgeois political economy 'defines the estranged form of social intercourse as the essential and original form corresponding to man's nature' (Marx 1974, p.217). It mistakes for the real essence of the human being that which is made of the person under the capitalist division of labour, a division of labour which 'transforms the worker into a cripple, a monster, by forcing him to develop some highly specialised dexterity at the cost of a world of productive impulses and faculties' (Marx 1974, p.381). In these criticisms we find the following idea suggested: that undistorted social inquiry will be guided by a true conception of human nature. If a further step is taken, and that conception is said to be one which cannot be empirically decided but which rests on an evaluative foundation, the undistorted social inquiry will be linked indissolubly with value commitments. It will appear that in order to reach the truth in social matters one will have to have a certain empirically inaccessible vision of human beings and that in order to gain access to that vision one will have to be of a certain evaluative disposition: what that disposition is may be left unanalysed but certainly it will involve rejecting those interests which wed a social scientist to the status quo.[7]

David Thomas develops the second line of argument in a recent work on the philosophy of social science (Thomas 1979). He argues as follows.

1 It is a fact that different philosophies of human nature have been responsible for the numerous different forms which the human sciences have taken.
2 'We just do take moral and political attitudes to the kinds of issues which enter the philosophical foundations of social sciences . . . we just do take positive and negative moral attitudes towards such statements as that people are creatively productive, that people are essentially equal, that people are divided between their biological instincts and their social soul, indeed that people have a fixed nature at all' (Thomas 1979, p. 144).
3 Although there is no logical link between an investigator's morality and his theory of human nature, the morality the social scientist holds 'tends to determine his theory of human nature and vice versa' (Ibid., p. 145).

There are two points at which any such argument for value-ladenness is likely to run into trouble. One is the claim that the conception of human nature which is said to guide the social scientist is not empirically determined, and the other is the thesis that the conception is based on evaluative commitments. The first claim is important to the argument since if the operative conception is selected by empirical considerations then there is no room for the intrusion of values. Equally, however, it is difficult to defend, especially if it is granted that empirical evidence may relate very indirectly to theories which it supports: it may bear out those theories only insofar as they belong to a web of beliefs which are unfalsified at those points where falsification is conceivable. Thomas does take a tolerant view of how empirical evidence gives support to theories and, that being so, it is not clear why the conceptions of human nature which he finds at the origins of social science have to be taken to be empirically undecided, or at least underdetermined.

But, even if this is granted, it is not clear why such a conception has to be chosen on an evaluative basis. Although it may be true that we just do take moral attitudes towards philosophies of human nature, the exact nature of the determining influence which those attitudes are supposed to exercise needs to be specified. That theories of human nature are only loosely linked to empirical considerations does not of itself render them undecidable on other than evaluative grounds. In fact the connection between moral attitudes and philosophies of human nature seems to be very tenuous indeed. A variety of moral beliefs have been held in conjunction with a number of views about human beings. The ethical altruist may reluctantly come to accept psychological hedonism, resigning herself to the non-ideal nature of reality. Again the political democrat may be brought to acknowledge the inevitability of oligarchy, her idealism turning thereby to sentimentalism or cynicism.

Like the first argument for the value-ladenness of social science this second fails to establish the desired conclusion although it does draw attention to an important aspect of social theorising. Finally then we come to the third attempt to show that social science is inextricably bound up with evaluative commitments. This argument takes its starting point from premises established earlier in our discussions. We have been arguing throughout the preceding chapters that what we describe as the orthodox conception of human beings is imposed on us willy nilly as we try to make sense of one another in our everyday exchanges or in social science. According to this conception human action is explained when, and only when, it is represented as an attempt on the agent's part to bring about a state of affairs which she desires or, as we may also say, believes to be desirable. It follows that in any enterprise of making sense of such action, and in particular in pursuing social science, we must get into the business of identifying the values which weigh with our subjects, the desires that move them to act.

That we have to ascribe evaluative beliefs to agents may not seem to raise the value-ladenness problem but a little reflection shows how, arguably, it does. In attributing non-evaluative beliefs to people we rely on a set of epistemological principles about what beliefs they are likely to have. We have a view about what is in the world, how different people are situated with respect to their environment, and what beliefs are liable to result from that situation. If the position were similar with the attribution of evaluative beliefs then we would be guided, in parallel, by our view of what values there are, how they may be perceived by different people, and what evaluative beliefs they are disposed to engender. This means that while we might be able to admit a certain divergence between the evaluative beliefs of our subjects and our own, we would have to rely on our own for determining which evaluative beliefs it was reasonable to ascribe. In other words, the enterprise on which we were embarked would be a deeply value-laden one. What we have to work out is whether the parallel holds between the attribution of non-evaluative belief and the attribution of evaluative which would yield such value-ladenness as a result.

In the first two chapters we argued that the ascription of belief and desire involved in the interpretation of utterances and the explanation of actions ought to be governed by the principle of humanity. According to that principle we should ascribe such mental states as minimise inexplicable error on the part of our subjects, whether error in their evaluative or non-evaluative beliefs: evaluative beliefs go proxy here and henceforth for desires, a desire for something always involving a belief that the thing in question is desirable. It appears then that we are committed to the view that in ascribing evaluative beliefs we should use our own beliefs as a touchstone, since it is only by reference to those beliefs that we can identify what we take to be error. In that case we would have to admit that the enterprise of making sense of people, and in particular social science, was inevitably value-laden.

This argument however is too quick. It is only on a certain conception of evaluative beliefs that the conclusion goes through. In order to illustrate the point consider the position we would be in if we took the view that a judgment of desirability was not, contrary to appearance, a judgment about some property inhering in the object judged to be desirable, that it was a judgment which was true or appropriate just in case the person judging had a certain positive feeling about the object. If we took such a subjectivist line with evaluative beliefs generally then we might not think that our own beliefs were any guide to the beliefs which it was sensible to ascribe to our subjects. We might hold that presented with any object for assessment our subjects are likely to have quite different feelings from those that we experience and that the evaluative beliefs which they form are likely therefore to diverge from those that we maintain. If we adopted such a line then applying the principle of humanity in ascribing evaluative beliefs would not mean bringing our own evaluative beliefs into play; it would not be a value-laden exercise, at least in that respect. We might still be concerned to ascribe only such evaluative beliefs as cohere with one another, and only such as derive from feelings which the background of our subjects makes intelligible, but this concern would not mean an intrusion of our own value commitments into the exercise.

Richard Wollheim makes the following comment on the explanation of actions. 'A thesis telling us how a moral agent acts is required at the same time to make sense of his action; it must render it intelligible. And, if it is to do this, the thesis must attribute to the agent a body of thoughts and feelings which, in the first place, are perfectly comprehensible in themselves and, secondly, are fully adequate to lead the agent to do the action in question' (Wollheim 1979, p.5). This remark gives nice expression to the principle of humanity. The second factor mentioned relates to behavioural rationality: the beliefs and desires, the thoughts and feelings, must be such as rationally to explain the action. The first factor bears upon attitudinal rationality: the beliefs and desires must be, as Wollheim says, comprehensible in themselves. The issue before us now is what it means for evaluative beliefs to be comprehensible in themselves. Does it mean that like non-evaluative beliefs they must display a responsiveness to inconsistencies and counter-examples? Or does it mean something less? If making evaluative beliefs comprehensible in themselves means the same as in the non-evaluative case, then we have to admit the value-ladenness of social science. If it does not, then we may not be forced to such an admission.

## 2 VALUE-LADENNESS UNDER VARIOUS ASSUMPTIONS

The conclusion yielded by the last section is that social science is value-laden if it is appropriate to impose the same constraints on evaluative as on non-evaluative beliefs in ascribing them to people. Whether it is appropriate to impose such constraints depends on whether evaluative beliefs are intentional states of the same kind as non-evaluative; in particular, it depends on whether they are cognitive states which are subject to the dictates of evidence and logic. In this section we shall consider a number of different views that may be taken of evaluative beliefs and in the case of each we shall raise the question of how far it likens them to non-evaluative and how far therefore it would support the claim that social science is value-laden. We shall start from the realist view which would maximise the similarity between the two sorts of belief and then we shall go on to consider various retreats from full-scale realism.

At a first level realism can be characterised as a general strategy in semantics. It prescribes that there is nothing against interpreting certain assertions in such a way that the following result goes through: that the assertions have truth conditions which outstrip our recognitional capacities, so that they may be true (false) even though we cannot tell that they are so. There are difficulties about this formulation of the doctrine, and about the connections between the doctrine and other theories, but we need not concern ourselves with them here.[8] What we are interested in is realism in the specific sense in which it has been applied to ascriptions of value and realism in this sense can be understood independently; indeed it may even be best understood in this way, since its relationship to the general doctrine is not straightforward. (See Pettit 1981 for an attempt to characterise the connection.)

Realism about values is well characterised, so far as moral values are concerned, by Mark Platts: 'moral judgments are viewed as factually cognitive, as presenting claims about the world which can be assessed (like any other factual beliefs) as true or false, and whose truth or falsity are as much objects of human knowledge as any other factual claims about the world' (Platts 1979, p. 243). If we are dealing with a statement to the effect that a certain object is desirable, whether unconditionally or in some particular respect, the thought is that the statement is true or false, as distinct from being merely appropriate or inappropriate in the manner of a prescription or an emotional expression; that it is true or false in virtue of how the object is and not in virtue of how the person making the judgment, or any other agent, feels about the object; and that whether it is true or false is an appropriate matter for cognitive inquiry, something as amenable as any factual issue to argumentative resolution.

If one is a full-scale realist about values then one assimilates evaluative beliefs to non-evaluative ones. In particular one takes such beliefs to be subject in just the manner of non-evaluative ones to the guidance of evidence and logic. This means that in fixing what evaluative beliefs someone has one will be concerned to ascribe beliefs such that the person does not have to be seen as unresponsive to more or less obvious counterexamples and inconsistencies. In the terminology which we introduced earlier, one will be anxious to find a pattern of attitudinal rationality in those evaluative beliefs of the kind that one expects in non-evaluative ones. Finding such a pattern will involve ascribing beliefs that one holds oneself, or at least ascribing beliefs which one thinks the evidence would lead one to hold in the situation of the person in question. Thus it inevitably brings one's own evaluative beliefs into play: it is inevitably a value-laden exercise.

It will be useful to look further into the effect which realism about values is liable to have on the enterprise of making sense of people's sayings and doings. Whether or not one is a realist, one will ascribe evaluative beliefs to one's subjects which in combination with their non-evaluative beliefs render their actions behaviourally rational: one will attribute such beliefs as make it possible to see the agents as acting with a view to securing outcomes that are found desirable. If one rejected totally the analogy between evaluative and non-evaluative beliefs one might regard the actions performed by one's subjects as the only source of evidence as to what they value. However if one is a realist and endorses that analogy then necessarily one allows a second source of evidence. This is constituted by the evidential circumstances of the agents, the opportunities they have for coming to learn about what is valuable and what not. As a realist one must find it outlandish, not just to ascribe evaluative beliefs which fail to represent one's subjects' actions as behaviourally rational, but also to ascribe evaluative beliefs which fail to represent those people as responsive to the evaluative realities with which one takes them to be confronted.

Granted these remarks, it should be clear that the realist may have to reject an ascription of beliefs, and a corresponding explanation of actions, which someone who rejected realism might regard as perfectly sensible. The realist may find that the evaluative beliefs among the set in question are ones which she cannot reasonably attribute: they are not beliefs to which she subscribes herself and neither are they beliefs to which she would subscribe were she confined to the evidential situation of her subjects. The realist will make a judgment as to whether a given set of beliefs can be attributed or not on the basis of her own intuitions about values: her own actual value commitments and the value commitments which she reckons she would be brought to make in the evidential circumstances of her subjects. Thus it can be seen that for the realist the acceptability of the explanation sponsored by that ascription of beliefs is value-dependent: whether it is found acceptable or not depends on what values are recognised by the investigator in question.

An example may help to show just how values affect explanation, if a realist theory is presupposed. Robert Mugabe's 1980 electoral victory in Zimbabwe called forth different explanatory attempts. The most natural explanation is that a majority of the electorate saw Mugabe as the best prospect for the country and that they therefore voted for him. If one rejected realism then regardless of one's own views about the prospect represented by Mugabe one might be happy to accept this account: even if one were of a right-wing colonial mentality, one might comment that there is no saying what people will fancy and happily endorse the explanation. If one is a realist however, and takes a jaundiced view of Mugabe, then that explanation may prove difficult to accept. At the limit one might be led to reject it, postulating instead that Mugabe's victory was due to electoral rigging. Failing that, one would have to go an explanatory level further and try to make sense of how the electorate could have come, as one sees it oneself, to have been so duped. Such a further explanation might be provided by a consideration of the evidence available to the people or, less flatteringly, by some hypothesis as to their evidential insensitivity.

That realism about values leads to the value-ladenness of social science should by now be clear. In the remainder of this section we consider how far that value-ladenness is reduced as assumptions about the reality of values are varied and a retreat is made from full-scale realism. There are two ways in which a retreat may be made from realism. One way is through contracting the domain of which the doctrine is maintained and the other is through modifying the content of the doctrine itself; one alters the scope of the doctrine, the other alters its substance. We shall look at each in turn.

The scope of value realism is diminished if a distinction is drawn between different sorts of value ascription and realism is only defended in respect of some of these. One distinction which is often maintained, although it may be drawn on different grounds, separates value ascriptions which express a general appreciation or depreciation of the matter evaluated and value ascriptions which express a definite decision for or against whatever is in question (see Wiggins 1976, Pettit 1981). Ascriptions of the first kind are not so closely related to action as those of the second and the two might be described respectively as evaluations and prescriptions. The distinction suggests a retreat from realism whereby evaluations would continue to be regarded as akin to factual assertions but prescriptions would not. Such a retreat might have us regard declarations as to the relative goodness or badness of anything as statements that should be assessed realistically, while leading us to see declarations on what is best or worst, what is right or wrong, as assertions not meriting such a treatment. It might have us deny the fact-value distinction, as we can call it, while maintaining the distinction between what is and what ought to be.

What effects would such a contraction in the scope of realism have on the value-ladenness of social science? In approaching this question we must distinguish the following possibilities: that evaluations have no effect on prescriptions; that evaluations partially determine prescriptions; and that evaluations determine prescriptions completely. The third possibility marks a collapse into full-scale realism, since if evaluations are treated realistically and prescriptions are a function of evaluations then prescriptions should be treated realistically too. Taking up the other possibilities, we have to consider how far the acceptability of action explanations ceases to be value-dependent under each.

If evaluations have no effect on people's prescriptions, if the way in which people value things has no influence on what they ultimately decide, then how one explains their actions will not depend on one's values. Consider the situation where one finds that a certain ascription of beliefs will explain what someone does, the beliefs including a prescriptive judgment to the effect that the outcome pursued is the best available. Suppose now that the prescriptive judgment, a species of evaluative belief, is not a judgment that one would maintain oneself. Does this have to constitute a problem on the scenario envisaged? Not at all. It would raise a difficulty if it was thought to arise from the agent's evaluations, those evaluations being taken realistically, for we would want to understand how the evaluations came to be different from what our own would be, determining a prescriptive judgment other than that which we would defend. As it is however, one can countenance any prescriptive judgment required for explaining what the agent does. One does not have to look to the agent's evaluations in explaining that judgment and one does not have to try therefore to account for differences as between those evaluations and one's own.

On the hypothesis that evaluations have no effect on prescriptions, a realism about evaluations will not make the enterprise of explaining actions value-dependent. Will such a realism free social science then from the value-ladenness? It will still make the ascription of non-prescriptive evaluative beliefs value-dependent, for one will want to ascribe only such beliefs as one finds defensible oneself, or would find defensible in the situation of one's subjects. This does not entail any serious value-ladenness however, since on the picture in question one will not be concerned very much with what evaluations are maintained by one's subjects. Those evaluations are said not to have any general effect on behaviour and so they need only be taken into account in interpreting the utterances which give them expression.

The hypothesis that evaluations have no effect on prescriptions is not a very plausible one. It would be plausible only if in every action circumstance the agent was faced with conflicting evaluations and it was denied that there was any objective procedure for resolving such conflicts and deriving a prescription. However it is likely that in some circumstances at least the evaluations will point to one particular prescription, all but one of the available courses of action being negatively evaluated. Thus the most serious scenario that we have to consider is that which arises when evaluations are said to determine prescriptions partially. Assuming that this is so we have to ask whether a realism about evaluations coupled with a denial of realism about prescriptions would make social science value-laden.

The answer is that it will do so always to some extent and that how far it involves the value-ladenness of social science depends on how much determination evaluations are said to exercise on prescriptions. The weakest determination is that countenanced when there is said to be no procedure for resolving conflict between evaluations. In that case evaluations have a determining influence only in circumstances where all conflict is lacking. Further degrees of determination are then allowed as ever more complete procedures for resolving conflict are said to operate. To give an example of such a procedure, it might be said that there is an objective ranking of importance as between different kinds of evaluations: say, that evaluations bearing on matters of human life and death are more important than those which relate to matters of social propriety, that these in turn are more important than evaluations bearing on matters of convenience and comfort, and so on. Such a ranking would resolve certain conflicts involving considerations of different kinds but would leave undecided conflicts in which evaluations of the same kind are engaged.

We have been considering the effect on the value-ladenness of social science of a certain sort of retreat from realism about values, specifically the retreat involved in restricting the scope of such realism. Finally we must turn to the effect of another sort of retreat from realism, the retreat which consists in revising the substance of the doctrine. In looking at this sort of revision we shall speak simply of modifying realism about values; we shall not distinguish between modifying a realism in respect of prescriptions and modifying a realism in respect of evaluations. The points which would emerge in a consideration of those two cases should be fairly obvious from our general discussion and it would be tedious to elaborate them.

The denial of realism about values, at its weakest, means the denial that the subject matter of evaluative discourse, or at least of all evaluative discourse, has the independence from human beings associated with that of ordinary factual assertions. The reality constituted by values may be said to be a construct of human beings, in some sense: a construct such as mathematical reality is held to be by constructivists or intuitionists (see Wiggins 1976). Constructivists hold that 'what makes our mathematical statements true or false is our own mathematical activity, which is essentially mental activity: mathematical reality is, therefore, not something existing independently of ourselves, though partially apprehended by us, but simply the product of our own "thought"' (Dummett 1977, p.382). A corresponding view of values would represent them as a reality answering to our evaluative activities. Such a denial of realism would have a concrete effect on the construal of ascriptions of value insofar as it would impose a constraint to this effect: that an ascription of value should not be taken to be true (false) when it is beyond our capacities to establish that it is true (false). It might lead for example to a distinctive view of the prescriptions which are in conflict in the case of moral dilemmas, suggesting that there is no sense in the thought that one of the prescriptions must be true and the others false.

How far would the denial of realism in question here affect the value-ladenness of social science? If evaluative activity is held to be common to human kind the answer must be, not at all. On the picture presented, values are the correlates of species-wide habits of thought and though they have no reality independently of those habits, they are still matters on which we must expect people in similar circumstances generally to agree. It follows that in accepting the ascription of evaluative beliefs involved in some action explanation, one must be persuaded that those beliefs are such as one would have formed oneself in the evidential situation of the agent. This means that in testing the acceptability of the ascription, and of the corresponding explanation, one must refer to one's own value commitments. And that is to say that the exercise must be value-laden.

The denial of realism about values usually takes a stronger form than the constructivist one, a form which we can generally characterise as subjectivist. Where the constructivist holds that the subject matter of value ascriptions is roughly as it appears to be, the subjectivist denies this. What she typically maintains is one or other of the following sorts of thesis: that at least some ascriptions of value are not statements which are capable of being true or false but non-assertoric utterances which express the utterer's subjective feelings, whether in the manner of a command or an exclamation, or that they are statements which are true or false, not in virtue of how their apparent subject matter is, but in virtue of how the utterer, or some other agent, feels about that subject matter. The first sort of subjectivist would say that a statement to the effect that something is desirable is really an expression of approval about that object in the manner of 'Wow!' or 'Bravo!' or a prescription to the effect that the object should be preferred to alternatives. The second sort of subjectivist would say that it is true or false not in virtue of any property in the object but rather in virtue of how the utterer or some other agent feels about that object.[9]

We are not concerned in this context with the difference between these varieties of subjectivism. What they have in common is the important matter for us: their refusal to acknowledge the reality of at least certain values. However before we can consider the question of whether subjectivism reduces the value-ladenness of social science we must introduce a further set of distinctions. The subjectivist, whatever precise thesis she defends, relativises the ascription of value to a non-cognitive state of feeling or will: the state non-assertorically expressed in the utterance or the state on which the truth of the utterance turns. Consistently with subjectivising values in this manner, she may be more or less universalist in her understanding of the sentiments with which they are correlated. She may take those sentiments to be similar across the species, arising on similar occasions and giving rise to similar responses. She may regard them as differing from culture to culture, although being similar within each culture. Or she may hold the view that they differ, or at least are liable to differ, from individual to individual.

What effect would subjectivism have on the value-ladenness of social science? The answer is that it would eliminate such value-ladenness, whether it relativises values to individual, culture or species. If the sentiments invoked by the subjectivist vary from individual to individual then in ascribing sentiments and evaluative beliefs to one's subjects, one will not have any reason to refer to the values that one recognises oneself: these are not going to give any clue as to the values by which others are guided. Thus the only source of evidence on which one will rely is the actions performed by the agents in question. The same will be true if the sentiments referred to by the subjectivist vary from culture to culture and one is involved in cross-cultural investigation. Again one will naturally take the people's actions as the only evidence of the values by which they are guided; one will not expect to learn anything from considering the evidential circumstances of the agents.

But there are two other cases where it may seem that subjectivism would not reduce the role of one's own value commitments in assigning evaluative beliefs to others and explaining their actions. Suppose the subjectivist's sentiments are said to vary from culture to culture but one is engaged in action explanation only within one's own culture. Or suppose that the sentiments are held to be species-wide. In either case it would appear that one will have to put one's own value commitments into play in divining the commitments of others. The appearance however is misleading. What will guide one in ascribing evaluative beliefs to others is not one's own value commitments but rather one's perfectly factual beliefs about the sentiments which people in one's own culture or people in general are likely to have on certain occasions. If one believes that sentiments are similar across the culture or across the species then that will be because one has begun to detect some pattern in them and what guides one in ascribing the sentiments will be one's view about that pattern. That view will have been formed partly on the basis of observing one's own evaluative responses but this does not make the exercise value-laden. Indeed, even if one always had to refer to one's own responses in divining the likely responses of others, this would not introduce value-ladenness. On the realist or constructivist scenario in which value-ladenness does arise, one's evaluative beliefs directly determine one's ascription of such beliefs, the possibility of error always being allowed for: one believes that a certain sort of prospect is desirable and that is prima facie evidence that one's subjects will find it desirable too. In the situation now envisaged, one's evaluative beliefs, one's subjective sentiments, do not play such a determining role. What plays that role is one's factual beliefs about the sentiments others are liable to have, beliefs which happen to be founded in observation of the sentiments one feels oneself.

This takes us to the end of our discussion. We have been concerned to see how social science remains value-laden under different assumptions about the reality of values. It appears that value-ladenness is guaranteed by realism but that it is reduced in some degree as the scope of realism is restricted. The denial of realism does not remove value-ladenness if a constructivist view is taken of values. However it does remove it if the view adopted is any form of subjectivism. With these points clear, the next topic of discussion would naturally seem to be the case for and against realism. Before we come to that topic however we pause to consider in the next section what exactly the problem is with value-ladenness. So far we have said nothing about why one might be concerned that social science should be value-laden and we must see whether such concern is appropriate.

## 3 THE PROBLEM OF VALUE-LADENNESS

It appears from the previous two sections that on certain assumptions social science is indeed value-laden: it is bound by evaluative commitments in an inescapable and distinctive manner. In this section we turn to the question of whether such value-ladenness is something which ought to worry us, whether it is a problem. The traditional discussions of social science assume a contrast between facts and values and assume that science is properly concerned only with facts: thus the conclusion is drawn that if social science is value-laden, it cannot claim to be science proper. The contact with values is taken as a sort of contamination which would undermine the social scientist's claim to speak on what there is in the world: that is, to speak the truth. What we have to consider now is whether there is anything to be said for this attitude.

There are three alleged facts any one of which might claim to constitute the problem of value-ladenness. The first is sociological in character, the second is epistemological and the third is ontological. In this section we consider each in turn. What we shall argue is that only the first two problems are genuine difficulties and that a curious logic ensures that we need not concern ourselves even with these. The reason we need not be worried about the difficulties is this: that if they exist they undermine the assumptions on which social science is value-laden. It turns out that any state of affairs which would make value-ladenness a problem is a state of affairs in which there would be no ground for thinking of social science as being value-laden.

The alleged sociological fact which would make value-ladenness a problem is the variability of evaluative beliefs. It is sometimes said that people vary in the things they value and that there is no hope of ever achieving a consensus on such matters: value commitments, on this picture, are as arbitrary and divergent as whim or taste. If such is indeed the case, then value-ladenness would make social science problematic. It would have the result that social scientists could not be expected to agree in their conclusions: as they each maintained different evaluative beliefs themselves, so they would naturally find it plausible to ascribe different beliefs to their subjects. Michael Lessnoff identifies the problem of value-ladenness in this sociological manner. He argues that even if the other problems which we shall mention did not exist, even if values were epistemologically and ontologically unexceptional, the diversity of evaluative opinion would make a value-laden social science problematic. 'Suppose that moral qualities of situations . . .are objective facts *sui generis* . . . the obvious difficulty is how to recognise them; for it remains true that different people judge differently whether they are present or absent in a given case' (Lessnoff 1974, p.138).

As against this claim it must be said that evaluative diversity is not as widespread as might at first be thought. If we distinguish between what we have called prescriptions and evaluations, then while people often do disagree on what they prescribe it must be conceded that just as often they are at one on how matters should be evaluatively characterised. What introduces prescriptive difference is not usually any difference of opinion as to whether something is good or bad in this respect or that; more often than not, it is a difference in the relative ranking of the evaluative pros and cons. Lessnoff may be accused of exaggerating the extent of divergence in identifying the problem of value-ladenness sociologically. It remains to be shown that there is any greater diversity of opinion in matters of value than there is in alleged matters of fact.

But this is not the point which we would like to emphasise in commenting on the first problem of value-ladenness. What is much more important to notice is that if the divergence alleged really did obtain, then it would be impossible to maintain a realist or even a constructivist view of values. Both views suppose that evaluative issues are moderately resoluble: otherwise the analogies, factual and mathematical, which they respectively maintain would be inappropriate. If Lessnoff were right, realism and constructivism would both have to be rejected and some form of subjectivism would have to be adopted in their place. In that case however social science would not be value-laden after all, for we have seen that subjectivism would free the enterprise of making sense of people from the influence of the theorist's value commitments. It appears that the sociological condition on which value-ladenness would be a problem is a condition on which it would also fail to arise.

Among the fathers of social science, Max Weber is the one outstandingly concerned to see that the discipline is not value-laden. It is interesting to note then that he was not himself impressed when his antagonist Schmoller argued that as a matter of fact there is a great deal of agreement among people on evaluative issues: that as a matter of fact there is no sociological problem. Weber pointed out in response that any such consensus must be regarded as accidental and that it remains in principle possible for there to be 'unbridgeably divergent ultimate evaluations' (Weber 1949, p.14). The possibility of such divergence would make social science problematic too. It would mean that the social scientist would not expect to win assent for her conclusions except insofar as she was fortunate enough to be dealing with an audience of her own evaluative dispositions.

Weber's response may be understood in either of two ways, depending on whether he is taken to make an epistemological or an ontological complaint against values. Taking the response epistemologically, we are pointed to the second alleged fact which would make value-ladenness a problem. This is the supposed fact that value commitments are not governed by observation or reason: that they are contracted on the basis of such non-evidential factors as impulse and decision, factors which vary with varying temperament and culture. If value-commitments are subject to variation independently of truth-relevant influences, and if they determine what conclusions social scientists reach, then value-ladenness really is a problem for social science.

Our response to the epistemological version of the problem of value-ladenness takes the form of our response to the sociological. It must first of all be said that it is far from obvious that value commitments are as epistemologically ungrounded as is alleged (see Wiggins 1976). But, more important for our purposes, what must also be noticed is that if such commitments were thought to be ungrounded, it would be impossible to take a realist or constructivist view of values and in that case there would be no reason to think of social science as bound by value commitments. The epistemological condition on which value-ladenness would be a problem for social science, like its sociological counterpart, is a condition on which value-ladenness fails to arise.

If Weber's complaint about values is understood ontologically, we are directed to the third alleged fact which might be said to make value-ladenness a problem. This is the fact, as it might be put, that values are not part of the hard stuff of reality, that they appear only when reality is viewed from a human perspective. The point is that even if people are said generally to agree about values, and even if this agreement is held to be evidentially grounded, it remains that values only come into view in the human being's interaction with what there is; they are recognised by anyone with the concerns of our species but a spectator with different concerns would be blind to them. If this is granted, then value-ladenness might be held to constitute a problem insofar as it would mean that social science was species-relative, that it represented how things are as seen from the human point of view, not how they must be admitted to be regardless of what perspective is adopted. At the source of such an objection to value-ladenness we can detect a distinctive conception of what there is in the world, according to which all that really exists is what cannot be denied, consistently with the evidence available, within any point of view. (On this conception see Williams 1978 and McDowell 1981.) The objection is that if social science is value-laden then it does not discourse on what there really is in the world, only on what appears there from a particular point of view.

In dealing with the alleged sociological and epistemological facts which would make a problem of value-ladenness, we argued that it was not clear that the facts obtained and, in any case, that if they did obtain they would undermine realism and constructivism and remove value-ladenness from social science. We cannot take a similar line with the ontological fact with which we are now dealing. For it does appear to be the case that values are species-relative in the required sense. And, what is more important, values can be held to be such consistently with the adoption of a realist or a constructivist view. The constructivist is explicit in saying that values are species-relative: this indeed is one of the main points in the constructivist theory. The realist can also maintain that thesis, for she may say that values have a certain independence, and are a proper object of cognitive inquiry, while admitting that they may be denied consistently with the evidence available within certain points of view: say, the point of view of the micro-physicist.

How then should we respond to the problem of value-ladenness in its ontological version? Our response is to say that what is identified in this third account is not something that needs to be considered a genuine difficulty. It would be a problem for the social scientist if she had to admit that her conclusions were reached on the basis of sociologically or at least epistemologically variable values. In that case she could not claim any sort of universal validity for her results. However it need not be considered a difficulty that the conclusions attained in social science bear only on the world as it presents itself in human perspective, and not on the world as it must be admitted to be within every point of view. The social scientist may happily acknowledge the species-relativity of her discipline, for she is free to deny either that what is relative to the point of view of our species is not therefore real in the most absolute sense; or that science proper is concerned only with what is real in that sense; or that social science is proper science on that particular understanding of the scientific enterprise.

The outcome of our reflections then is this. The value-ladenness of social science does not cause a problem on the grounds of the ontological feature just mentioned: the species-relativity of values. On the other hand it would be a source of difficulty if value commitments were sociologically or epistemologically variable. However were either such condition realised we would have to reject realism and constructivism as ways of looking at values. And if realism and constructivism had to be rejected, social science would have to be said not to be value-laden after all. Thus value-ladenness does not raise a problem on the grounds of any ontological peculiarity in values, whereas if it were said to raise a problem on the grounds of sociological or epistemological peculiarity, that very distinctiveness would be a reason for denying that social science is value-laden.

This line of thought dissolves the so-called problem of value-ladenness. However it does not release us from an obligation to think carefully about the nature of values, and the place of values in social inquiry. The reason is that how we think about social science is deeply affected by whether we are realists or not in our conception of value commitments. If we are realists, or indeed constructivists, we make social science a species-relative discipline, for the acceptability of our explanations turns on what values are recognised by the scientist and values, as we have seen, are a species-relative reality. This conception of social science has a negative and a positive side. Negatively, it means that we cannot think of the enterprise as interest-free in the way in which, rightly or wrongly, natural science is often conceived; we cannot think of the practitioner of the discipline as the unmoved observer who puts her own values entirely aside in the pursuit of truth. Positively, the conception means that we must think of social science as something which personally involves the inquirer, as she tries to come to terms with the value perceptions of her subjects, and in particular with those perceptions that do not agree with her own. It means that the inquirer cannot treat the variant perceptions of her subjects as exotica, that she must find some explanation of why they differ from her own or that she must look to her own to see whether she is really sure of what she believes.

Since our conception of social science depends on whether we are realists, or at least constructivists, about values, we turn to consider the argument pro and con realism in the next section; constructivism we do not consider separately, since so far as most of the arguments given are concerned it stands or falls with realism. The discussion of the arguments will be critical but it will not lead us to a definitive conclusion. The issue is one of the debated questions in contemporary philosophical writing and we do not see how it can be resolved.

## 4 REALISM AND VALUES

In this section we review some of the arguments for and against a realist view of values. Two points about the discussion are worth noting. The first is that we do not distinguish generally between a realism in respect of evaluations and a realism in respect of prescriptions. This is because the same sort of arguments are relevant in both cases, even if they may be thought to apply more clearly in the one case than in the other. The second point to note about the discussion is that realism is cast in a defensive role and subjectivism in an offensive; as mentioned, we do not discuss constructivism. The reason for this role-casting is that realism is the less established view and the first thing that needs to be done in promoting it is to show that it can resist dominant subjectivist assumptions. Our discussion will be divided into three sub-sections, in each of which we shall consider how well realism can defend itself against a particular subjectivist view. It will not take us to a definitive conclusion but at least it will show how the argument goes between the rival doctrines.

*(i) Values and action*

One source of subjectivism lies in Humean psychology, in particular in the claim that 'reason alone can never be a motive to any action of the will: and . . . it can never oppose passion in the direction of the will' (*Treatise* Book II Section III). The assumption is that moral judgments provide us with at least prima facie reasons for acting; that our cognitive 'faculties', in providing us with beliefs about how the world is, can never impel us toward one action rather than another; and that the moral judgments therefore are not themselves the result of reason alone: they are derivative from our desires. These desires propel us to act, and Humean subjectivism makes what is seen as valuable depend upon such driving desires. If we believe that values exist independently of the cognising subject, this is due to the projection of values onto the world, such a projection having no grounding in fact. (For an outline of this argument, see Mackie, 1977, pp.40-41.)

The realist response takes two forms (see Platts 1979, pp.225-58, 1980, pp.73ff, McDowell 1978, pp.18-19). Where the subjectivist wants to maintain that driving desire is always present in the motivational account of every action, the realist claims that this is either phenomenologically false or unsupported theoretical dogma. That we do not experience such a desire as present every time we act was recognised by Hume, who invented the 'calm passions' to explain this phenomenological absence. However the invention is warranted only if it is true that actions must be generated by driving desires and since this proposition is precisely what is at issue it cannot non-circularly support the postulation of calm passions. Thus the realist may reasonably claim that the psychological thesis of the subjectivist is unproven. She will admit that a full action explanation always refers to desires but she will deny that these have to be thought of as driving motivational states: after all they may simply consist in perceptions of what is valuable.

The other side of the realist reply is a positive thesis about the motivational power of reason. To claim that reasons do, in themselves, influence the will is in effect to maintain that the world is not 'motivationally inert'. 'The idea of the world as motivationally inert is not an independent hard datum. It is simply the metaphysical counterpart of the thesis that states of will and cognitive states are distinct existences: which is exactly what is in question' (McDowell 1978, p.19). Other kinds of fact may not move us to action but this does not inhibit the realist maintaining that certain evaluative facts do.

The argument around the subjectivist's psychological thesis bogs down very quickly. What the subjectivist takes as self-evident- that driving desire is an essential element in motivating our actions- the realist dismisses as unsupported psychological dogma. No independent leverage on the argument can be obtained by speculating on the relative primacy of belief and desire, for it is possible to depict beliefs as certain sorts of desires (that the world satisfy a certain sort of description) and desires as certain sorts of beliefs (about what is desirable). Thus we are left with two opposed theories as to what is required for the genesis of action, neither of which can offer definitive objections to the other.

One recent realist argument is worth considering however. Platts (1980) has argued that for the subjectivist the motivating force of non-experiential desire - desire which lacks a phenomenological quality- must be mysterious. The subjectivist, as defined, sees the source of the desirability of an object in her desire for that object: the object is not intrinsically desirable. Given the view of desires which the subjectivist has - that they are, in Hume's phrase, 'original existences' and hence not answerable to reason - it must be possible for an agent to have desired something other than she does: to have desired not-p instead of p. The claim made by Platts is that if the agent reflects on this possibility (that not-p is desirable), then on subjectivist premises the desire that p will be eliminated.

> If this is right, then, for such an agent, reflection will eliminate the motivating force of his desire; and since, ex hypothesi, his desire lacks any phenomenological quality, his desire will then cease to be as the motivating force ceases to be. For a reflective being with a nature like ours, the price of abandoning moral realism can be the end of desire (Platts 1980, p.79).

The subjectivist's conception of desire, it is thought, is liable to kill off all the desires which aren't felt as such, these being 'empty of motivation'.

Unfortunately this argument is also inconclusive. It may simply be that, for reflective beings operating with a subjectivist conception of value and desire, some desires will appear quite arbitrary and replaceable by others, but that subjectivism nonetheless is correct. Moderate moral nihilism may result - moderate because not all our desires are like that - but this will not be acceptable as an objection to the relevantly-described position. It may also be the case that the objection to the subjectivist is too strong, in the sense that similar reflections about beliefs may render them inefficacious as well. The thought here is that reflecting upon our beliefs and the historical contingencies surrounding them - we have the beliefs we do as a result of living at a certain time, in a certain society and so on - might induce in us a scepticism which erases those beliefs. In particular, one 'Feyerabendian' reflection could do this: it is true that nearly all scientific beliefs of a theoretical kind have been proven false in the past, so it is inductively highly likely that present scientific beliefs will be proven false. Therefore we have good evidence that they are false and so, for any such present scientific belief, we should not believe it! Instrumentalism or some other 'scientific' counterpart to evaluative non-realism results.

The recognition that reflective reason has this corrosive power was a hallmark of Hume's philosophy, one which led him to proclaim the primacy of passion over reason. Platts's suggestive remarks indicate that passion or desire may be equally baseless, and that the recognition of this fact may lead to the dimming of desire. It is not clear however that the value-voluntarist, the person who believes that values enter into the world because of our desires, cannot remain faithful to Hume, emphasising with him the role of habit in protecting us against reflective criticism. The force of habit doesn't require for its efficacy the presence of phenomenological desire, nor is it necessarily broken by the recognition of that habit's being replaceable. Thus motives to act may remain despite the efforts of reflection. This line of thought leaves the argument in much the same position as before: tangled. It requires more work in the philosophy of mind to unravel the knots, work which could not be done here, even if we were quite clear about how to complete the job successfully.

*(ii) The status of values*

Related to the issue in the philosophy of mind is the question as to what kind of entity values are, what kind of status they have. The realist places them firmly 'in the world', existing independently of a cognising subject and perhaps capable of transcending the subject's recognitional capacities. The moral qualities of states-of-affairs and actions are not, of course, just like other qualities; for one thing, they are related to action in providing us, when they are discerned, with a prima facie reason to act. This very difference, however, renders them suspect as bona-fide entities of the (material) world, especially if the subjectivist can explain both their apparent and real location. An 'error' theory of moral beliefs suggests such an explanation, attempting to show why we mistakenly take moral qualities as being in the world independently of us, when they are really to be located in ourselves (Mackie 1977). The explanation might be, that if the function of moral beliefs is to be the cement of the social universe, then they can best serve that function by obscuring their subjective origin.

The two ontological positions traditionally opted for by realists are: simply accepting the peculiarity of the non-physical status of moral qualities (intuitionism), or reducing these qualities to physical properties (naturalism). A third option is that provided by supervenience without reducibility. This allows for the fixing of moral facts by physical facts - no moral difference is possible as between two states without an accompanying physical difference - but does not raise the problems associated with reductions (see Chapter 3, Section 2). The idea is that the physical characterisation of anything determines its moral or other evaluative characterisation, thus ensuring that there is no moral difference without a physical one, but that there may be no disjunction of physical predicates available to us which gives all the different physical ways in which a given moral predicate may be satisfied. There may be no biconditional law available which tells us, not just that when one or another physical configuration occurs, such and such a value is realised - the action, if action is in question, is cruel or kind, blameworthy or praiseworthy - but also that only when one of a given set of physical configurations occurs, is the value realised (see Kim 1978). In other words, our moral predicates may give us a way of classifying and characterising a physical reality, and a way which is responsive only to physical differences, without the conclusion following that for every moral predicate we can find a physical one that applies just when it applies.

The most likely way for the realist at once to maintain the distinctiveness and the respectability of values is to adopt the view just characterised which maintains the supervenience but non-reducibility of value predicates in relation to physical ones. We cannot complain that such a view is incoherent, since we have suggested ourselves that institutional predicates may be supervenient on certain individualistic ones and yet not be reducible to them (see Chapter 3, Section 2). However where the institutional-individualistic claim was allowed by way of concession to the collectivist, the realist's claim must be examined more closely for what can be said in its defence: it may be coherent without being convincing. And here it must be remarked that argument is lacking as to how value predicates can come to be physically supervenient without being physically reducible. Thus the subjectivist may well feel that the supervenience claim is a deus ex machina introduced to rescue the realist from the charge of countenancing entities whose status is unclear.[10]

In bolstering the realist position, recourse may be had to the idea that whereas what has to be admitted within all points of view to be in the world must be said to determine all that is perceived there, it may be that some perspective-relative accounts are not derivable within the 'absolute' one. To take our species-relative distinctions of colour for example, Bernard Williams points out that while these will not appear in an account of how the world absolutely is, they are nonetheless responsive to the nature of things: they are not radically relative as between observers, and arguments can take place about what is and is not of such and such a colour (Williams 1978). The perception of colours is taken by David Wiggins as a model for the perception of values, as this is understood by the realist (Wiggins 1976). Our perception of colours is explained on the one hand by how the world (absolutely) is, and on the other by our perceptual apparatus. The role of this apparatus makes the category of colour anthropocentric and ensures that it will not appear in an absolute account of what there is. Wiggins suggests that we should see value terms in a parallel manner. They are relevant when things are surveyed from the point of view of human concerns and they are used in response to how things (absolutely) are, but they would not appear within an absolute account of reality.

There is a problem with the colour analogy, and that is precisely that colours are not merely supervenient. Colour qualities are reducible to light waves, so it is possible for us to identify the colour of a surface with a feature of the spectral reflection curve. (See Dummett 1979, for a discussion of the possibility of such an identification). Thus even if colours do not figure in an 'absolute' conception of our world, that conception should contain within it the resources to explain our experience of colour, and the (systematic) variation of that experience. More generally, as Williams puts it,

> the absolute conception should explain, or at least make it possible to explain, how the more local representations of the world can come about - it is this that would enable us to relate them to each other, and to the world as it is independently of them (Williams 1978, p.245).

The moral subjectivist, it should be noticed, claims to have just such an explanation of values and of any varying perception of them: the values are tied, more intimately than the realist would allow, to our interests, or to our experience of pleasure and pain, or to our cultural conditioning, and so on.

It appears then that the colour analogy plays into the subjectivist's hands rather than serving as a bolster to realism. Consistently with the distinction between absolute and relative conceptions of what there is, the subjectivist can describe our value perceptions as valid only relative to us and then proceed to show how that relative representation can be made sense of in absolute terms. On the other hand the realist can only make partial use of the distinction. She can characterise value perceptions as relative but she must deny that they can be explained within the absolute account in the manner favoured by the subjectivist. Once again we reach stalemate. As the psychological issue dividing the realist and the subjectivist was left undecided, so the issue about the status of values must also remain unresolved.

*(iii) Values and knowledge*

The subjectivist view of values is nurtured in great part on the assumption that values are liable to vary across cultures, and even across individuals; if there is ever consensus, that is put down to sociological accident. The diversity of value systems is taken by the subjectivist as a reason for questioning the realist picture. It is invoked to raise doubts about the realist claims that value questions are matters for cognitive resolution. If such resolution is available, it is asked, how do people come to hold such widely divergent value commitments?

In discussing the sociological version of the problem of value-ladenness, we saw that the diversity alleged by the subjectivist can be questioned: if there is variation in the prescriptions defended by people, for example, there may yet be a good deal of consensus on evaluations. Questioning the diversity will mean arguing for example that despite the differences in institutional practices across societies, we can detect common underlying attitudes, similar ideals and even precepts. Suppose twins are sacrificed in some culture. That may only testify to a mistaken non-evaluative belief, to the effect that such sacrifice benefits the society: it need not indict members of the society as having radically different intuitions about the value of human life. Suppose again that widespread adultery occurs in some other culture. That need not betoken a deep moral difference either, since if adultery is widespread it need not cause hardship or hurt in the individual case.

> *Bukoniam* was not an accusation heard often, for adultery was everyday practice and was not in any way considered reprehensible. In using it as he did, and I asked him why, Atum explained that he had been pointing out that she had slept well but not wisely; she had in fact been wasteful, there had been no profit (Turnbull 1974, p.206).

The important question to raise about diversity in value systems is whether we can envisage being led to ascribe such different evaluative beliefs to people in a foreign culture that, if we were realists, we would have to charge them with wholesale error. If we can envisage this, and if the error we would have to ascribe is so wholesale as to be barely explicable, then subjectivism may be able to cull support from the diversity in question. Let us begin then with a concrete case. There is hardly a more shocking account of a society which from our point of view is evaluatively deviant than that provided by Colin Turnbull in his description of the Ik (see Turnbull 1974). In dealing with these people his own moral instincts caused him to be outraged at the selfishness, mendacity, cruelty and dishonesty which seemed to pervade the society. Given this behaviour, however, he found his own behaviour gradually changing. Instead of sharing his food with others, he took to eating it furtively, away from the prying eyes (and hands) of the starving Ik. One example of apparently extreme cruelty will suffice to indicate the problem of appropriate moral description. It is best to quote at length, as Turnbull's description is crucial.

> It was there, while I was nursing Loriangorok, that there was a sudden exodus from the village, distant shouts of laughter, and then someone running back to tell me to come quickly . . . It was someone else whom I had never seen before, dead Lolim's widow, Lo'ono. She too had been abandoned, and had tried to make her way down the mountainside. But she was totally blind and had tripped and rolled to the bottom of the gulf and there she lay on her back, her legs and arms thrashing feebly, while a little crowd standing on the edge above looked down at her and laughed at the spectacle.

Turnbull rescued the starving and thirsty Lo'ono, giving her food and water, after which she requested to be allowed to walk on, towards her son's village. As her son had already driven his father out of the village, so that he died just outside, Turnbull felt she wouldn't be welcome, but she insisted, wanting at least to be near her son when she died.

> So we gave her more food and made her eat and drink all she could, put her stick in her hand and pointed her the way she wanted to be pointed, and she suddenly cried . . . she was crying, she said, because all of a sudden we had reminded her that there had been a time when people had helped each other, when people had been kind and good (Turnbull 1974, pp.187-8).

The example is useful for the following reason. The observer-anthropologist is able to distance himself sufficiently from the scene in order to give an accurate description of what happened. But anthropology is not just such description; a deeper understanding of the events is required. It is at this point that Turnbull finds it difficult to characterise the Ik's actions. Are the Ik wilfully cruel? Or do their actions simply exemplify a different moral code? Or are they cruel in a way which is explicable and even excusable? The replies to these questions reinforce the point made earlier, that the realist will provide explanations of the Ik's actions other than those of the subjectivist. That an action is cruel provides a fairly strong prima facie reason against doing it. If the Ik are, by our lights, characteristically cruel, some explanation is required as to why they have overridden the prima facie reason for not so acting. The subjectivist can take refuge in denying that, for the Ik, the cruelty has any normative significance. The descriptive difference between cruel and kind actions remains: what is put in question is whether it must be the case, the virtue of it being forced upon us by 'the world', that cruel actions, thus descriptively identified, are to be condemned (see Mackie 1977, pp.16-17). On the subjectivist account, we agree to describe certain actions as cruel but it is illicit of us to go further and assume a condemnatory force in the description. We should prevent ourselves from making the illicit force transference, and allow for the possibility that the Ik do not condemn cruel actions and see no prima facie reason not to act in a cruel way. Having taken this step, the subjectivist is freed from supplementary explanation.

It appears that the realist about values will be forced to impugn the Ik with wholesale moral error. Even someone who was a realist only about evaluations would have to face this prospect, for evaluations cover the values which the Ik appear not to recognise: values such as kindness, honesty, loyalty, generosity, and so on. According to the realist the Ik would have false beliefs of a kind particularly difficult to understand. The disagreement that arises on non-evaluative questions usually has to do with more theoretical matters; it is not disagreement as to the nature of the evidence. Judgments about cruelty, kindness, generosity are not theoretical: they are not inferred in an inductive manner from some other description which attaches to the actions or people judged. It is thus more difficult to understand, on realist lines, the perceptual blindness which seems to be associated with the Ik's actions.

And yet even if understanding is difficult, it may not be impossible. The harsh environmental conditions of the Ik must be taken seriously into account in trying to make sense of their behaviour and attitudes. When taken into account, they open up the possibility of seeing the Ik as a people reconciled to starvation and death, even to the point of finding a despairing sort of amusement in things which would ordinarily be rare enough to be tragic. Turnbull himself follows such a line of thought and ends up condemning his own well meant interventions on behalf of Lo'ono.

> I thought of other old people who had joined in the merriment when they had been teased, knocked over or had a precious morsel of food taken from their mouths. They knew that it was silly of them to expect to go on living, and having watched others, they knew that the spectacle really was quite funny. So they joined in the laughter. Perhaps if we had left Lo'ono, she would have died laughing, happy that she was at least providing her children with amusement . . . . At the time I was sure we were right, doing the only 'human' thing. In a way we were - we were making life more comfortable for ourselves, confirming our own sense of superiority . . . In the end I had a greater respect for the Ik, and I wonder if their way was not right (Turnbull 1974, p.188).

It is hard to imagine a case where we would have to attribute more wholesale evaluative error than we naturally tend to do with the Ik. Nonetheless it seems that even here the error can be made sufficiently intelligible to avoid a forced retreat from realism. That thought is given further support when we consider the sort of error that must be ascribed. It need not involve a misperception: a belief to the effect that it is not cruel to treat Lo'ono in the way described. All that may be involved is inattentiveness to the cruel aspect of such actions, or underweighing of the cruel aspect in relation to other considerations. Neglect of the cruelty factor in either of these senses would be more easy to make sense of than the error of thinking actions such as the treatment of Lo'ono not cruel. We can see how in the conditions under which the Ik lived, it would cease to matter as much as it normally does that certain actions are cruel, and it might begin to matter much more that they are a source of merriment, or whatever. We might or might not consider that the change in priorities was right - we might or might not think that the change raised a matter of right or wrong - but we would certainly be able to make sense of it.

Like the subjectivist's first two complaints against realism, it appears that this last one is not definitive, and may even be misplaced. Even evaluative diversity such as we find as between ourselves and the Ik might be explained consistently with a realist view of value commitments. In conclusion it is worth making a

comment on the role which the diversity issue played in the encouragement of subjectivism, and in particular a relativist subjectivism, among anthropologists. Anthropological relativism about values was originally a reaction against a certain moralistic brand of Victorian anthropology, within which 'primitives' were represented as morally inferior beings. This reaction towards relativism was understandable since it meant that the recognition of difference no longer led to condemnation, moral rules being seen more in terms of convention than of universal moral imperatives.
As in the case of etiquette, it is impossible for a vast majority to be 'wrong' about the code of conduct to be followed: the rules of etiquette are a distillation of the manners of the majority and a moral code, viewed analogously, would not be damned because it differed from ours. Members of another culture could act in a manner which would systematically violate our moral precepts without meriting our condemnation. The adoption of relativism was buttressed by the humane desire to be tolerant, and not to be placed in the position of playing moral judge on a whole society.

Is it the case that in rejecting relativism about values, the realist might have to countenance the condemnation of a whole culture for supporting a certain sort of behaviour? Do we have to condemn the Ik if we adopt a realist view of values and charge them with being indifferent to cruelty, whether through misperception or mere neglect? The answer, clearly, is that we do not. If we could make out a case for misperception on the part of the Ik, we might complain of their perceptual carelessness but we certainly could not condemn them for acting in a manner explained by their misperception. If we charged them with neglect of the cruelty factor, we would move closer to condemnation but here too we would stop short of pronouncing an anathema for, as we have seen, the ascription of such neglect across a whole culture would only be sensible if we could go some way towards explaining it. To understand all is to forgive all and to understand in part would be to forgive in part.

But finally it should be noticed in any case that if the desire to criticise the condemnation of other cultures leads to a comprehensive relativism about values, it succeeds only in undercutting itself. The principle of tolerance motivating the relativist criticism is something like this: 'Nobody should presume to interfere with the moral beliefs of people in other cultures'. If a culture of Victorian anthropologists did not respect what are seen as the demands of tolerance, if they did not recognise tolerance as a virtue, this principle could be invoked to criticise them only insofar as it is understood as binding across cultures: for our purposes, insofar as it is taken realistically. The strict relativist makes it impossible to criticise the intolerant practice of such a group, unless it can be shown that the practice is inconsistent with other aspects of their code (see Harman 1977, Ch.8). It may be that we shall gird ourselves most effectively against cultural intolerance, if we adopt that realist view of values which has seemed to many to lie at its source.

# NOTES

INTRODUCTION

1 There are some problems which we are ignoring on the grounds that they are complicated but not overwhelming. One such problem arises with questions that begin with 'what', 'which', 'who', and so on, for unlike yes-no questions these do not have straightforward indicative counterparts.

2 The introduction of the concept of truth does not prejudge the issue between realism and anti-realism. The anti-realist holds that it is epistemologically scandalous so to interpret a class of assertions that the following result goes through: that an assertion is capable of being true or false even when the appropriate evidence for or against it is unavailable in principle. In order to mark his position terminologically the anti-realist may speak of assertibility rather than of truth; but he need not do so (see Pettit 1981).

3 We say 'something like' because in order to cater for indexical sentences which use words such as 'I' and 'you', 'here' and 'now', a T-sentence will have to be relativised to speaker and context: '"S" is true in language L for speaker s at time t if and only if . . .' (see Davidson 1967).

4 The requirement is sometimes described, in a phrase of Tarski's, as convention T. This way of referring to it is not altogether fortunate, since Tarski was not concerned with semantics, but rather with the definition of truth, and meant something different by convention T. (See Platts 1979, Ch.1, for a discussion of Tarski's theory.)

5 To assume such rationality, it may be noticed, is to assume in a certain measure what is sometimes described as the holism of the mental. It is to take it that an agent's beliefs are connected with one another in such a way that to attribute a single belief is always implicitly to attribute others. One does not believe that London is the capital of England if one believes that London is not a city, or that England is not a country. Indeed, assuming that one has some beliefs on the matter, it is positively required that one believes that London is a city and that England is a country.

CHAPTER 1 CROSS-CULTURAL UNDERSTANDING

1 Quine draws from this epistemological underdetermination the ontological lesson of indeterminancy: that there is no unique meaning in the utterances of the natives which our translation manuals try to capture, no fact of the matter as to which of the manuals possible is correct.

2 The doctrine characterised makes the mental supervenient on the physical but not reducible to it. On supervenience see Chapter 3, Section 2. The individualist slant of the doctrine needs amendment in the light of Burge 1979 but the crucial point remains: that, loosely characterised, the physical determines the mental.

3 An additional uncertainty made famous by Quine is whether the general term 'Anzo' refers to dogs, spatio-temporal dog-slices, universal doghood, or whatever (see Quine 1960, Ch.2).

4 Richard Grandy has formulated it as follows: it is the condition that 'the imputed pattern of relations among beliefs, desires, and the world be as similar to our own as possible' (Grandy 1973, p.443). The stress is on the 'as possible'. That Davidson's description of the principle of charity is not much different seems apparent if one compares the above to his qualification that agreement must be 'subject to considerations of simplicity, hunches about the effects of social conditioning, and of course our common sense, or scientific, knowledge of explicable error' (Davidson 1974a, p.19).

Notice that in our formulation we do not speak of minimising unintelligible agreement, unintelligible correctness in the beliefs of interpretees. We might have done, for we are assuming that such agreement as is identified, such correctness as is ascribed, will turn out to be explicable. The assumption is not unreasonable, since ascribing unintelligible agreement on certain matters will affect how much agreement is ascribed overall and, if it is unintelligible, will hardly maximise overall agreement. Our formulation heightens the continuity between the principle of humanity and the principle of charity.

5 The most obvious way in which such a disposition will come to be assumed will be through crediting our subjects with general beliefs from which particular beliefs are derived. Notice however that we do not have to attribute general beliefs unless these are linguistically expressed. Chopping down trees for firewood can be explained either as the effect of an inductively-arrived-at general belief 'All wood from trees is good firewood' and a particular belief 'This is tree-wood' or, on Carnapian lines, as the result of an inference from the singular belief 'The last treewood chopped was good firewood' to another singular belief 'This treewood will be good firewood'.

6 Notice that the test which the interpreter is to perform is not that suggested by Colin McGinn of seeing 'whether the subject behaves as one would of whom that theory were true' (McGinn 1977, p.534). This suggested test bears only on the appropriateness of propositional attitudes to action; it does not relate to the mode of acquisition of those attitudes.

7 This is a strict reading of psychoanalysis. On a revisionary reading, it might be said that the psychoanalytic story does not postulate unconscious beliefs but merely accounts for why the hand-washer finds washing so attractive: what would be unconscious thus is not a belief, or even a desire, but only the source of a desire. On such a revisionary reading psychoanalysis would not offer the same challenge to our notion of agent rationality; and neither, on a parallel reading, would the symbolist approach.

8 For a full discussion of the issues that arise in trying to make sense of the relativist thesis see Williams 1974-5. We skirt such a discussion because we are more interested in the matters raised later in the section.

9 Difficulties can be raised a priori about what genuinely alternative logics amount to but these we ignore. See S. Haack 1974 for a discussion.

10 Horton does not put this down as a consequence of the lack of alternatives, he simply says it is 'directly connected' to that lack. The connection is being construed by us as 'causal consequence'. The belief in the causal efficacy of conceptual change is characterised by Skorupski as the result of not diffentiating between effects which obtain as the result of certain conventions operating in a society, and effects which are causal consequences. So, for example, when the social status of an individual is changed by some ceremonial action, an ontological change is believed to accompany the social change (see Skorupski 1976, part 11, especially chapter 7).

11 The solution, it can be objected, is still only partial as it leaves open the question as to why some societies are literate and others oral. This is admitted, but (a) it still goes beyond previous explanations, and (b) it goes beyond them in a direction consistent with our starting point.

The importance of modes of communication for other developments in the culture of a society has been recently emphasised by Alvin Gouldner, in a manner sympathetic to Goody's conclusion. See Gouldner 1976. It has also been suggested that a reason for the non-development of science in China is to be found in the nonexistence of printing in China, which in turn is explained by its ideographic and non-alphabetic script. See Eisenstein 1979.

## CHAPTER 2 THE UNDERSTANDING OF INDIVIDUALS: HUMANISM VERSUS SCIENTISM

1 Strictly speaking, it enables us to say this only when the agent's state of mind was responsible for A 'in the right way'. Consider this possibility: that my desire to be rid of someone combined with my belief that I may do

so by appearing flustered distracts me and causes fluster. Here the state of mind explains my appearing flustered, but not intentionally (see Davidson 1971).

2 Here we are opting for the method of individuating actions defended in Davidson 1971, according to which one and the same action may instantiate different properties and have different descriptions. For an opposing point of view see Goldman 1970, chapter 1. The debate about the individuation of actions is surveyed in Davis 1979, chapter 2.

3 We ignore the question of whether descriptions of an action as projected that give us aspects under which the agent foresaw the event, but not aspects under which he particularly desired it, are to be counted as intentional. It seems in any case that such descriptions cannot be made to serve an explanatory purpose, not engaging a pro-attitude in the agent.

4 Our account of non-nomothetic explanation makes it out to be something very close to what is called 'holistic' explanation in Peacocke 1979; the similarity will be clearer from the discussion later in Section 6.

5 Here we see a sense in which the Wittgensteinian may claim that a rationalising mental state is logically connected to the action it is invoked to explain: see the discussion towards the end of Section 5. What still fails to follow however is the further claim that the mental state and the action are not really distinct, and not therefore causally connected.

6 As mentioned earlier, such a judgment, by the account offered in Davidson 1978, is nothing other than the act of intending the action. Notice that, in discussing Churchland's formula, Davidson reads it in such a way that it does not preclude the failure of practical reasoning which occurs when an agent wants something and believes that a particular course of action is the best way to get it but fails to put these two things together (see Davidson 1971). On our reading such failure, like moral weakness, is precluded. Notice also that the principle precludes the possibility of the action's arising 'in the wrong way'; this, because of the competence clauses 5 and 6. (See note 1.)

7 The picture suggested is that the assumption of behavioural rationality, the contextually *a priori* principle at the heart of our orthodox conception of agents, is sufficient with certain other contextually *a priori*, or at least not normally questioned, premises to entail the truth of the principles that guide us in explaining particular actions. The assumption is that every action issues from a rationalising state of mind and together with the assumptions that M is a rationalising state of mind for action A, and that rationalising states of mind are deterministic causes, it entails the truth of 'If M, then A'. Notice that the deeply embedded principles in the conception of things underlying regular event explanations, contextually *a priori* though they may be, do not normally entail the truth of regular explanatory principles, save by the addition of purely empirical premises. Thus the orthodox conception of agents is distinctive in fitting the traditional rationalist, as distinct from empiricist, image of theory (see Hollis 1977).

8 Our position, it should be noted, is close to that of Donald Davidson when he argues that rationality is a constitutive ideal in making sense of people and that it undermines the possibility of countenancing psychophysical laws (see Davidson 1970). The principles of action explanation are treated by us as laws but, being without firm indices, they are not liable to raise problems for the assumption of (attitudinal) rationality: where an agent would be inexplicably irrational (attitudinally) if we subsumed an action under a principle that initially seemed to apply, we are free to decide that the principle did not bear on the case after all; the agent did not have the beliefs and desires which it mentions (see Davidson 1974b). Notice that in contrast to action principles, psychophysical principles which were thought to link agent circumstances, behavioural responses or brain conditions to mental states in a lawlike way would put the ideal of rationality at risk. Thus Davidson argues that we must disavow such principles and take the mental and physical to be related only in a non-lawlike or 'anomalous'

way: in particular, if we take the mental and the physical to be one and the same realm- for example if we take mental events to be physical events under mental descriptions- the monism we thus embrace must be an 'anomalous monism'.

## CHAPTER 3 THE UNDERSTANDING OF INSTITUTIONS: INDIVIDUALISM VERSUS COLLECTIVISM

1 The characterisation of practices as concrete, continuant objects is more contentious than the parallel account of groups: this, because practices are made up of items which are not themselves objects. We recognise that the characterisation of both sorts of entity requires fuller discussion than that which we can provide here, and that attention to detail might suggest something more sophisticated than the assimilation of groups and practices to material objects. One justification for the line we take is that we wish to give a fair hearing to the idea, considered in Section 3 below, that institutions have causal powers of their own: although we reject that idea we would not wish to undermine it just by categorising institutions as causally inefficacious abstractions.

2 The ambiguity is reflected in the fact that while Lewis 1969 is concerned with norms in the sense of objective regularities Ullman-Margalit 1977, ostensibly dealing with related topics, is concerned with norms in the sense of social regulations.

3 Our claim that the orthodox conception of action is irreplaceable and unrevisable may seem to render reference to the mental indispensable and thus to force us into psychophysical dualism. The impression is misleading, for it is still possible that any particular action should be explained in this way: the action is describable as so and so superveniently on being such and such a neurophysiological response and that response is to be accounted for by reference to certain brain conditions. The availability of such explanations is compatible with our claims for the orthodox conception because it is still possible that there are no laws for identifying actions with neurophysiological responses and laws of this kind would be required for replacing psychological explanations systematically. One may deny such laws by holding that the psychological characterisation of actions is supervenient on, but not reducible to, their neurophysiological description. On this see the end of section 3 and notes 5 and 6 below.

4 Attitudinal contexts can also be rendered in such a way that a term which originally occupied a non-referring slot is transferred to a referring one: this happens when we render 'He believes that X is a so-and-so' as 'He believes of X that he is a so-and-so'. It is sufficient for our claim that we are able to adopt the first formulation in ascribing attitudes in respect of institutions; difficulty would arise only if the second was shown for some reason to be obligatory or even more appropriate. The second is often thought to be more appropriate when the X in question enters into causal interaction with the subject in producing the belief in question but, as we go on to show, institutions do not occasion beliefs about them in this way.

5 Notice that the picture of the relation between the psychological and the neurophysiological is one defended in Donald Davidson 1970. Where the parallel breaks down is in the further claim on Davidson's part that there are no psycholophysical laws of any kind. Supervenience without reduction disallows laws relating phenomena described from the higher perspective with phenomena described from the lower but not laws which do the converse. Thus there is no reason why we should not have laws relating individualistic conditions to institutional ones. See also Chapter 2, note 8.

6 As against this last suggestion, it may be thought that to allow what we might call supervenience laws would be to run the risk of implying full-scale reducibility. That risk would be real however only if the set of supervenience laws were recursively enumerable and there is no reason to think that this condition must be fulfilled: as mentioned in section 2, it seems that there is an open-ended number of individualistically describable ways in which an institutional predicate may be fulfilled. On this matter see

Hellman and Thompson 1975, pp.562-3, Kim 1978 and Peacocke 1979, footnote pp.122-3.

6 It should be noticed that apart from the event-explanatory criterion of ontological autonomy described in section 3, we might also characterise a law-explanatory one. On such a criterion we would say that one sort of entity X exists over and beyond another sort Y if and only if the following condition is fulfilled: that the addition of terms by means of which we refer to X-type things enables us to give explanations of regularities that we cannot account for in a language with terms for referring to Y-type items. What we argue in this section is, in effect, that institutions are no more autonomous on this criterion than they are on the event-explanatory one.

7 Notice the pivotal role which the orthodox conception of agents is naturally made to bear in the assessment of putative laws that have a relevance to behaviour. It is because of holding the conception firm that Donald Davidson argues that neurophysiological laws cannot be systematically related to psychologically characterised states and events: this psychophysical anomalousness protects the orthodox conception against subversion from below. See Chapter 2, note 8. Similarly it is because of adhering to that conception that we argue that macro-sociological laws are naturally not taken seriously unless they can be explained by reference to individuals: and that if they had to be taken seriously for some reason such as empirical salience, they would inevitably be regarded as anomalies or miracles. Taking this line, we protect the orthodox conception against overthrow from above.

8 Miller 1978 claims that the rationalistic version is that which is upheld in the tradition of methodological individualism associated with Hayek, Popper and Watkins. We do not make a judgment on this issue.

CHAPTER 4 TRUTH AND VALUE

1 Popper's attack on inductivism appears in (inter alia): Popper (1959) and Popper (1963). The impossibility claim rests on Carnap's use of the probability calculus, whereby all universal sentences have a zero probability.

2 Popper's attack is aimed primarily at the positivists but much of his characterisation of their position is caricature, not reflecting the diversity of views held by the positivists: e.g. the difference between Schlick and Carnap (under the influence of Neurath) concerning the nature of 'basic statements' (see Ayer 1959).

3 This is, implicitly, to assume that the position adopted by Popper, and criticised by Kuhn, is naive falsificationism, i.e. the doctrine that a theory should be rejected if it has even one 'false' consequence. Whether Popper ever held this view is doubtful, but some of his statements suggest it (e.g. that we know a theory to be false if it has a false consequence). The text magnifies the difference between Kuhn and Popper, but that difference is still real and centres on the desirability of wholesale adoption of a falsificationist methodology. For a survey of Popperian positions see Lakatos (1970).

4 Whether Marx thought of his social science as value-laden is a moot point but it is worth mentioning that he often eschewed evaluative considerations in setting up his theoretical principles. Thus he makes the following comment on his way of defining the value of labour power by reference to the labour time necessary for the production (and reproduction) of the article in question - the worker. 'This method of determining the value of labour power arises out of the necessities of the case, and to complain that it is a brutal one is a piece of cheap sentimentalism' (Marx 1974, p.161). Surplus-value, and hence exploitation, is defined in a similarly 'scientific' manner.

5 A recent commentator has suggested that science can be included in the 'base' (the forces of production) itself, since labour-power, one of the forces of production, includes the skill of the workers and such skill can include technological and scientific knowledge. See Cohen 1979.

6 This may seem to suggest that social science is impeded if there is any appearance-reality split, whereas Cohen has argued that if there is no

divergence between appearance and reality, then social science will 'wither away' (Cohen 1979). That social science depends on some such divergence can be conceded whilst the claim is made that it is impeded by the particular sort of split mentioned in the text.

7 The best rebuttal of the claim that Marx rejected all views of human nature is to be found in Ollman, 1971. See also Marx's comments on Bentham:

> To know what is useful for a dog, we must study dog nature. This cannot be excogitated from the 'principle of utility'. Applying the same considerations to man, he that would pass judgment on all human activities, movements, relations, etc. in accordance with the principle of utility, must first become acquainted with human nature in general, and then with human nature as modified in each specific historical epoch (Marx 1974, p.671).

8 They are discussed, though not at great length, in Pettit 1981. It should be noticed in particular that the denial of realism should not be conflated with reductivism, as it appears to be in McGinn 1979b. See Dummett 1979, pp.3-7.

9 These options correspond respectively to the instrumentalist and reductivist strategies described in Pettit 1981. The constructivist approach corresponds roughly to the redescriptivist strategy mentioned in that paper.

10 Our discussion in Chapter 2 would offer an argument, as mentioned in footnote 8 there, for treating psychological predicates as perhaps supervenient on physical ones but not reducible to them. See also Chapter 3, footnote 5. It is such an argument that is wanting in the realist's arsenal.
Notice however that if psychological characterisations are physically supervenient without being physically reducible, and if value characterisations supervene on these (whether or not they reduce to them), the value characterisations also supervene on physical without reducing to them. The realist will want to deny the reducibility of the valuable to the psychological whereas this is precisely what the subjectivist upholds: here we see that a supervenience without reducibility claim in respect of the valuable and the physical may also be made by the realist's opponent. The problem will then turn on how the realist's denial can be argumentatively supported.

# BIBLIOGRAPHY

Abel, Theodore (1948) The operation called 'Verstehen', 'American Journal of Sociology', vol. 54 reprinted in Dallmayr and McCarthy (1977).
Adorno, T.W. (1976) Introduction to 'The Positivist Dispute in German Sociology', tr. by G. Adey and D. Frisby, Heinemann, London.
Alexander, Peter (1962) Rational Behaviour and Psychoanalytic Explanation, 'Mind', vol. LXXI.
Althusser, L. (1977) 'Lenin and Philosophy and other essays', 2nd edn, New Left Books London.
Anscombe, G.E.M. (1963) 'Intention', 2nd edn, Blackwell, Oxford.
— (1971) 'Causality and Determination', Inaugural Lecture, Cambridge University Press, Cambridge.
Ayer, A. ed. (1959) 'Logical Positivism', Collier Macmillan, Toronto.
Berlin, Isaiah (1976) 'Vico and Herder', Hogarth Press, London.
Brand, Myles, ed. (1976) 'The Nature of Causation', University of Illinois Press, London.
Brodbeck, Mary (1958) Methodological Individualisms: Definition and Reduction, 'Philosophy of Science', vol. 25, repd. in O'Neill (1973).
Burge, Tyler (1979) Individualism and the Mental, in French, P., Uehling, T., Wettstein, H. (eds), 'Midwest Studies in Philosophy', vol. IV, University of Minnesota Press, Minneapolis.
Churchland, Paul (1970) The Logical Character of Action Explanations, 'Philosophical Review', vol. 79.
— (1979) 'Scientific Realism and the Plasticity of Mind', Cambridge University Press, Cambridge.
Coleman, James (1974) 'Power and the Structure of Society', Norton, New York.
Cohen, G. (1979) 'Marx's Theory of History', Oxford University Press, London.
Cooper, David (1975) Alternative Logic in Primitive Thought, 'Man', vol. 10, no. 2.
Dallmayr, Fred and McCarthy, Thomas (1977) 'Understanding and Social Inquiry', University of Notre Dame Press.
Danto, Arthur (1973) 'Analytical Philosophy of Action', Cambridge University Press, Cambridge.
Davidson, Donald (1963) Actions, Reasons and Causes, 'Journal of Philosophy', vol. 60.
— (1967) Truth and Meaning, 'Synthèse', vol. VII.Page reference to Davis, Hockney and Wilson (1969).
— (1969a) True to the Facts, 'Journal of Philosophy', vol. 66.
— (1969b) On Saying That, in Davidson, D., and Hintikka, J. (eds), 'Words and Objections', Reidel, Dordrecht.
— (1970) Mental Events, in Foster, L. and Swanson, J. (eds), 'Experience and Theory', Duckworth, London.
— (1971) Agency, in Binkley, R. Bronaugh, R. and Marras, A. (eds) 'Agent, Action and Reasons' Blackwell, Oxford.
— (1973a) Radical Interpretation, 'Dialecta', vol. 27.
— (1973b) In Defence of Convention T, in Leblanc, H. (ed.) 'Truth, Syntax and Modality' North Holland.
— (1974a) Belief and the Basis of Meaning, 'Synthèse', vol. 27, nos 3/4.
— (1974b) Psychology as Philosophy, in Brown, S. (ed.), 'Philosophy of Psychology', Macmillan, London.
— (1975) Thought and Talk, in Guttenplan, S. (ed.), 'Mind and Language', Oxford University Press, London.
— (1977) Hempel on Explaining Action, 'Erkenntnis', vol. 10.

— (1978) Intending, in Yeovel, Y. (ed.), 'Philosophy of History and Action', Reidel, Dordrecht.
Davis, J.W., Hockney, D., and Wilson, W. (1969) 'Philosophical Logic', Reidel, Dordrecht.
Davis, Kingsley and Moore, Wilburt (1945) Some Principles of Stratification, 'American Sociological Review', vol. 10.
Davis, Lawrence (1979) 'Theories of Action', Prentice Hall, N. Jersey.
Dennett, Daniel (1973) Mechanism and Responsibility, in Honderich, T. (ed.), 'Essays on Freedom of Action', Routledge & Kegan Paul, London.
Donnellan, Keith (1967) Reasons and Causes, in Edwards, P. (ed.), 'Encyclopedia of Philosophy', Crowell Collier and Macmillan, New York.
Douglas, Mary (1973) 'Natural Symbols', Penguin Books, Harmondsworth.
Dray, William (1957) 'Laws and Explanation in History', Oxford University Press, London.
Dummett, Michael (1973) 'Frege: the Philosophy of Language', Duckworth, London.
— (1977) 'Elements of Intuitionism', Clarendon Press, Oxford.
— (1979) Common Sense and Physics, in G.F. Macdonald (ed.), 'Perception and Identity', Macmillan Press, London.
Durkheim, Emile (1915) 'The Elementary Forms of the Religious Life', Allen & Unwin, London.
— (1933) 'The Division of Labour in Society', Macmillan, New York.
— (1938) 'The Rules of Sociological Method', Collier-Macmillan, London.
Eisenstein (1979) 'The Printing Press as an Agent of Change', Cambridge University Press, Cambridge.
Elster, J. (1979) 'Ulysses and the Sirens', Cambridge University Press, Cambridge.
Evans, Gareth and McDowell, John (eds.), (1976) 'Truth and Meaning', Clarendon Press, Oxford.
Evans-Pritchard, E. (1936) 'Witchcraft, Oracles and Magic Among the Azande', Oxford University Press, London.
— (1956) 'Nuer Religion', Oxford University Press, London.
— (1965) 'Theories of Primitive Religion', Oxford University Press, London.
Gadamer, Hans Georg (1970) 'Truth and Method', Sheed & Ward, London.
Geach, P.T. (1972) 'Logic Matters', Blackwell, Oxford.
Geertz, Clifford (1975) 'The Interpretation of Cultures', Hutchinson, London.
Giddens, Anthony (1976) 'New Rules of Sociological Method', Hutchinson, London.
Goffman, Erving (1969) 'The Presentation of Self in Everyday Life', Allen Lane, Harmondsworth.
Goldman, A.I. (1970) 'A Theory of Action', Princeton University Press, Princeton.
Goodman, Nelson (1973) 'Fact, Fiction and Forecast', 3rd edn, Bobbs Merrill, Indianapolis.
Goody, Jack (1977) 'The Domestication of the Savage Mind', Cambridge University Press, Cambridge.
Gouldner, A.W. (1976) 'The Dialectic of Ideology and Technology', Macmillan, London.
Grandy, Richard (1973) Reference, Meaning and Belief, 'Journal of Philosophy', vol. LXX, no. 14.
Grice, H.P. (1957) Meaning, 'Philosophical Review', vol. 66.
— (1975) Logic and Conversation, in Cole, P., and Morgan, J. (eds), 'Syntax and Semantics 3: Speech Acts', Academic Press, New York.
Gustafson, D. (1973) A Critical Survey of the Reasons Versus Causes Arguments in Recent Philosophy of Action, 'Metaphilosophy', vol. 4.
Haack, S. (1974) 'Deviant Logic', Cambridge University Press, Cambridge.
Habermas, J. (1972) 'Knowledge and Human Interests', Heinemann, London.
Hacking, Ian (1975) 'Why Does Language Matter to Philosophy', Cambridge University Press, Cambridge.
Hare, R.M. (1952) 'Language of Morals', Oxford University Press, London.
Harman, G. (1977) 'The Nature of Morality', Oxford University Press, New York.

Hart, H.L.A. (1948-9) The Ascription of Responsibility and Rights, 'Proc. of Aristotelian Society', vol. XLIX.
Hayek, F.A. (1942-3) Scientism and the Study of Society, in 'Economica', reprinted in (1973) O'Neill (ed.), 'Modes of Individualism and Collectivism', Heinemann, London.
Hellman, G. and Thompson F. (1975) Physicalism: Ontology, Determination and Reduction, 'Journal of Philosophy', vol. 72, no. 17.
Hempel, C.G. (1965) 'Aspect of Scientific Explanation', Free Press, New York.
Hesse, Mary (1974) 'The Structure of Scientific Inference', Macmillan, London.
Hodges, H.A. (1944) 'Wilhelm Dilthey, An Introduction', London.
Hollis, Martin (1977) 'Models of Man', Cambridge University Press, Cambridge.
Horton, Robin (1970) African Thought and Western Science, in Wilson (ed.), 'Rationality', Blackwell, Oxford.
Hume, David (1902) 'An Enquiry Concerning the Human Understanding', ed. L.A. Selby-Bigge, Oxford University Press, London.
James, Susan (1978) Holism in Social Theory: the case of Marxism, Ph. D. Dissertation, Cambridge University.
Jeffrey, Richard (1965) 'The Logic of Decision', McGraw Hill, New York.
Kenny, Anthony (1963) 'Action, Emotion and the Will', Routledge & Kegan Paul, London.
Kim, Jaegwon (1978) Supervenience and Nomological Incommensurables, 'American Philosophy Quarterly', vol. 15.
Kripke, Saul (1972) Naming and Necessity, in Davidson, D, and Harman, G. (eds.) 'Semantics of Natural Languages', Reidel, Dordrecht.
Kuhn, T.S. (1970) 'The Structure of Scientific Revolutions', 2nd edn. University of Chicago Press, Chicago.
Lakatos, I. (1970) Falsification and the Methodology of Scientific Research Programmes, in Lakatos, I. and Musgrave, A. (eds), 'Criticism and the Growth of Knowledge', Cambridge University Press, Cambridge.
Lessnoff, M. (1974) 'The Structure of Social Science', Hutchinson, London.
Lewis, David (1969) 'Convention', Harvard University Press, Cambridge, Mass.
— (1974) Radical Interpretation, 'Synthèse', vol. 27, nos. 3/4.
Lewis, G. (1980) 'Day of Shining Red', Cambridge University Press, Cambridge.
Louch, A.R. (1967) 'The Explanation of Action', Blackwell, Oxford.
Lukes, Steven (1973) 'Individualism', Blackwell, Oxford.
Lyons, John (1968) 'Introduction to Theoretical Linguistics', Cambridge University Press, Cambridge.
Mackie, J.L. (1974) 'The Cement of the Universe', Oxford University Press, London.
— (1977) 'Ethics', Penguin Books, Harmondsworth.
Malinowski, B. (1944) 'A Scientific Theory of Culture and Other Essays', University of North Carolina Press, Chapel Hill.
Mandelbaum, Maurice (1955) Societal Facts, 'British Journal of Sociology', vol. 6.
Marx, Karl (1974) 'Capital' vol. 1, J.M. Dent & Sons, London.
McDowell, John (1976) Truth-Conditions, Bivalence and Verificationism, in Evans, Gareth and McDowell, John (1976).
— (1978) Are Moral Requirements Hypothetical Imperatives, in 'Aristotelian Society Suppl.', vol. LII.
— (1981) Non-Cognitivism and Rule-Following, in Holtzman, S. and Leich, C. (eds), 'Wittgenstein: To Follow a Rule', Routledge & Kegan Paul, London.
McGinn, Colin (1977) Charity, Interpretation and Belief, 'Journal of Philosophy', vol. LXXIV, no. 9.
— (1979a) Action and Its Explanation, in Bolton, N. (ed.), 'Philosophical Problems in Psychology', Methuen, London.
— (1979b) An A Priori Argument for Realism, 'Journal of Philosophy', vol. LXXVI, no. 3.
Melden, A.I. (1961) 'Free Action', Routledge & Kegan Paul, London.
Mellor, D.H. (1976) Probable Explanation, 'Australasian Journal of Philosophy', vol. 54.

Mellor (Forthcoming) The Reduction of Society, 'Philosophy'.
Merton, R.K. (1957, 1968) 'Social Theory and Social Structure', Free Press, Chicago.
Milgram, Stanley (1974) 'Obedience and Authority', Tavistock, London.
— (1977) 'The Individual in a Social World', Addison & Wesley, London.
Miller, Richard (1978) Methodological Individualism and Social Explanation, 'Philosophy of Science', vol. 45.
Nagel, Ernest (1961) 'The Structure of Science', Routledge & Kegan Paul, London.
Nordenfelt, Lennart (1974) 'Explanation of Human Actions', University of Uppsala Publication, Sweden.
Nozick, Robert (1977) On Austrian Methodology, 'Synthèse', vol. 36.
Ollman, Bertell (1971) 'Alienation', Cambridge University Press, Cambridge.
O'Neill, John, ed. (1973) 'Modes of Individualism and Collectivism', Heinemann, London.
Outhwaite, William (1975) 'Understanding Social Life: The Method Called Verstehen', Allen & Unwin, London.
Papineau, David (1978) 'For Science in Social Science', Macmillan, London.
Parsons, Talcott (1951) 'The Social System', Free Press, Chicago.
— (1958) Authority, Legitimation and Political Action, in Friedrich, C. (ed.), 'Authority Nomos I', Harvard University Press, Cambridge, Mass.
Peacocke, Christopher (1979) 'Holistic Explanation', Oxford University Press, London.
Peters, R.S. (1958) 'The Concept of Motivation', Routledge & Kegan Paul, London.
Pettit, Philip (1975) The Life-World and Role Theory, in Pivcevic, E. (ed.), 'Phenomenology and Philosophical Understanding', Cambridge University Press, Cambridge.
— (1976) Making Actions Intelligible, in Harre, R. (ed.) 'Life Sentences', Wiley, London.
— (1978) Rational Man Theory, in Hookway, C. and Pettit, P. (eds), 'Action and Interpretation: Studies in the Philosophy of Social Science', Cambridge University Press, Cambridge.
— (1979a) Rationalization and the Art of Explaining Action, in Bolton, N. (ed.) 'Philosophical Problems in Psychology', Methuen, London.
— (1979b) 'Philosophy and the Human Sciences', Inaugural Lecture, University of Bradford Publication.
— (1980) 'Judging Justice: An Introduction to Contemporary Political Philosophy', Routledge & Kegan Paul, London.
— (1981) Evaluative Realism and Interpretation, in Holtzman, S. and Leich, C. (eds), 'Wittgenstein: To Follow a Rule', Routledge ' Kegan Paul, London.
— (forthcoming) On Actions and Explanations in Antaki, L. (ed.), 'The Psychology of Ordinary Explanation', Academic Press, London.
Platts, Mark (1979) 'Ways of Meaning', Routledge & Kegan Paul, London.
— (1980) Moral Reality and the End of Desire, in Platts, M. (ed.) 'Reference, Truth and Reality', Routledge & Kegan Paul, London.
Pompa, Leon (1975) 'Vico', Cambridge University Press, Cambridge.
Popper, Karl (1957) 'The Poverty of Historicism', Routledge & Kegan Paul, London.
— (1959) 'The Logic of Scientific Discovery', Hutchinson, London.
— (1963) 'Conjectures and Refutations', Routledge & Kegan Paul, London.
— (1976) The Logic of the Social Sciences, in 'The Positivist Dispute in German Sociology', tr. by Adey, G. and Frisby, D., Heinemann, London.
Putnam, Hilary (1977) 'Two Dogmas' Revisited, in Ryle, G. (ed.), 'Contemporary Aspects of Philosophy', Oriel Press, London.
— (1978) 'Meaning and the Moral Sciences', Routledge & Kegan Paul, London.
Quine, W.V. (1951) Two Dogmas of Empiricism, 'Philosophical Review', vol. 60.
— (1960) 'Word and Object', M.I.T. Press Cambridge, Mass.
— and Ullian, J.S. (1978) 'The Web of Belief', 2nd edn, Random House, New York.

Quinton, Anthony (1975-6) Social Objects, 'Proceedings of the Aristotelian Society', vol. 75.
Radcliffe-Brown, A.R. (1952) 'Structure and Function in Primitive Societies', Cohen & West, London.
Rickman, H.P. (1976) 'Wilhelm Dilthey. Selected Writings', Cambridge University Press, Cambridge.
— (1979) 'Wilhelm Dilthey', Elek, London.
Salmon, Wesley (1971) 'Statistical Explanation and Statistical Relevance', University of Pittsburgh Press, Pittsburgh.
Skinner, B.F. (1953) 'Science and Human Behaviour', Macmillan, New York.
Skorupski, John (1976) 'Symbol and Theory', Cambridge University Press, Cambridge.
Sosa, E., ed. (1975) 'Causation and Conditionals', Oxford University Press, London.
Sperber, Dan (1975) 'Symbolism Revisited' Cambridge University Press, Cambridge.
Stinchcombe, Arthur (1968) 'Constructing Social Theories', Harcourt, Brace & World, New York.
Stoutland, Frederic (1970) The Logical Connection Argument 'American Philosophical Quarterly Monograph no. 4', Blackwell, Oxford.
Strawson, P.F. (1950) Truth, 'Proceedings of the Aristotelian Society', Suppl. vol. XXIV.
— (1962) Freedom and Resentment, 'Proceedings of the British Academy'.
Taylor, Charles (1964) 'The Explanation of Behaviour', Routledge & Kegan Paul, London.
— (1971) Interpretation and the Sciences of Man, 'Review of Metaphysics', vol. 25.
— (1978) Language and Human Nature, Alan B. Plaunt Memorial Lectures; Mimeo.
Thomas, David (1979) 'Naturalism and Social Science', Cambridge University Press, Cambridge.
Turnbull, Colin (1974) 'The Mountain People', Pan Books, London.
Turner, J. and Maryanski, A. (1979) 'Functionalism', Benjamin/Cummings, London.
Ullman-Margalit, Edna (1977) 'The Emergence of Norms', Oxford University Press, London.
— (1978) Invisible Hand Explanations, 'Synthèse', vol. 39.
Von Wright, G.H. (1971), 'Explanation and Understanding', Routledge & Kegan Paul, London.
Watkins, J.W.N. (1952) Ideal Types and Historical Explanation, 'British Journal for the Philosophy of Science', repr. in O'Neill (1973).
— (1954) Methodological Individualism: A Reply, 'Philosophy of Science', vol. 21, repr. is O'Neill (1973).
Weber, Max (1949) 'The Methadology of the Social Sciences', tr. and ed. by Ghils, H., and French, H., Free Press, Chicago.
Wiggins, David (1976) Truth, Invention and the Meaning of Life, British Academy Philosophical Lecture, University Press, Oxford.
Williams, Bernard (1973) 'Problems of the self', Cambridge University Press, Cambridge.
— (1974-75) The Truth in Relativism, 'Proceedings of the Aristotelian Society',
— (1978) 'Descartes', Penguin Books, Harmondsworth.
Wilson, Bryan ed. (1970) 'Rationality', Blackwell, Oxford.
Wilson, N.L. (1959) Substances Without Substrata, 'Review of Metaphysics', vol. 12.
Winch, Peter (1958) 'The Idea of a Social Science', Routledge & Kegan Paul, London.
— (1964) Understanding a Primitive Society, 'American Philosophical Quarterly', vol. 1. repr. in Wilson, Bryan (ed.), (1970); page references to latter.
Wollheim, R. (1979) 'The Sheep and the Ceremony', Leslie Stephen Lecture, Cambridge University Press, Cambridge.
Woodfield, Andrew (1976) 'Teleology', Blackwell, Oxford.

# INDEX